Library of Arabic Linguistics

The reasons behind the establishment of this Series on Arabic linguistics are manifold.

First: Arabic linguistics is developing into an increasingly interesting and important subject within the broad field of modern linguistic studies. The subject is now fully recognised in the Universities of the Arabic speaking world and in international linguistic circles, as a subject of great theoretical and descriptive interest and importance.

Second: Arabic linguistics is reaching a mature stage in its development benefiting both from early Arabic linguistic scholarship and modern techniques of general linguistics and related disciplines.

Third: The scope of this discipline is wide and varied, covering diverse areas such as Arabic phonetics, phonology and grammar, Arabic psycholinguistics, Arabic dialectology, Arabic lexicography and lexicology, Arabic sociolinguistics, the teaching and learning of Arabic as a first, second, or foreign language, communications, semiotics, terminology, translation, machine translation, Arabic computational linguistics, history of Arabic linguistics, etc.

Viewed against this background, Arabic linguists may be defined as: the scientific investigation and study of the Arabic language in all its aspects. This embraces the descriptive, comparative and historical aspects of the language. It also concerns itself with the classical form as well as the Modern and contemporary standard forms and their dialects. Moreover, it attempts to study the language in the appropriate regional, social and cultural settings.

It is hoped that the Series will devote itself to all issues of Arabic linguistics in all its manifestations on both the theoretical and applied levels. The results of these studies will also be of use in the field of linguistics in general, as well as related subjects.

Although a number of works have appeared independently or within series, yet there is no platform designed specifically for this subject. This Series is being started to fill this gap in the linguistic field. It will be devoted to Monographs written in either English or Arabic, or both, for the benefit of wider circles of readership.

All these reasons justify the establishment of a new forum which is devoted to all areas of Arabic linguistic studies. It is also hoped that this Series will be of interest not only to students and researchers in Arabic linguistics but also to students and scholars of other disciplines who are looking for information of theoretical, practical or pragmatic interest.

The Series Editors

Language variation and change in a modernising Arab state

Library of Arabic Linguistics

Series editors
Muhammad Hasan Bakalla
King Saud University, Riyadh, Kingdom of Saudi Arabia
Bruce Ingham
School of Oriental and African Studies, University of London

Advisory editorial board
Peter F. Abboud *University of Texas at Austin*
M.H. Abdulaziz *University of Nairobi*
Yousif El-Khalifa Abu Bakr *University of Khartoum*
Salih J. Altoma *Indiana University*
Arne Ambros *University of Vienna*
El Said M. Badawi *American University in Cairo*
Michael G. Carter *University of Sydney*
Ahmad al-Dhubaib *King Saud University (formerly University of Riyadh)*
Martin Forstner *Johannes Gutenberg University at Mainz*
Otto Jastrow *University of Erlangen-Nürnberg*
Raja T. Nasr *University College of Beirut*
C.H.M. Versteegh *Catholic University at Nijmegen*
Bougslaw R. Zagorski *University of Warsaw*

Clive Holes
University of Salford

Language Variation and Change in a Modernising Arab State

The Case of Bahrain

Monograph No. 7

Routledge
Taylor & Francis Group
LONDON AND NEW YORK

First published 1987 by
Kegan Paul International

Published 2016 by Routledge
2 Park Square, Milton Park, Abingdon, Oxon OX14 4RN
711 Third Avenue, New York, NY 10017, USA

Routledge is an imprint of the Taylor & Francis Group, an informa business

First issued in paperback 2015

Transferred to Digital Printing 2010

British Library Cataloguing in Publication Data
A catalogue record for this book is available from the British Library

ISBN 978-1-138-97431-9 (pbk)
ISBN 978-0-7103-0244-1 (hbk)

Publisher's Note
The publisher has gone to great lengths to ensure the quality of this reprint but points out that some imperfections in the original copies may be apparent. The publisher has made every effort to contact original copyright holders and would welcome correspondence from those they have been unable to trace.

To 'Ali Ibrāhīm Hārūn of Bani Jamra
and 'Isa al-'Arādi of 'Arād

Editor's Note

This book appears at a time when two other studies of language variation in Bahrain have also recently been published: Theodore Prochazka's "The Shi'i dialects of Baḥrain and their relationship to the Eastern Arabian dialect of Muḥarraq and the Omani dialect of al-Ristāq", *Zeitschrift für arabische Linguistik, vi, 1981, pp.16–55,* and one in this series, Mahdi Abdalla al-Tajir's *Language and linguistic origins in Baḥrain: the Baḥārnah dialect of Arabic,* London, 1982.

These three works take quite different approaches. Al-Tajir's is basically a correlation of present-day language variation with traditional genealogy based on an examination of Arabic historical sources. Prochazka's is a three-way comparative study between the Shi'ite dialects of Bahrain, the Sunni dialect, and a dialect of nearby Oman, advancing historical explanations for the present situation. All three concentrate on phonological and morphological variation of high incidence in the language, and in this follow a precedent set by Haim Blanc in his pioneering work *Communal Dialects in Baghdad* (1964) in which he examined the separate dialects of Muslims, Jews and Christians in Iraqi urban centres and explained their historical relationship to dialect groups outside the immediate area.

In some ways the picture in Bahrain is similar, namely an influx of population from central Arabia has created a relic area of part of what was once a larger dialect band which is now cut off from the main areas where such dialects are spoken. In this case the Shi'ite (Baḥārina) is the older dialect related to parts of Oman and to a lesser extent al-Hasa, while the Sunni dialect is related to the Najdi group. As Holes points out in an earlier work (1983a, p.15) Blanc's classification into so-called "sedentary" and "nomadic" dialect types is broadly applicable to the Bahraini situation with of course many differences of detail, and is indeed applicable to other areas well outside Mesopotamia.

The present work differs widely in approach and methodology from the previous two. The author is probably the prime exponent of the Labovian sociolinguistic approach in the Arabic field and this present study is the culmination of years of work on the dialects of Bahrain, following his four previous articles on the subject: "Variation in Bahraini Arabic: the (j) and (y) allophones of /j/" (1980), "Bahraini dialects: sectarian differences and the sedentary/nomadic split" (1983a), "Patterns of communal language variation in Bahrain" (1983b), and "Bahraini dialects: sectarian differences exemplified through texts" (1984). In approach, he has taken the "taxonomic" method of Blanc in describing Arabic communal dialect differences a step further, bringing in the techniques begun by Labov (1964) and later developed further by him (1963, 1966, 1972), and also by De Camp (1971, 1973) and Bickerton (1973). It differs from the earlier approach in taking account of variability in the language of individual speakers both in the direction of the spoken dialects and in the direction of Classical Arabic. This is captured best in the words of the author (p.7):

> Patterned variability is at the heart of natural speech data, whether at the individual or community level, and requires a dynamic rather than a taxonomic linguistic model to handle it.

And further:

> Variation in dialectal Arabic ... should not be discussed ... as "interference" from the standard, but incorporated into dialectological description, since from the speaker's point of view it is every bit as much a part of his speech behaviour as "the dialect".

The author's approach takes into account factors of nationality, religious group affiliation, and occupational class in the selection of linguistic variables and is thereby squarely in the camp of the sociolinguists. However it is interesting to note that, as he points out in Chapter 2, such judgements as "educated/non-educated", when based on speech variables, have to be defined for the individual state, since the demographic history and politico-social structure of each state is different even in an area as (relatively) small and intimate as the Gulf litoral. So that, for instance, the exponent /y/ for Old Arabic *jīm* marks "uneducated" speech in a formal context in Kuwait and is thus stigmatized, while in Bahrain the same exponent /y/ marks Sunni speech vs. Shi'a speech which has /j/ and bears no stigma. The Arabic speech communities considered by Holes are in a state of rapid social and linguistic change and this study attempts to (p.8)

> explain how a selected range of phonological elements and morphophonological patterns are becoming the subject of variation and ultimately change within the Arabic-speaking community of Bahrain.

Bruce Ingham
Series Co-Editor
School of Oriental and African Studies
London, July 1986

Contents

PREFACE xiii

ACKNOWLEDGEMENTS xvi

TRANSCRIPTION AND TRANSLITERATION SYSTEMS xvii

1 VARIATION IN SPOKEN ARABIC 1
1.1 The traditional dialectological approach 1
1.2 Studies of interdialectal conversation and the stylistic continuum 5
1.3 The present work 8

2 BAHRAIN: THE SOCIAL AND CULTURAL BACKGROUND 10
2.1 Geographical and historical sketch 10
2.2 Sect and ethnicity 11
2.3 Linguistic consequences of social change 16

3 DATA COLLECTION METHODS 21
3.1 Selection of speakers 21
3.2 Interview methods 25
3.3 Comparability of data between groups of speakers 26
3.4 Intra-speaker variability: contextual styles 28
3.5 Presentation of the analysis of variation 29

4 THE SOCIAL DISTRIBUTION OF SOME BA PHONEMES 32
4.1 The linguistic background 32
4.2 The dialect of the 'Arab 34
4.3 The dialects of the Baḥārna: the village/urban split 38
4.4 Summary of consonantal correspondences 42

5 PHONEMIC VARIATION: ANALYSIS AND INTERPRETATION 48
5.1 Introduction 48
5.2 Measurement of variation 48

5.3 Type 1 variables: the data base 49
5.4 Type 2 variables: the data bases for PV3 and PV4 62
5.5 Type 3 variables: the data bases for PV5 and PV6 62
5.6 Summary 65
5.7 Levels of "dialectalness" 66
5.8 Summary 80
5.9 Implicational scaling as a data-displaying device 81
5.10 Interpretation of trends in the scaled data 88
5.11 Inter-rule relationships 91
5.12 Rule formulation: some issues raised by the data 95
5.13 Summary of conclusions: 'phonetic variation' 104

6 THE SOCIAL DISTRIBUTION OF SOME BA MORPHOPHONEMIC PATTERNS 106
6.1 Introduction 106
6.2 Socially distributed morphophonemic differences: some examples 107
6.3 Selection of variables for investigation 111
6.4 The variables 112
6.5 Summary 122

7 MORPHOPHONEMIC VARIATION: ANALYSIS AND INTERPRETATION 124
7.1 Introduction 124
7.2 Syllable structure and stem-type 125
7.3 Analysis of quantified data 140
7.4 Summary of trends in the data 174

8 MORPHOPHONEMIC RULE FORMULATION 176
8.1 Notational problems 176
8.2 Implicational scales and DMR constraints 186
8.3 Implicational relationships between DMRs 195
8.4 Dialect-type and social network 200
8.5 Conclusions 202

BIBLIOGRAPHY 203

INDEX 208

GLOSSARY OF TECHNICAL TERMS 212

Preface

In essence, this book is an updated and substantially revised version of the PhD thesis completed at the Department of Linguistics, University of Cambridge, in 1981. The thesis was a contribution to the debate on how variation in language form should be incorporated into linguistic description. As such, it fell into the category of what Ingham (1982:xvi) describes as 'theory-oriented' Arabic dialectology, as opposed to the 'data-oriented' approach represented by such works as Johnstone 1967 and Al-Tajir 1982.

My main concern in the thesis was to examine how well the formalisms of modern correlational sociolinguistics were able to account for the variation which could be observed in a large corpus of natural speech data which I had tape-recorded over an 8 month period of field-work in Bahrain. This involved an examination of the advantages and disadvantages of the two approaches to correlational sociolinguistics which dominated the literature in the 1970's. On the one hand, following Labov (1972) and Cedergren and Sankoff (1974), speakers can be selected and classified on a range of socioeconomic crieteria, and their speech then sampled in a number of artificially created, but supposedly 'naturalistic' contexts. The correlation of social and contextual variables with linguistic variation, whether inter-speaker or intra-speaker is then analysed and the probability of a particular rule (e.g. final consonant cluster reduction in the Black English Vernacular) applying in given sets of environments (linguistic, contextual) is computed for the community as a whole. Unconscious knowledge of the ordering of environments in which such a rule is progressively more or less likely to apply is conceived of as part of communal linguistic competence: whatever the differences in the observed number of times one speaker as opposed to another applies the rule, the relative likelihood of it being applied in a context A as opposed to context B as opposed to context C is claimed to be the same for all speakers. According to this theory, many of the socially significant linguistic choices which speakers make are probabilistic rather than absolute, and, crucially, contingent upon their social identity as expressed by classical sociological indices (educational level, employment, sex, etc.).

A different view is taken by another group of sociolinguists represented by Bickerton (1971, 1973a, b), Bailey (1973), De Camp (1971, 1973) and Anshen (1975). These scholars argue that the primary aim of sociolinguistics should be to draw up ranked 'implicational' scales of the minimally differing grammars (or 'lects') which data analysis indicates exist within any speech community. On this view, speakers are not seen as varying with respect to fixed communal norms, but rather as constantly moving up and down ranked scales of grammars as the demands of context require. Speakers are seen as 'multi-lectal', that is, able to adjust their speech to meet communal criteria of communicative appropriacy through the simultaneous operation of large numbers of implicationally related rules which cut across all linguistic levels, resulting in what is conventionally termed style-switching. While it is true that speakers with a certain social identity, as defined by a Labovian approach, may tend to operate these rules in such a way that they use only a certain limited repertoire of styles (or 'lects'), there is no necessary connection, implicationalists would argue, between social identity as defined by non-linguistic indices, and the range of lects which a speaker makes use of. What is important, on their view, is to uncover all the permissible lects used in a given community (the 'pan-lectal grammar'), rather than to attempt to link variability to specific non-linguistic factors to which it may be only indirectly related. Nor is any special significance given to the quantification of variation: speakers are conceived of as either applying a rule categorically, never applying it, or applying it optionally. The difference between one lect and another may simply be that a categorical rule in lect A is optional in lect B; in a third lect C this rule may not operate at all, and some other rule, categorical in both A and B, may be optional.

Recent work, notably that of Milroy (1980) and Milroy and Margrain (1980) has provided a much more sophisticated means of relating linguistic repertoire to social identity through the concept of 'social network', that is, the nature and density of the social relationships which an individual contracts with other individuals inside and outside his/her community. Using the notion of differences in social network types, it has been possible to explain why some speakers, who according to standard sociological criteria, belong to the 'same' community or group, differ markedly from each other in the use they make of particular linguistic variables (or, put another way, why they make use of different parts of the 'pan-lectal grammar' of their community).

Issues in the methodology of sociolinguistic research, and the debate about what kinds of formalism provide the most descriptively and explanatorily adequate model for capturing the patterns of variation in linguistic form provide the backdrop to the present work, though not, I hope, in such a way that it becomes unintelligible to the Arabic dialectologist with no background in these subjects. My prime aim in writing this book is to elucidate the motivations and mechanisms of dialectal change in an Arab state undergoing rapid social and technological change. This aim can be achieved, I hope, without engaging in a lengthy weighing of the pros and cons of rival theories which might prove a hindrance rather than a help in understanding the mechanism of variation and change. At certain points, issues of a general nature, which I believe my data throw light on, are taken up, e.g. the legitimacy of positing historically attested phonological forms as underlying synchronic variation, and the lexical diffusion theory of phonological change. However, the Arabic dialectologist who has no interest in these issues is under no obligation to read those sections of the book.

A number of the phonological and morphophonological variables dealt with in Chapters 4 - 7 have been the subject of recent papers published in _Zeitschrift für arabische Linguistik_, _Language in Society_, _International Journal of the Sociology of Language_, _Anthropological Linguistics_ and _Transactions of the Philological Society_.

Acknowledgements

I owe an enormous debt of thanks to a great many people both in Baḥrain and in Britain for the help and encouragement they gave me in the preparation of the thesis out of which the present work grew.

Financial help, without which no research would have been possible, was provided by the (then) SSRC in the form of a Research Fellowship covering the period 1976-9. Additional funding was also generously provided by the same source for field-work travel in 1977-8. In Britain, I have to thank Dr. Steve Levinson of C.U. Linguistics Dept. for his valued and perceptive criticism throughout the period of my research, and also express my debt to the late Professor Tom Johnstone who was especially helpful during the initial planning and ground-clearing phase.

In Bahrain, there are far too many people who gave freely of their time for me to be able to thank each individually. In general, I should like to thank the Baḥraini Ministry of Education, and especially its Director of General Education, Dr. Ḥassan al-Mehri, whom I have known as a colleague and friend since I first made my acquaintance with Baḥrain as a teacher of English at Nu'ēm School in 1969-71. Especial thanks go to Graham Ness, Representative of the British Council during my field-work in 1977-8, and to Shawqi Zayāni, who very kindly provided me with a place to stay. I also owe a debt of gratitude to the Baḥrain Ministry of Agriculture's Experimental Research Station at Budayya', whose staff allowed me to accompany them on innumerable visits to farms and villages. All of them were quick to grasp the point of my research and on so many occasions engineered access to language data which it would have been quite impossible for me to get at without their help. In particular, 'Ali Ibrāhīm Hārūn, of Bani-Jamra village was a mine of information on Baḥarna cultural and language attitudes, with an unrivalled personal knowledge of farmers and village communities in Baḥrain. He was a tireless and perceptive critic and helper for the whole period of my field-work. To him, and to 'Isa al-'Arādi of 'Arād village, who spent many hours helping in the transcriptions of miles of often impenetrable taped conversation, go my greatest thanks.

Transcription and transliteration systems

The transcription of spoken Arabic used in this book reflects only those distinctions between Baḥrain's dialects at the phonological level which happen to be significant for its aims. Place names, where they form part of the data for analysis are given in a phonemic transcription of how they are actually pronounced by the people who live in them, rather than in the literary form in which some of them appear when written (e.g. Muḥarrag not Muḥarraq). Within the narrative text, however, proper names are transliterated according to the orientalist custom, (e.g. Al-Manāma), while they are transcribed in a phonemic transcription if they occur as part of an actual spoken text (il-mana:ma). Where there are differences in the way a word is pronounced (e.g. 'Arab /ga:l/, village Baḥārna /ḳa:l/, the text always indicates unambiguously which group uses which variant.

The phonemic transcription is not that of IPA but a system which can be handled by a normal typewriter keyboard with the addition of super- and sub-scripts. In the rare cases where a narrow transcription is needed, standard IPA symbols are used. Special symbols used in the Arabic transcription are:

CONSONANTS

ṯ	voiceless interdental fricative
ḏ	voiced interdental fricative
š̱	voiceless palato-alveolar fricative
j	voiced palato-alveolar fricative
x	voiceless uvular fricative
gh	voiced uvular fricative
q	voiced or voiceless uvular plosive
ḥ	voiceless pharyngeal fricative
9	voiced pharyngeal fricative
'	glottal stop (rarely used)
ṭ	voiceless alveolar plosive, pharyngealised
ṣ	voiceless alveolar fricative, pharyngealised
ḍ	voiced alveo-dental plosive, pharyngealised

ḏ voiced interdental fricative, pharyngealised
č voiceless palato-alveolar affricate
ḳ voiceless retracted velar plosive

In addition to the above the symbol [G] is used where a voiced variety of /q/ needs to be distinguished, and the symbols [ɟ] and [ ] (respectively voiced and voiceless palatal affricates) are used in the description of the speech of some Baḥārna speakers from the village of 'Āli (see Chapter 5).

VOWELS

The main object of this study is to examine the conditions under which variation in consonantal segments and syllable structure patterns are retained or replaced synchronically. Although historical processes such as the affrication of velar stops and the resyllabication of certain nominal and verbal forms both arose as a result of the vocalic environment and changes which occurred in it (see e.g. Johnstone 1965, 1967 passim), there are no grounds whatever for supposing that such processes are still synchronically operative. All the evidence points in the opposite direction: that these are 'dead' processes. For example, while synchronic /č/ arose in very many lexical items as a result of a historical k→č change in which /k/ was in contiguity with a high, front vowel, its present-day susceptibility to vary with /k/ has nothing to do with phonetic environment, to judge from the data: susceptibility to variation is rather a question of the 'lexical status' (Chapter 5) of the word in which /k/∼/č/ occurs. Similarly, variation in the 'Arab dialect between pairs of syllable structure variants like /drisat/∼/dirsat/ 'she studied' and /aktibah/∼/a:kitbah/ 'I write' is explainable by reference to morpho-syntactic factors which seem to be causing a synchronic redistribution of available dialect syllable types to form classes. The point is that this synchronic process has nothing to do with the historical process which caused the rival form-types to arise.

For the reasons given above (viz. that this is not a diachronic study, although some brief comments are to be found in Chapter 4), no detailed attention needs to be paid to vowel quality. The system of transcription employed in the text distinguishes three short vowels /i/, /a/, /u/, and five long ones /i:/, /a:/, /u:/, /e:/ and /o:/. /ə/ indicates reduced unstressed vowels.

Readers interested in a more detailed account of vowel quality differences between the Baḥraini dialects which are ignored by the transcription system used here are referred to the literature (e.g. Al-Tajir 1982; Holes 1983a, 1983b).

1 Variation in spoken Arabic

This chapter is a brief review of work in descriptive Arabic dialectology relevant to a sociolinguistic study of Bahraini Arabic, and of studies whose aim has been to describe how speakers of Arabic, of whatever provenance, shift between different styles as the topic and social context of conversation change. Both of these types of study are germane to this work, which attempts to describe and explain the process of variation and change in one particular Arab society. My object in reviewing these works is not so much to criticise their findings, but rather to examine the data collection principles on which they are based and the descriptive procedures used to present results.

1.1 The traditional dialectological approach

If one thing has been learnt from the intense work in sociolinguistics over the last twenty or so years, it is that data collection techniques - what is collected, how it is collected, who it is collected from and who collects it - deserve the greatest attention if an accurate description (let alone explanation) of the vernacular speech forms used by any social group is to be made. The type of data collected, the physical and social contexts surrounding collection, and the identity of the researcher (native/non-native) and the choice of subjects - all of these will have a direct bearing on what kind of language data is produced. Arabic-speaking speech communities are no different in this respect from any others. The researcher needs to be aware, through long-term participant observation in the community under study, of the linguistic effects which the factors mentioned above can have, if he is to build them into his research design and ultimately be able to explain the large amount of at first sight unmotivated variation in the spoken Arabic of his subjects, whether considered as individuals or groups.

The problems which arise from a failure to take adequate account of immediate context variables on the one hand, and the social structure of the community and the individual speaker's place in it, on the other, affect traditional dialectological approaches to the study of spoken Arabic as much as they can more linguistically orientated ones. Some specific problems are highlighted below.

First of all, there is the question of what Ingham (1982:32) has referred to as the 'multivalency' of dialectal features. It has been observed (e.g. in Johnstone 1963, 1965, 1967; Al-Tajir 1982) that dyadic variables such as k/č, j/y, and even triadic ones such as q/g/j occur widely throughout the Gulf. The traditional dialectological approach has been to record such variation without any attempt at an explanation either of what social values the use of one or other variant has in any particular Gulf community, or at considering whether j/y variation in one country (say Kuwait) follows the same principles, and has a similar social or contextual significance to what it has in another (say Baḥrain). In the absence of any research methodology aimed at discovering which type of speaker says what, to whom, when (and ultimately why), the dialectologist is reduced to simply listing the forms which happened to show up in his data, and describing the least standard forms as 'typical of the dialect' (e.g. y<OA/j/) and the corresponding variant form (/j/<OA /j/) as betraying the influence of 'other dialects' or MSA. While it may be true that variation of the k/č or j/y type arose historically through the operation of the same phonological processes in all of the present day Gulf states, it is also true that the phonological conditioning on these processes differed from one area to another, and more importantly, that the present-day *social significances* of the use of the resultant forms (and hence their susceptibility to variation and ultimate replacement) differ considerably from Gulf state to Gulf state both because of differences in the distribution of 'the same' non-standard forms among high and low prestige social groups from one country to another and because of differences in the degree to which non-local forms of Arabic may have affected these countries' populations (through the relative availability of modern education and television, for example). Thus, in Kuwait, the 'normal' dialectal reflex of MSA *jīm* for most native Kuwaitis in most circumstances is now an alveolar affricate /j/. The palatal glide /y/ may be frowned upon as 'uneducated' even though it is extensively used when Kuwaitis talk to each other. Thus for a Kuwaiti, /y/ signifies simply an uneducated or informal mode of speech. But in Baḥrain, while /y/ is certainly regarded by all speakers as 'non-standard', it is also basically a local marker of Sunni as opposed to Baḥārna (=local Shi'i) speech, which has 'standard-like' /j/ where the Sunnis have /y/. It is very noticeable that /y/ is retained by even highly educated Baḥraini Sunnis in all but their most classicized spoken styles, despite the pressure of MSA /j/. The explanation seems to be that a switch by a Sunni to /j/ could only be interpreted in the Baḥraini context as a *cross-dialectal* switch to Baḥārna speech norms (Holes 1980, 1983b). This, as an observer of the Baḥrain social scene would confirm, is a most unlikely event: where it does occur, it is in joking imitation of the Baḥārna

dialect. Thus it will be appreciated that j/y variation is the 'same' phenomenon in Kuwait and Baḥrain only in the sense that some of the population of the territories which these two modern states occupy were once affected by a historical j→y change; but subsequent population movements and social developments have resulted in variation between /j/ and /y/ acquiring different social meanings.

A second problem with traditional Arabic dialectology is the assumption that the 'most dialectal' forms are to be found amongst the oldest and least educated members of a community, and indeed, the assumption that there is a stable set of 'basic' forms shared by them. This has been shown to be fallacious by many recent studies in other languages. No speaker in any community in which in-depth sociolinguistic research has been done (e.g. Labov 1966 (New York City English), 1972 (Black American English); Trudgill 1974 (Norwich English); Bickerton 1973a (Montreal French); Jahangiri & Hudson 1982 (Tehrani Persian); Russell 1982 (Swahili)) has been shown to be 'single-style'. Whilst it is true that speakers may differ in the extent to which their speech changes as a concomitant of changes in some aspect of speech context, and that they may differ somewhat in the features they change, the major finding is that all speakers in all communities display some degree of variability (Hymes 1967:9). Even the oldest, most uneducated informant, it seems, has a repertoire of variant forms none of which can be considered more basic to him (whatever their historical status) than any other. All speakers, in short, appear to be 'multi-lectal' (to borrow a term from creolist linguists). If then, multi-lectal grammars are to be accurately described, data will need to be gathered in a variety of contexts which are different from each other, or in a single context in which there is a change in contextual factors.

A forthcoming study by Holes (1987) shows how, in the speech of a group of non-literates, pronominal enclitic forms show regular patterns of co-variation with changes in communicative intent, even in the space of a single ten-minute conversation. Such variation appears unmotivated and inexplicable if communicative intent is disregarded, just as, in the example quoted earlier, /j/ and /y/ variation in Baḥraini can only be described and explained properly if the social values associated with each variant are understood. Some old and uneducated speakers may, because of their age and isolation from or imperviousness to modern influences, preserve 'old-fashioned' forms of speech, but this preservation is likely to be partial and to differ in extent from speaker to speaker. Older and illiterate speakers, just like any others, are part of the speech community and more or less receptive to the changes occurring in it. They do not necessarily form a linguistically homogeneous group.

The purpose of these remarks, let me make it clear, is not to cast aspersions on the value of traditional dialectology as a separate and autonomous branch of linguistics, with its own tried and trusted methodology. Its chief advantage (e.g. Cantineau 1936, 1937, Johnstone 1967 for the Gulf and contiguous regions) is that it can provide a description of the characteristics of the dialects over a very large geographical area, which is useful in two main respects: the historical links of the dialects to Classical Arabic can then be investigated, and the typological links to neighbouring or more distant dialects (e.g. the sedentary/nomadic distinction)may be illuminated and may ultimately provide evidence for a demographic history of the area under study. But it is precisely because of its inevitably static, historical orientation to language study that traditional dialectology is methodologically ill-equipped to describe the linguistic variation and change which are the concomitants of present day social change, in anything more than an anecdotal manner.

The sociolinguist Dittmar claims that a major task for any theory of human language is to explain:

(a) how speech realisations are <u>evaluated</u> (privileged versus stigmatised status of speech forms);

(b) how languages <u>change</u> on the basis of such evaluations (revaluation versus devaluation of standard languages, dialects, speech behaviour of minority groups);

(c) to what extent language systems coexistent in the same community <u>interfere with one another</u> on the phonological, syntactic and semantic levels;

(d) how languages are <u>acquired</u>, <u>conserved</u> and <u>modified</u> on these levels;

(e) on the basis of what relationships language systems <u>coexist</u> and come into social conflict.
(Dittmar 1976: 104-5)

Aims such as these are not on the agenda of traditional Arabic dialectology, but clearly need to be addressed if any sense is to be made of the mass of co-existing and varying forms which characterise any extended piece of Arabic conversation. Dittmar's concern is clearly <u>explanatory</u> rather than <u>descriptive</u>: he is arguing that we need to get at the mechanisms which underlie observed behaviour, rather than merely describe and classify what we observe on particular occasions. But if we now turn to work done on spoken Arabic which is outside the traditional dialectological paradigm, we find very few studies which have gone beyond taxonomy and attempted explanation. The reasons, it seems to me, have again to do with research design, data collection methods and the lack of suitable frameworks for the description of both context and linguistic variation.

1.2 Studies of interdialectal conversation and the stylistic continuum

Blanc's (1960) study of interdialectal conversation was the first attempt to grapple with the problem of describing what speakers of Arabic whose native dialects are different do when they talk in order to ensure that they understand each other. On the basis of his data, which was a twenty-minute tape-recording of four Arab students at a U.S. university talking to each other on a pre-set topic, Blanc proposed a spectrum of stylistic formality ranging from 'plain colloquial' at the most dialectal end, through 'Koineized colloquial' to 'semi-literary' to 'modified classical' to 'standard classical' at the opposite extreme. Blanc's data showed that, while the dialects at their most local diverge markedly from each other, the need to communicate clearly in an inter-dialectal situation leads speakers to suppress localisms in favour of more widely understood terms (not necessarily those of the interlocutors' dialect(s)). Speakers are depicted as moving up and down this stylistic spectrum as the demands of the situation change.

There are, however, a number of difficulties with this approach. Blanc's division of the gradient of formality into five blocs seems to have little a priori justification, (c.f. Versteegh 1984:32). As Blanc recognises, no inventory of the variants which belong to each bloc can be given, since some of the variables (e.g. vowel quality) are continuous rather than discrete and where variables are discrete (e.g. phonemic choices like /t̲/ versus /t/, or lexical pairs), the constituent variants cannot be unequivocally assigned to one part or another of the gradient: it is usually a question of a particular variant occurring more or less in one part of the gradient, rather than always or never. Style in spoken Arabic seems to be largely definable not in terms of the absolute presence or absence of particular linguistic features, but by the number of times features actually occur as a proportion of the times they could have occurred. The choice of one rather than another constituent variant of a variable does not, of course, happen in isolation. Spoken style is a set of mutually compatible (or as some sociolinguists would put it, implicationally ranked) choices which cut across all linguistic levels. Blanc, however, does not attempt to show how the choice of one variant might favour or constrain the choice of another. Talmoudi (1984), in a recent replication of Blanc's work, but this time using North African speakers, again steers clear of the problem of describing the linguistic rules which underlie the 'hybrid' forms which are thrown up in cross-dialectal conversation.

Perhaps the most interesting recent work in the description of 'medial' Arabic is that done by the Leeds-based group of the 1970's (e.g. Mitchell 1978; El-Hassan 1978, 1979; Sallam 1979, 1980), and in particular that of Meiseles (1980). Meiseles identifies three types of combinational process in structural mergers between MSA and vernacular elements. Firstly, there is the development of 'symbiotic' forms, in which for example, Egyptians combine dialectal verb prefixes such as /b/ - with MSA in an additive process, e.g.

wa naḥnu *binaqu:l* 'anna
hal *bta9taqidu:n* 'ann

Secondly, there is the *mingling* of dialectal and MSA elements in words which belong to both codes:

MSA	dialectal			
9arafa	9irif	(Cairo)	⟶	9arif
ṭari:q	ṭri:'	(Damascus)	⟶	ṭari:'
kuntu	činit	(Badhdad)	⟶	kinit

Thirdly, there are *hybrid* phrases based on the fact that expressions exist in MSA and the dialects which have the same immediate constituents but different surface realisations, e.g.

MSA		Cairene
laysa huna:ka ḥall ↘	ma huna:k ḥall	↙ ma fiš ḥall
lastu wa:fiqan ↘	ana ma wa:fiq	↙ ana muš wa:fi'

Meiseles considers (1980:132) that such blends are '(at least partially) controlled by a certain regularity. In other words, the blend belongs in part to the level of *langue*'

The examples above are clearly pitched at the standard end of the speech continuum. But there are many kinds of occasion when a more 'dialectal' feel is aimed at for social and communicational reasons. A case in point in Gulf speech communities is the language used on the radio in children's programmes concerned with encouraging road-safety, regular school attendance, etc. The vocabulary in these admonitory pieces is largely standard, but the phonology and, to some extent, the morphology (especially demonstratives and negatives) is, it would appear, deliberately dialectal, in order to give more of a friendly feel to the warning. Here is an example:

/u ha:ḏi ḥdaṯat bilfi91/
'and this in fact happened'

Here the syllable structure of the verb is dialectal, though the verb itself is not (/ṣa:rat/ would be the dialectal equivalent); the demonstrative is morphologically dialectal; and /bilfi91/ is standard. The whole phrase appears to be a dialectalisation of /wa ha:ḏihi ḥadaṯat bilfi91/ through the application of dialectal morpho-phonological rules, where this is possible. Data of this type are interesting in so far as they can tell us a little about the linguistic strategies which speakers employ in just one of a wide range of speech contexts where neither a purely standard, nor purely dialectal variety of Arabic is communicatively appropriate. But to date, to my knowledge, no-one has attempted to collect extensive corpora of data in the variety of contexts within one speech community which would be necessary to build up a complete description of that community's 'rules of use'. In the absence of such a comprehensive description, the behaviour of particular speakers on a particular occasion will remain uninterpretable in many key respects.

To sum up, it seems to me that progress in the description of modern Arabic, whether in areal dialectology or in the description of hybrid varieties, is being hampered by a number of common problems.

Firstly, there is a need to recognise that patterned variability is at the heart of natural speech data, whether at the individual or community level, and requires a dynamic rather than a taxonomic linguistic model to handle it. Martinet reviewing the necessity and utility of the "homogeneity hypothesis" commented over twenty years ago (1963:vii) "There was a time when the progress of research required that each community should be considered linguistically self-contained and homogeneous....By making investigators blind to a large number of actual complexities, it has enabled scholars, from the founding fathers down to the functionalists and structuralists of today, to abstract a number of problems, to present for them solutions perfectly valid in the frame of the hypothesis and generally to achieve...some rigor in a research involving man's psyche....But we shall have to stress the fact that a linguistic community is never homogeneous, and hardly ever self-contained." Weinreich, Labov and Herzog (1968: 101) take this argument a stage further, claiming that the detailed study of the data of large number of speakers leads inevitably to the conclusion that "nativelike command of heterogeneous structures is not a matter of multidialectalism of 'mere' performance, but is part of unilingual competence. One of the corollaries of our approach is that in a language serving a complex (i.e. real) community, it is the absence of structured heterogeneity that would be dysfunctional." Variation in dialectal Arabic in other words, should not be discussed, for example, as 'interference' from the standard, but incorporated into dialectological description, since from the speaker's point of view it is every bit as much a part of his speech behaviour as 'the dialect'.

Secondly, there is a need to recognise and control the effect of contextual factors in data collection. Much apparent 'variation' is the result of subtle changes in the context of utterance which go undetected. This in turn argues for a much broader data-base in terms of the amount of data collected, the number of speakers from whom it is collected and the range of natural contexts in which it is collected. Data collection methods calculated to sample the range of speech styles, and dynamic models to handle the resultant data have been available in general sociolinguistic literature for some considerable time (e.g. Labov 1963, 1966, 1972; De Camp 1971, 1973; Bickerton 1973 to name only a few) and could easily be adapted to Arabic-speaking communities, whose linguistic homogeneity in terms of the use of self-contained codes (Ferguson 1959) increasingly appears as a convenient but unhelpful fiction.

1.3 The present work

This study is intended as a small step down the road of applying the methods of theoretical sociolinguistics to Arabic-speaking communities which are in a state of rapid social and linguistic change. The primary aim, is not to provide an exhaustive description of the typical features of BA dialects but rather to describe and explain how a selected range of phonological elements and morphophonological patterns are becoming subject to variation and, ultimately, change within the Arabic speaking community of Baḥrain as a whole. In the first instance, the variables were selected because their constituent variants were found to be typical of one self-contained community or another within Baḥrain (that is, they are recognised as communal stereotypes). Susceptibility to change in the Baḥrain context, however, does not turn out to be merely a question of the status of a dialectal variant - whether 'high' or 'low' status socially. Some variants which have traditionally been associated locally with low-status social groups can theoretically, be considered "prestigious" because of their similarity to MSA norms; conversely some dialectal stereotype forms associated with a socially 'high-status' group are obviously non-standard in the sense that they are clearly not MSA-like. The forces of standardisation and local prestige thus sometimes pull in different directions and set up linguistic tensions, particularly in the case of educated, by socially low-status speakers. Such speakers frequently state that their native dialect is more 'correct' (in the sense of more similar to MSA norms) than that of traditionally higher status speakers, but nonetheless show clear indications in their shift towards the dialectal forms associated with this higher status group, and away from the technically 'correct' forms of their own dialect, that local linguistic pressures can be stronger than those of the supradialectal standard. In the case of other variables, as we shall see, the forces of local and supradialectal prestige pull in the same direction. But in either case, it is important to establish exactly what the dialectal stereotypes of each community are, before it is possible to see how these match up with the norms of MSA.

The present study accordingly proceeds along the following lines:

(i) the establishment of the basilectal norms on a number of variables for each community within Bahrain through the analysis of the natural conversation of the oldest illiterate members least exposed to outside influences

(ii) the collection of conversational data from educated speakers from the same communities (in some cases the same families) as in (i)

(iii) the comparison of the data gathered in (i) and (ii) in order to establish the extent to which educated speakers maintain or avoid the norms of their illiterate fellows

(iv) the explanation, in both linguistic and social terms, of why certain variables seem to be more susceptible to variation (and ultimately change) than others.

The main aim of this work is thus to provide a fully worked out example of how data-based sociolinguistic work in an Arab community might be executed. The methodology of data collection could obviously be applied in a much wider context than Baḥrain, which merely serves as an example of an Arab society in transition; similarily, the reader should not be misled into assuming that the peculiar features of Baḥrain's social structure, which at many points in this study are shown to be intimately articulated with the direction of linguistic change, limit the general validity of the analysis presented here. The point is that in all Arab societies, some kind of local pecking-order of dialectal prestige exists, which is overlaid by another linguistic prestige system, that of MSA. I would claim that the points of convergence and conflict between these two systems constitute the motive force behind linguistic variation and change in many Arab societies; and further, that only through a prolonged period of participant observation is it possible to get a clear idea of how these forces work, because it is first necessary to establish accurately the local network of inter-group status relations in any community, the status of variant linguistic forms, and hence the linguistic 'pecking order'.

In short, my purpose in presenting this study is to answer the essential questions posed by sociolinguists about all societies, and listed in Dittmar's summary form on page 4 above, in regard to one Arabic-speaking society. The method of arriving at the answers, rather than the answers themselves, is, I hope of general applicability to a socially-oriented Arabic linguistics.

2 Bahrain: the social and cultural background

2.1 Geographical and historical sketch

The state of Baḥrain, which achieved its formal independence in 1971 on termination of its treaty relationship with the Crown, lies some 10 miles off the eastern coast of Saudi Arabia and approximately 250 miles south-east of the mouth of the Shaṭṭ-al-'Arab. Physically, it consists of more than 30 small islands, all but four of which - Muḥarraq Island, Nabīh Ṣāleḥ, Sitra and the main island itself, Baḥrain - are uninhabited. In 1942, the mile of sea which separates Muḥarraq and Baḥrain Islands was bridged by a causeway, and in 1976 Sitra and Nabīh Ṣāleḥ were also physically linked to the main island. The Baḥrain islands are low and flat: the land rises to a high point of only 400 feet above sea-level. The total surface area is about 552 sq. kilometres, two-thirds of which is waterless uninhabited desert. All of the population lives in the northern third of the main island (or on one of the other islands mentioned above), where there is plentiful fresh water, and where all industrial and agricultural activity is centred.

In 1972, the population was 216, 078, of whom 178,193 were Baḥrain nationals (State of Baḥrain Statistical Abstract: 8). The remainder comprised expatriate workers from the Indian sub-continent, other Arab states and western Europe. Some 130,934 Baḥrainis, or 73.5% of the indigenous population, were living in the three major urban centres. In order of size and importance these are:Manāma, the capital and seat of Government, Muḥarraq the former capital, and Madīnat 'Isa, a new town recently completed and situated 4 miles south-west of Manāma. The remaining 47,259 Baḥrainis were living in more than sixty hamlets scattered over the islands (Nakhleh 1976: 18).

Until the discovery of modest quantities of oil in the mid 1930s, the mainstay of Baḥrain's economy was the pearl trade. Baḥrain was also a thriving entrepôt because of its convenient position on east-west trade routes and its easy marine access.

Cottage industries such as weaving and pottery flourished in the villages, and the abundance of water in northern Baḥrain promoted farming and animal husbandry. Many villages specialised in fishing. Although the discovery of oil did not change the basis of the economy overnight, the decline of the old system accelerated after the Second World War, and the discovery in Japan in the late 1940s of a method for producing cultured pearls cheaply and quickly had a radical effect. By 1969 no one was regularly employed as a pearl-diver. The ex-divers had been almost entirely absorbed by the oil-company as manual labourers. The attractions of a regular wage were also strongly felt by agricultural workers, potters and fishermen to the point where, by the early 60s, the oil company was the single biggest employer in Baḥrain. Recently there has been a certain amount of industrial diversification as the oil stocks have begun to run low, and the new factories employ the unskilled labour which in former times would have been employed in fishing, farming or pearl-diving.

The modern history of Baḥrain began with the invasion of the islands by the Āl-Khalīfa branch of the Bani 'Utūb in about 1783 (Wilson 1954: 245ff). Prior to this, the political history of the islands is obscure. Until the early 16th century Baḥrain was held by Arabs, when it was captured by the Portuguese. In 1622, however, the Persians evicted the Portuguese and held Baḥrain, apart from a short period of 'Omani occupation in 1718, until the Āl-Khalīfa invasion. The Āl-Khalīfa, who are tribally related to the ruling family of Kuwait, the Āl-Sabāḥ, have ruled Baḥrain uninterruptedly ever since.

2.2 Social structure: sect and ethnicity

Baḥrain is an overwhelmingly Muslim state, but the salient feature of its social composition is the division of the native population into two roughly numerically equal religious groups - Sunni (orthodox) Muslims and Shi'i Muslims. Like the other Arab states in the Gulf region, Baḥrain is a Sunni-ruled country, but it is unlike them in that approximately half its population is Shi'i. There are, it is true, Shi'i enclaves in Kuwait, Saudi Arabia and Qatar, but in each of these countries they are small minorities.

A further important division in Baḥraini society cross-cuts that of sectarian affiliation - ethnic origin. Both sects have adherents of Arab and Persian origin living in Baḥrain who are mostly Baḥraini from the point of view of nationality. The Sunnis count among their community both the descendants of the Bedouin invaders of Baḥrain who arrived with the Āl-Khalīfa, known as 'Arab (roughly 'tribal Arabs'), as well as the descendants of settlers from the Persian side of the Gulf known as Ḥwala ('Arabised Persians'). These Ḥwala are originally of Arab stock, town dwellers who migrated to southern Iran over a period of centuries, attracted by the opportunities for commerce. In the

19th century, many of them were driven out of Iran and they returned to settle in their original home, the coastal regions of eastern Arabia. In the Baḥrain of today, the 'Arab and Ḥwala are virtually indistinguishable in speech, dress and customs. As co-religionists, marriage between them is commonplace. One still hears "tribal" Arabs occasionally use the somewhat disparaging term Ḥwala, however, or more politely Bastakiyya (after the town of Bastak in southern Iran where many of them formerly lived). The Ḥwala are dominant in the Baḥrain business community, while most of the major political offices are held by 'Arab - the Āl-Khalīfa and their kinsmen (Rumaiḥi 1976:27).

The Shi'is are similarily split into two ethnic sub-groups, though here the differences between the two are much more evident. The major ethnic group, which is purely Arabic-speaking, refers to itself (and is referred to by other groups) as Baḥārna (sing. Baḥrāni). This term can be roughly translated as "Shi'i Arabic-speaking inhabitants of Baḥrain, or of any neighbouring territories in which their kinsmen live" (Lorimer 1908:208). The terms Baḥārna and 'Arab have no political meaning. They simply denote mutually exclusive social groups. Baḥrainiyyīn, on the other hand, is a neutral political term which refers to anyone carrying a Baḥraini passport, be he of Sunni or Shi'i origin. Although the terms 'Arab and Baḥārna convey no pejorative overtones, and are used by each group to refer to itself and the other, they have come to acquire different sets of associations. The Baḥārna point to the common etymology of Baḥrain and Baḥārna to underpin their claim that they are the "original" inhabitants of Baḥrain whose rights were usurped by the invading 'Arab. The 'Arab, by contrast, associate themselves, by the use of this name, with the complex tribal structure of Arabia proper of which their ancestors formed part. Their culture reflects this in its emphasis on the Bedouin virtues of independence, manliness and self-reliance. The Baḥārna, on the other hand, do not have the tribal traditions of the 'Arab and have always pursued a sedentary, unwarlike way of life (Lorimer 1908: 248).

Though the 'Arab have long since forsaken the Bedouin way of life, they still share the nomad's disdain for certain kinds of work. Many consider it beneath their dignity to earn their living by any form of buying and selling, farming, barbering or tailoring (Sergeant 1968: 487). Such jobs are 'ayb ("disgrace", "shame") and are only performed by the Baḥārna or by non-Baḥrainis. The Baḥārna, especially those from the villages, are aware of this stigma, and in self-defence tend to point to the religious backsliding and moral laxness which they feel many 'Arab are guilty of as a result of their generally greater affluence. They themselves are in general fiercely devout and more socially conservative than the 'Arab (see, e.g. Khuri 1980: 146 on rural Baḥārna attitudes to the education and employment of women).

The other Shi'i group is the Iranian Shi'a, referred to disparagingly by 'Arab and Baḥārna alike as 'Ajam ("Persians"). Despite their common religious convictions, the 'Ajam and Baḥārna do not form a coherent social group in the same sense as the 'Arab and Ḥwala. For one thing many of the 'Ajam are relatively recent arrivals whose first language is Farsi and who speak only very broken Arabic. They are the butt of many jokes because of this. But there is also a group of longer established wealthy businessmen. The economically underprivileged Baḥārna regard this prosperous merchant class of 'Ajam with a good deal of resentment, while the poorer 'Ajam are regarded as rivals for employment in the factories, docks and building trade (Rumaiḥi 1976: 30). From this point on we shall be dealing mainly with the Arabic-speaking 'Arab and the Baḥārna, which are by far the largest social groups in Baḥrain. In this chapter the term Shi'a is used to refer to all Baḥrainis who profess Shi'ism, whether Baḥārna or other origin.

In recent censuses, the sensitivity of the religious and the ethnic issue was reflected by the fact that no enquiries were made into the religious affiliations of the populace. It would almost certainly have shown that the 'Arab are in a minority. The last year for which figures are available is 1941, when there were 46,359 Shi'is and 41,984 Sunnis (Rumaiḥi 1976: 26).

One of the most striking features of Baḥrain society, small as it is, is the extent to which the 'Arab and Baḥārna have segregated themselves geographically (see maps). The 'Arab mainly live concentrated in towns - Muḥarraq town, Ḥidd, East and West Rifāʿ- and in a few large villages - Qalāli, Budayya', Jaw, 'Askar, Zallāg and Jisra. The Baḥārna live in a large number of tiny villages and are in a large majority in Baḥrain's capital, Manāma. While it is true that a small number of Baḥārna live in Muḥarraq town, and a somewhat larger group of 'Arab live in Manāma, the physical separation between the sects is still generally maintained. The 'Arab live in certain quarters, and the Baḥārna in others. Only in Madīnat 'Isa, the new town, do the two groups live mixed together in what appears to have been a deliberate attempt at social engineering.

In recent years, this voluntary segregation has begun to be broken down by the development of a non-sectarian national education system, and modern industry in which 'Arab and Baḥārna work side by side: "the first result of the new system of work was to bring together those sections of the community formerly divided by relgion, namely the Shi'a and the Sunnis. Naturally enough, changes did not occur overnight, and at first workers who were obliged to live near their work used to gather on a village, kinship or sectarian basis....The Sunni elements, descended from semi-tribes,learnt to accept orders from the Shi'a who had previously been regarded as inferior. They also learnt to accept manual work, something which had been regarded as degrading. The change however has been gradual and is still going on. As yet there is no clear-cut class consciousness." (Rumaiḥi 1976: 148)

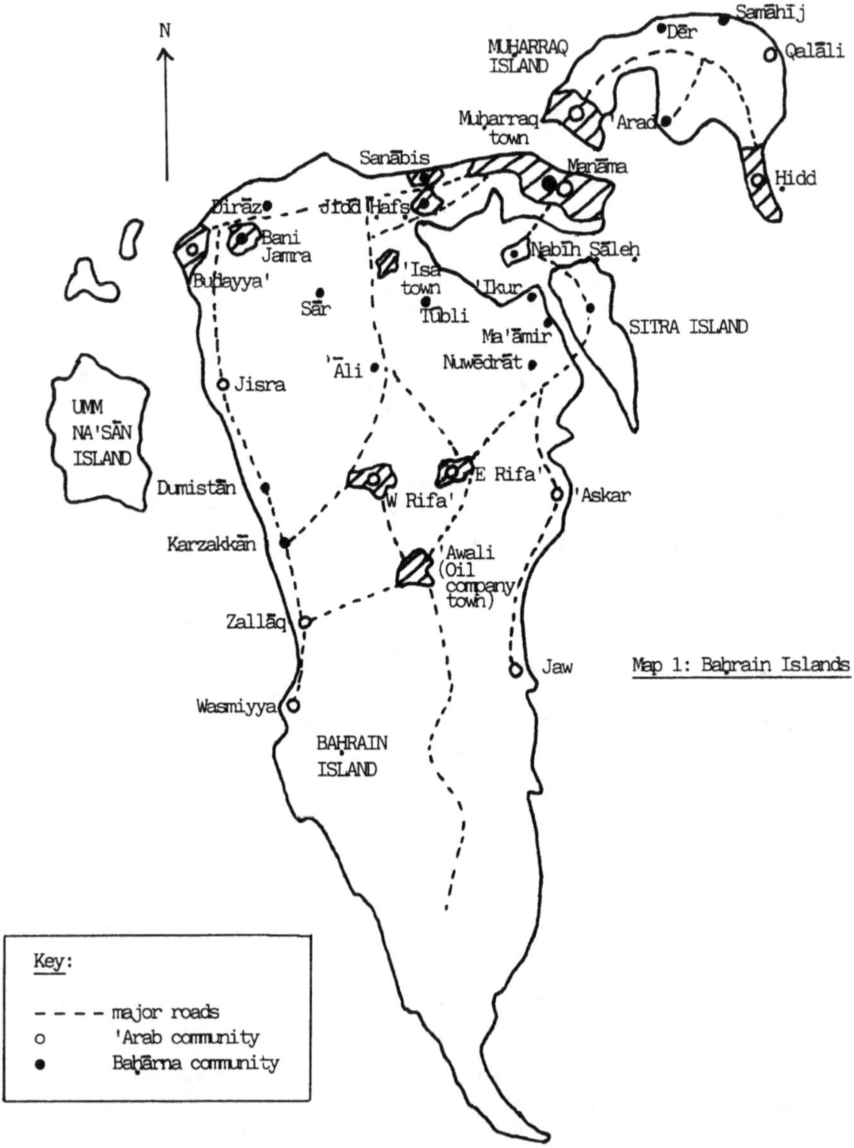

Map 1: Baḥrain Islands

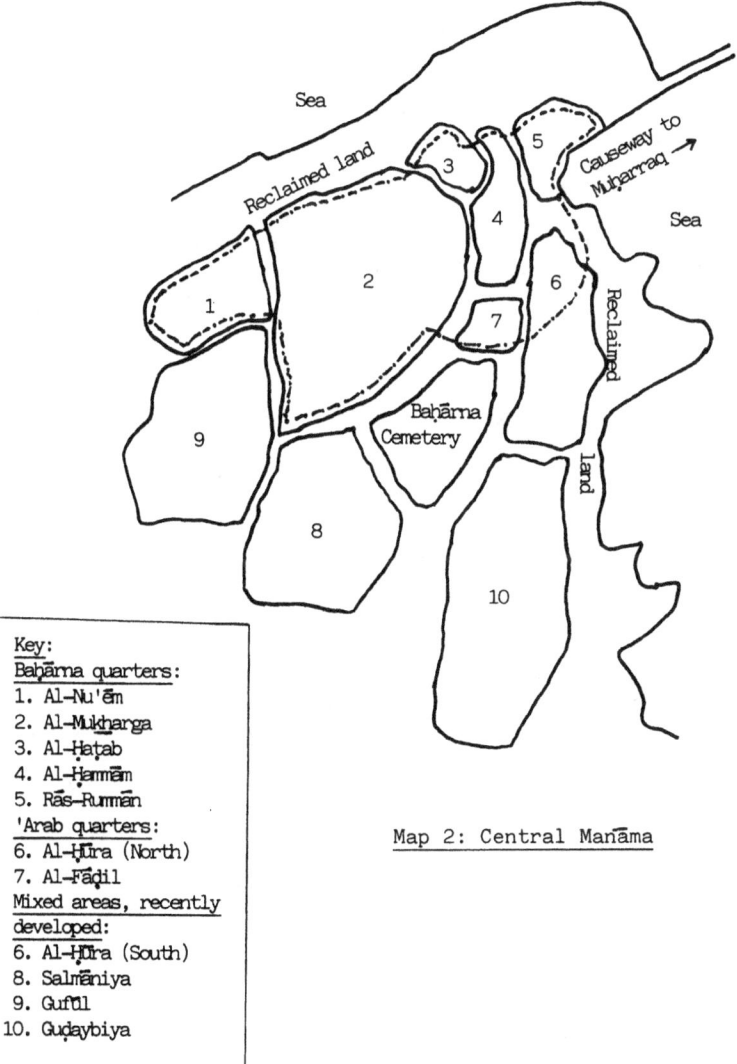

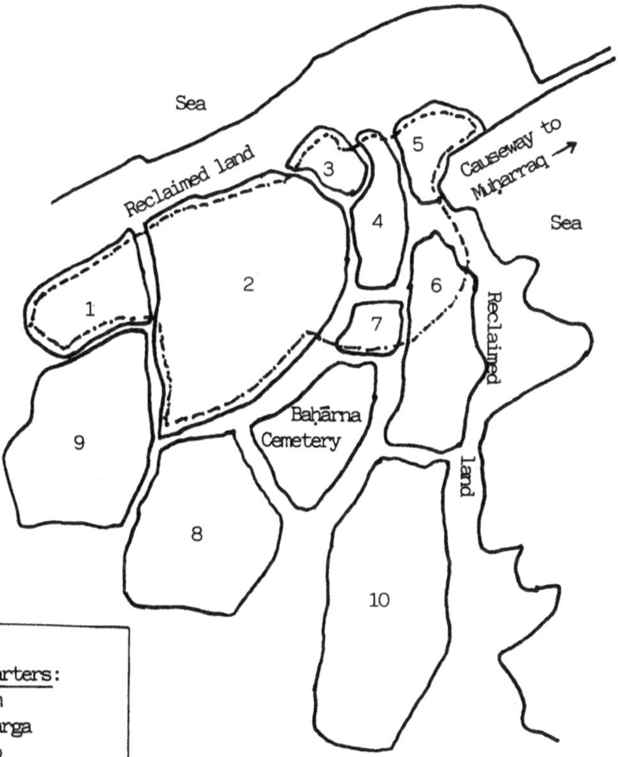

Key:

Baḥārna quarters:
1. Al-Nu'ēm
2. Al-Mukharga
3. Al-Ḥaṭab
4. Al-Ḥammām
5. Rās-Rummān

'Arab quarters:
6. Al-Ḥūra (North)
7. Al-Fāḍil

Mixed areas, recently developed:
6. Al-Ḥūra (South)
8. Salmāniya
9. Gufūl
10. Guḍaybiya

Broken line indicates approximate limit of original town

Map 2: Central Manāma

Marriage between 'Arab and Baḥārna is still rare, even between the better educated, and there is recent evidence to suggest that sectarian loyalties are still the strongest bonds beyond those of the immediate family: voting patterns in the first Baḥraini elections held on 1 December 1972, when analysed by area, showed clearly that Shi'is everywhere cast a bloc vote for the Shi'i candidates (Nakhleh 1976: 154).

Although relations between the two groups are now good, there is still a certain amount of suspicion and distrust between them, and many Baḥārna over the age of forty have vivid memories of Sunni persecution which led to the voluntary evacuation of whole villages to southern Iraq, where similar communities of pastoral Shi'is live. The discord and tension between the two sects have been chronicled in articles by Hakken (1933) and Qubain (1955). During the course of data collection for this research, several older Shi'is gave vivid accounts of the Sunni attack on the Shi'i village of 'Āli in 1923 (Holes 1984) which resulted in the expulsion by the British political advisor of the Sunni Dawāsir tribe from Budayya' to Dammām in mainland Arabia.

2.3 Linguistic consequences of social change

The linguistic consequence of the social segregation of 'Arab and Baḥārna, and the group solidarity of each, has been the preservation over a period of two hundred years, in an area no bigger than a medium-sized English city, of two distinct varieties of Arabic. Clear and consistent differences exist in the phonology, morphology and lexicon of these two varieties. Such sharp communal differentiation, though not unknown elsewhere in the Arab world (c.f. Cadora 1970 on urban/rural dialects in Ramallah) is unusual in having been preserved so clearly. According to Blanc's typology of communal dialect differentiation in Arabic, Baḥrain can be classified as an area of 'major communal differentiation' in that dialect differences "(a) permeate the whole phonology and grammar of the dialect (b) correlate fully with community membership" (Blanc 1964: 12-16). But with the change in Baḥrain's economic system, social forces have been unleashed which have directly affected this simple correlation of sect membership and dialect. Chief among these forces are the greater mixing which has resulted from the development of modern industry; the gradual rehousing of people in 'unsegregated' new towns; and most important of all, the compulsory education of children in state schools which draw from both communities. The rapid spread of radio and television in the last fifteen years has also had a deep effect in making the population more aware of its national identity and in de-emphasising parochialism and sectarianism.

Nonetheless, the social dominance of the 'Arab is linguistically reflected in a number of ways. In all attempts, spoken or written, at representing "typical" or "ordinary" Baḥraini speech, it is 'Arab dialectal forms which are predominantly used. On radio and television, soap-operas, women's programmes and children's hour are all acted or presented in the 'Arab dialect. The same is true of popular literature - stories, poetry and drama which have a local setting are written in an orthography which gives an approximation of 'Arab speech. Newspaper cartoonists put 'Arab speech forms such as/ḥaṣṣale:t/ 'I got' (Shi'i /ḥaṣṣalt/), /wa:yid/ 'a lot' (Shi'i /wa:jid/) into the mouths of "typical" Baḥrainis. And this is despite the fact that something over half of the listeners/readers speak a dialect in many important respects different from this "typical" form of BA.

An aspect of 'Arab linguistic dominance with which this work will be concerned is the non-reciprocal nature of dialectal borrowing. The details of this process will be one of our main focusses, but at this point we draw attention to the significant fact that, where small groups of Baḥārna speakers have, because of historical accident, found themselves surrounded by 'Arab, they have quickly adopted 'Arab speech forms; but where small groups of 'Arab live isolated among Baḥārna, and are known to have done so for decades, there is no evidence to suggest that they have adopted Baḥārna forms. An example of Baḥārna assimilation is in the Muḥarraq quarter of Al-Ḥiyāč, where a group of Baḥārna sail-makers from the west of Baḥrain have settled within the last fifty years. Their dialect is now quite indistinguishable (even to 'Arab) from that of the Muḥarraqi 'Arab who surround them. But the old 'Arab minority living in the Manāma quarters of Al-Fāḍil and Dhawāwida, though they have been conversely surrounded by speakers of a Baḥārna dialect for at least the same length of time, do not show typical Baḥārna features in their speech and cannot normally be distinguished from 'Arab from other parts of Baḥrain.

The major effect of universal schooling has been to create a new and important distinction in Baḥrain between those literate in a non-local form of Arabic, Modern Standard Arabic (henceforth MSA) and those who only speak a dialect of Baḥraini Arabic (BA). Tables 1 and 2 below show the percentage of the population which was illiterate in 1971, by sex and location (Nakhleh 1976: 18).

We shall see from these Tables that a major split in the population comes at age 20 - 24: over the age of 25, no group, whether defined by sex or location, has less than 45% of its members illiterate, and the level of illiteracy rises to 95.6% in the case of females over 45. In terms of the distribution of population, across these age groups, the 10 - 20 age-group accounts for 25% of the total population, while the under 10-group, which will eventually reap the benefit of recently improved educational facilities, accounts for no less than 33% of the total population. If literacy is a potent force for linguistic change in the Arabic-speaking world, it is to be expected that rapid changes will occur in the linguistic situation over the next 10-20 years as Baḥrain changes from a predominantly illiterate to a literate society. Paradoxically, however, (see Ch. 7 below and Holes 1986a) this does not necessarily mean the supplanting of non-literary by literary forms, but rather a re-evaluation and re-structuring of existing dialectal linguistic resources.

Age	Male	Female	Total
10–14	16.7	34.4	25.4
15–19	15.5	38.7	26.5
20–24	31.7	55.8	41.8
25–29	45.7	67.7	55.1
30–34	53.9	76.5	63.2
35–44	63.0	86.6	73.1
45+	77.6	95.6	85.3
Mean:	44.6	63.3	52.9

Table 1: Illiterate population by age-group and sex in Baḥrain

Age	Urban	Rural	Total
10–14	20.9	51.7	25.4
15–19	23.0	49.2	26.5
20–24	39.8	57.1	41.8
25–29	52.4	76.6	55.1
30–34	60.8	83.3	63.2
35–44	70.8	89.6	73.1
45+	84.0	93.7	85.3
Mean:	50.3	70.6	52.9

Table 2: Illiterate population in urban and rural areas of Baḥrain

It is clear from Table 1 that women have a higher rate of illiteracy than men, and from Table 2 that the rural population has a higher rate of illiteracy than the urban. These figures reflect the negative attitudes to the education of women of a partriarchal society and the conservatism of the villages as compared with the towns. Moreover, since the village population is very largely Baḥārna, it is clear that, as a group, village Baḥārna are less literate, and in general less well-educated than the 'Arab and urban Baḥārna. Although attendance at state schools is becoming more acceptable in rural Baḥrain for girls as well as boys, and the school-building programme has been extended to cover outlying villages, it is still unusual for Baḥārna girls to continue their education after the age of puberty. The feeling that modern schooling has a corrupting effect on young people is still common in rural Baḥārna areas. Since 1974, however, the government of Baḥrain has been offering adult evening literacy programmes which have proved popular with the many married women who were forced to leave school early to get married, or who never went to school at all. Attitudes to education are changing slowly, however, and the transition from the inward-looking tradition-bound, non-literate society of the pre-oil era to a literate technocracy is proving to be a more gradual one than in some of Baḥrain's richer neighbours.

An interesting side-light to this study was the attitudes to change expressed by the speakers from whom the data were collected. These data were gathered in nearly two hundred recorded conversations in which recent environmental and social changes in Baḥrain were recurrent themes. The differences in attitude between those who approved or disapproved of the changes correlated closely with the level of education and literacy (and to some extent sect). The young literate of both sects spoke approvingly of what they called the recent tamaddun ("civilisation") of Baḥrain: in particular the new roads, land reclamation and building work, the less strenuous white-collar jobs which their education had qualified them for, and (among the 'Arab) the freer relationships between the sexes. The illiterate speakers, who were on average older, expressed their dislike of the materialistic bent of the younger generation, their religious backsliding and the weakening of family ties. The Baḥārna group was, generally speaking, more outspoken in expressing these latter sentiments than the 'Arab, and the villagers more so than the town-dwellers.

From a sociolinguistic point of view, the dialect differences between 'Arab and Baḥārna, and between sub-groups within the Baḥārna community, were most obvious in the speech of the older illiterates (who tended to be strongest in their condemnation of tamaddun). They had not had consistent exposure to different varieties of Arabic during their formative years and, in fact, the only education most of them had received was at Quranic school under the supervision of religious teachers who in some cases were themselves able to read but not write. The older speakers, especially the women, were also less mobile both physically and socially, and their work was usually conducted in the immediate vicinity of their homes (c.f. Hansen 1967: 175). During the course of this research the writer came across octogenerian women living in villages ten miles distant from Manāma who had never been to the capital during the first sixty years of their lives.

The question of how the acquisition of literacy by most of the younger Baḥrainis has affected their speech - and in particular what effects it may have had, in concert with the greater degree of social mixing and mobility, on sectarian dialect distinctions - is a major object of enquiry of this work. A second focus is to test current theories of variation and change in the light of linguistic variation which this study suggests is being thrown up as an effect of educational and social changes.

3 Data collection methods

The achievement of descriptive accuracy in sociolinguistic studies is constrained by two main factors: the depth of knowledge of the community which the researcher brings to his task (since this provides his prime orientation to the social variables which are likely to be reflected by variation in the language system); and his ability to overcome the practical difficulties involved in obtaining a truly representative sample of natural speech behaviour in an exotic society. In this chapter, I shall briefly review the problems posed by conducting a data-based study in an Arab society, paying particular attention to these two constraints on sociolinguistic field-work.

3.1 Selection of speakers

No sociological survey of Baḥrain exists of the type used by sociolinguists such as Labov (1966: 154-199) in their studies of N American urban communities. It is in any case doubtful whether the ready-made indices of class-membership, developed by Western sociologists, have much relevance to an Arab society such as Baḥrain. Faced with such a society, which has developed until recently along lines quite alien to the industrialised West, the sociolinguist has, *faute de mieux*, to rely on his own experience of the cultural milieu, or on reports such as Rumaiḥi (1976), Nakhleh (1976) to provide the initial framework for field-work. Prior to beginning field work in 1977, I was fortunate in having had the benefit of a two-year working stay in Baḥrain in 1969-71. The knowledge gained during this period informed the early part of data collection, and largely determined the social profiles of the speakers whose speech it initially seemed important to investigate. Only later did analysis of actual data collected from speakers who conformed to these profiles reveal how far the initial assumptions about society-language relationships were correct.

It was assumed at the outset that the social variables listed below - some discrete, some continuous - would be worth examining as potentially related to linguistic variation:

1. socio-sectarian affiliation (Arab/Baḥārna)

2. literacy (literate/illiterate in MSA)

3. sex (male/female)

4. region (town/village)

5. age (old/young)

Baḥrainis anecdotally recognise each of these variables as a major or minor source of linguistic variation: the speech of the old and illiterate is often labelled /hamaji/ ("barbarous"); women have their own speech forms which they use with each other (/ḥači n-niswa:n/ - "women's speech"); village Baḥārna, known somewhat disparagingly as /ḥala:yil/ are caricatured by townsmen because of their "incomprehensible"(/ghalaj/) speech; and pre-eminently, the Baḥārna and 'Arab are acutely aware of the close correlation of sect and dialect.

Some of these variables of course, overlap with each other. For example, owing to the rapid development of education in recent years, age and literacy in both the 'Arab and Baḥārna communities are closely associated (See Tables 1 and 2, Chapter 2). On the other hand, the geographical distinction between town and village, which is associated with a difference between an agriculture-based and a non-agriculture-based means of earning one's living, applies only to the Baḥārna community; the 'Arab of Baḥrain have never engaged in agriculture and the urban/rural distinction is not recognised as an important parameter within their social group.

The linguistic correlates of social differences did not start to become clear until some time after field-work had started. At this point, a decision was made about which factors were to be the main focus of attention. This was a simple decision to make, since it became rapidly clear that factors 1, 2 and 4 of the list above were the prime social variables with which language variation was associated. "Women's speech" did show certain special intonational and lexical characteristics worthy of separate study, and it is probably true that,as a socially isolated group, their speech tended to extremes of "dialectalness" on the variables examined in this study; but there were nothing like the gross and consistent phonological and morphological differences between the sexes that there were between social groups divided along sect, literacy or regional lines.

The sources for the BA speakers who eventually formed the representative sample were as follows:

Literate speakers

(a) British Council students

Some 500 students following English courses at the British Council evening institute were sent a questionnaire asking if in principle they would be willing to participate in a research project into the "dialects of Baḥrain". Each student was asked to give information about his age, sex, date and place of birth, present place of residence, job and level of education. No enquiry was made into the students' sectarian affiliation but this was unnecessary in any case, as it was readily apparent from a combination of place of residence - whether he/she lived in an 'Arab or Baḥārna area - and from his/her given and family names.

Some 455 affirmative replies were received, which proved to be a valuable data-bank, facilitating the selection of a cross-section of literate speakers from all parts of Baḥrain. 25 students were eventually selected for informal interview, the selection covering a variety of educational levels, job-types and ages, roughly equally divided by sex and sect.

The social profiles of those who refused to participate in the research - some 35 students - provided a first insight into the sensitivity of certain parts of the Baḥrain speech community to linguistic investigation. Although the 480 replies received to the questionnaire were roughly equally divided between speakers from 'Arab and Baḥārna areas, all 35 who refused to participate in the research were apparently Baḥārna, 27 of them from villages. This indicated a degree of suspicion about possible "ulterior motives" of the research and hinted at the linguistic insecurity of some Baḥārna, who, as we saw in Chapter 2 have traditionally been more socially conservative, inward-looking and educationally disadvantaged than the 'Arab. As research proceeded, this suggestion of linguistic insecurity became a clear and consistent feature of the Baḥārna "literate" data.

(b) The Teacher Training Colleges

A group of 20 literate speakers, all student teachers at the Government Mens' or Womens' Teacher Training Colleges were also interviewed. The reason for this was partly that there were some areas of Baḥrain which were under-represented by literate speakers in the British Council sample, and that these gaps needed to be filled. But, more importantly, the help of these students was canvassed in interviewing certain categories of non-literate speakers to whom the writer did not have easy access (see below).

Illiterate Speakers

Unlike sex or sect, literacy is a non-discrete, continuous variable. Though the description "fully literate" is accurate when applied to the speakers selected from the British Council evening classes and the Teacher Training Colleges (in the sense that, to be able to perform their daily work, they had to be able to read and write MSA to acceptable standards), it was not always possible to be so certain about the classification of a speaker as "illiterate". In fact, almost all of those eventually classified as such showed some evidence of marginal literacy in a limited range of controlled situations. For example, "illiterate" farm-labourers could read receipts for fertiliser purchased from the Government Agricultural Research Station; "illiterate" housewives could read electricity bills. Some older "illiterates" were capable of "reading" the Qur'an, though this "reading" often seemed to be a rote-learned recitation triggered by certain key words which they had retained from their days at Qur'anic school. They were quite unable to transfer this "reading" ability to a simple newspaper article written in a grammatically identical form of the language (MSA). Marginal reading abilities of the type described here were not considered evidence of functional literacy; in fact the classificatory rule-of-thumb used was whether a speaker had ever attended a modern State school, even to the end of the Primary stage. If he had, he was classified "literate", otherwise, unless there were special circumstances, he was considered "illiterate".

(a) Farm workers

A large proportion of the Baḥārna male village population is still employed on the land as allotment owners, tenants or day-labourers. Because of the suspicion and conservative traditions of the Baḥārna villagers (Hansen (1967) passim), it was thought that obtaining a representative sample of their natural speech might prove a considerable difficulty; the Muslim taboos on photography and sound-recording are still strong in their communities.

In the event, the problem was overcome with the help of the Government Agricultural Research Station, an organisation with which the farmers have frequent contact. Over four months, I was allowed to accompany one of the Station's muršidīn ("advisers") on his rounds, helping in the delivery of fertiliser, seedlings, cement, etc., to virtually every village in Baḥrain. Since the adviser was well-known to the farmers, and respected as a successful ex-farmer and pillar of the Baḥārna community, ease of access to these villages was assured. At the time of my field work, a research project on the profitability of allotment farming was being run by the Station, and I was given the job of recording the farmers' replies to various questions put by the muršid and doing various calculations which gave an extra air of authenticity to the muršid's explanation that I was working as an expert at the Station. The farm visits were in fact as much social as business calls and always involved extended conversation over coffee and dates in the farmers' huts, or visits to their nearby houses. The small cassette recorder which was left running during these conversations was rarely noticed among the other paraphernalia of the Western "expert": calculator, notebooks, pens, pencils, etc. In this way some 70 farmers from almost every village in Baḥrain were recorded in extended natural conversation in their place of work or at home.

(b) Students at literacy centres

At the time field-work was in progress, the Baḥraini Education Department was running an extensive illiteracy-eradication programme. This had proved particularly popular with village women, a selection of the population to which the writer, as a male European non-Muslim would have had no access in normal circumstances. There was no question of the writer himself interviewing the women in these Centres, but the teaching staff were trained to do this by proxy. In this way, illiterate females from a dozen small rural communities were recorded.

(c) Literate speakers' illiterate relatives

The 20 literate speakers from the Teacher Training Colleges whom I interviewed were asked to conduct similar interviews with illiterate family relatives - usually aunts/uncles or grandfathers/grandmothers. The stipulation was that the interviewee should be at least one generation removed from the interviewer and illiterate in terms of the definition above. With these interviews, an adequate coverage of all communities in Baḥrain, in terms of the five parameters listed, was completed.

3.2 Interview methods

The literate speakers were interviewed individually by me, with a tape-recorder in view, for about half-an-hour each. These interviews normally took place in a classroom or office set aside for the purpose with only the writer and the interviewee present. A set pattern was followed in each case: each speaker was asked for his/her opinion on the old versus the new way of life in Baḥrain, marriage customs old and new, religious festivals, work, personal interests and interesting or dangerous personal experiences. At the end of each interview, by which time he/she had usually become quite relaxed, the speaker was asked if he knew any typically Baḥraini jokes or traditional stories which he/she could relate.

As far as possible, the same topics were covered with the illiterate speakers interviewed by the teachers in the Literacy Centres, and by the Teacher Training College students who interviewed relatives or neighbours. Each interview was a one-to-one between interviewer and interviewee lasting about half-an-hour.

Although both the literate and illiterate interviewees were told at the outset that the research was concerned with the "Baḥrain dialects", they were encouraged to think that the main object of the interview was to find out about old Baḥraini customs and about their opinion on recent changes in Baḥrain society. Their attention was never directed towards linguistic forms _per se_, though many speakers made unsolicited comments which provided useful insights into commonly-held language attitudes.

The data from the farming communities were collected in a rather different way. The muršid whom I accompanied was fully briefed on the real point of the research and was able, in the most unobtrusive way, to direct conversation towards the same set of topics which were discussed in the interviews. Sometimes, for the sake of plausibility, the writer was introduced as not only an agricultural "expert" but also an Arabist curious about local customs. By and large, however, I contributed little to the farm conversations beyond formal greetings and leave-takings.

The literate Baḥārna speakers were noticeably less relaxed and forthcoming in interviews than were the literate 'Arab. This manifested itself in their unwillingness to voice opinions on topics of the moment, their pleading ignorance of customs they must have known about and their reluctance to discuss religious or associated "sensitive" matters. Many seemed hesitant in their delivery, measuring their words in a way that the fluent, uninhibited 'Arab did not. The illiterate Baḥārna, by contrast, like the illiterate 'Arab, answered all questions with a bluntness which belied no insecurity about their status.

3.3 Comparability of data between groups of speakers

The speech-style of the literate speakers was probably influenced to some degree by a number of special factors: the fact that a tape-recorder was visibly in operation, that the interlocutor, though a fluent BA speaker, was obviously a foreigner, and the fact that the question-and-answer routine of an interview bore little resemblance to natural conversation. The interview in any Arabic-speaking society is a context where the influence of MSA might always be expected to be felt; in Blanc's (1960) terminology, we would expect to find evidence of both "levelling" and "classicizing" stylistic tendencies. While these expectations were to some degree fulfilled - especially in the choice of lexical items - the Arabic used by the literate speakers was nonetheless unquestionably Baḥraini in its major phonological and morphological characteristics.

The drawbacks (if such they are) of artificially controlling the physical context and topic of recorded conversation are compensated for by increased inter-speaker data comparability and clarity of recording. All speakers perform in more-or-less identical circumstances, and this makes comparison between them easier; we can be reasonably certain that we are comparing one speaker's "formal" style with that of another. The differences noted - especially if a consistent pattern of co-variation with social factors such as sex, sectarian affiliation or regional provenance emerges - can provide insights into the status of dialectal forms which may be variably replaced by "standard" or other borrowed dialectal forms, or completely zeroed out.

This approach, of course, presupposes that it is possible to identify what the dialectal "norms" for each Baḥraini community are. I do not mean to imply by the use of this term that there are speakers in any community who set, as it were, standards of dialectal purity from which literate speakers deviate. All speakers, as Labov has convincingly shown, have a range of styles, which cover different parts of the spectrum of variation possible in their community. What I wish to show is how wide or narrow the gap is between the speakers least exposed to outside influence in the form of education, contact with other dialects, etc. and the speakers most exposed to it: that is, how homogeneous the speech of members of one community (e.g. "village Baḥārna", "urban Baḥārna", 'Arab) is compared to another; how far educated speakers have "moved away" from the speech forms of still extant illiterates living in the same community, and on what linguistic variables dialect replacement is more or less pronounced. To answer these questions we need to establish "dialectal baselines" for each community - a concept similar to the "basilect" of Creole studies. We define the "baseline" for each community as that set of variant forms, on a number of commonly occurring variables, which native Baḥrainis regard as the "stereotype" of the dialect of that community. Surreptitious recording of older illiterate speakers in a number of representative localities verified that adherence to the "baseline" set of variants could be remarkable consistent - 100% in many cases on all 20 variables examined in this study.

The speech sample for illiterate speakers was gathered in altogether more "naturalistic" circumstances. There was clearly a practical purpose to the farm visits, and, although the literacy-centre teachers and the trainees at the Teacher Training Colleges conducted interviews rather than recorded natural conversation, the fact that they were all Baḥrainis well known to their interlocutors, or even close relatives of them, was almost certainly reflected in a more "informal" style of speech. Just as literate speakers were likely to have adopted a "formal" style precisely because of the circumstances in which recording took place, so the illiterates were likely to have adopted a correspondingly "informal" style for the same reasons.

The effect of the inevitably different methods of data collection employed with literate and non-literate speakers was probably to exaggerate linguistic differences between them; if it had been possible to record speakers from the same areas, in the same circumstances, matched on other social factors, but differing only on the literacy variable, the results of our investigation would probably have indicated less strikingly divergent behaviour. Put another way, in the terminology of implicational analysis, I probably sampled lects at either end of a scale of pan-lectal grammars which would accommodate all BA lects: "literate speakers speaking formally" at one end of the scale, and "illiterates speaking informally" at the other. Nonetheless, a good deal of variation was revealed within each group on a variety of phonological and morphological variables, and I would contend that the practical constraints on data collection in no way invalidate the description and conclusion about how variation in BA works. It is obvious that no study can hope to provide a complete description of synchronic variation in any speech community; the presumption which the investigator makes is that the general principles according to which it operates will be immanent in any sufficiently large and varied corpus of data recorded in that community; it makes little difference therefore, which parts of a community's pan-lectal grammar are subjected to analysis, since the forces for variation and change which produce it are community-wide, though perhaps more strongly pronounced in some parts of the community, in some speech styles, than in others.

3.4 Intra-speaker variability: contextual styles

The methods by which Labov induced his subjects apparently to vary their speech-style in the interview situation (Labov 1972b: 70–109) have been criticised by Gal (1979: 92–5) as based on too simple a view of the psycho-social forces which trigger style-switching. Whatever the merits of that argument, it is clear that there are other severe drawbacks to Labov's methods if applied to an Arabic-speaking society. Various kinds of reading tests were used by Labov to get at the "formal" end of speakers' phonological repertoires. But, as already noted, there is a clear distinction drawn in all Arabic-speaking societies between the vernacular, in its varying forms, and MSA. Only the latter has a written form – there is no standard way of rendering many of the dialectal equivalents of MSA forms. The focus of this study is in fact on precisely how and in what conditions dialectal phonological and morphological forms come to be replaced by standard equivalents; the construction of reading tests aimed at sampling more "formal" styles of spoken Arabic would inevitably involve the test-constructor in pre-empting the speaker's choice between such alternative forms, even if the speaker could accept the artificiality of the test. For example, there is no equivocal way of writing the Arabic word for "how much" which would not condition the speaker's choice: either /kam/= كم or (BA) /čam/ (sometimes written چم to indicate colloquial speech in newspaper cartoons, etc.) must be written, and no "neutral" form, which leaves the choice of pronounciation to the speaker, is possible. The way variation between phones such as k and č works must be investigated through the analysis of more naturally produced speech-data since performance variation in a reading test is pre-empted by the facts of Arabic orthography and the expectations which the literate speaker brings to the task. A further practical constraint on this kind of experimental technique is that a large proportion of the population in all Arab countries (and Baḥrain is no exception as we have seen from Tables 1 and 2 in Ch.2) is illiterate.

Because of the relatively loosely controlled method of data collection - the farm interviews in particular could be very discursive and even in the "literate" interviews conducted by the writer not all topics were discussed with all speakers - each interview was treated for analytical purposes as "single-style" and not broken down into separate episodes such as "personal experiences of danger", "jokes", etc. The literate data was certainly affected by the context of the recording and its effects may have been uneven across groups and within each interview. Most 'Arab literates, though curious and helpful at the start of the interview, tended to use a somewhat classicized lexicon until they realised that the writer could talk to them in their own dialect. From that point on, usually about one to two minutes into the interview, they tended to slip into a gradually more uninhibited and dialectal speech style. The literate Baḥārna as already noted, maintained a classicized style throughout, only intermittently letting the mask slip to allow "Baḥārna" dialectal forms through, and showing some interesting cross-dialectal borrowing which was almost certainly triggered by a desire to present themselves as "speaking like 'Arab". This in itself was an interesting spin-off of the mode of data-collection: it probably simulated real situations in which Baḥārna feel on the defensive. 'Arab frequently commented that, for example, Baḥārna from Muḥarraq island villages tried to imitate 'Arab speech when shopping in the predominantly 'Arab-run and 'Arab-frequented markets of Muḥarraq town. The reverse process - 'Arab cross-dialectal borrowing of Baḥārna forms - was not recorded, and nor did Baḥrainis claim it ever occurred.

3.5 Presentation of the analysis of variation

The data bank built up from the programme of field-work we have described consisted of cassette recordings of conversations of interviews with 180 native speakers of BA, divided roughly equally into blocks by sect, sex and literacy, who came from almost every named locality in Baḥrain, and who ranged in age from 13 to 70. The bulk of this data (approx. 350,000 words) was eventually transcribed, much of it with the assistance of native speakers of BA, before my departure from Baḥrain.

From this initial corpus, some 87 speakers were eventually selected as representative of common combinations of social variables in the community (Table 3 below) e.g.:

male 'Arab literate
male 'Arab illiterate
female Baḥārna illiterate town-dweller
female Baḥārna illiterate villager

and so on.

Recording clarity inevitably played a part in the selection of speakers for the final sample: in the conditions in which some of the recording was done (particularly in the Literacy Centres and by the Teacher Training College students) external noise, interruptions, poor acoustics and defective equipment reduced the value of a proportion of the data and excluded it from further consideration.

The 87 speakers can be broken down as follows:

Sect/ Region	Male		Female		Total N
	Literate	Illiterate	Literate	Illiterate	
'Arab	10	7	7	10	34
Baḥārna (town)	6	6	3	4	19
Baḥārna (village)	8	7	8	11	34
Total N	24	20	18	25	87

Table 3: Speaker sample analysed by sect, region, literacy, sex.

The sect/regional distinctions of Table 3 coincided closely but not exactly with many major linguistic distinctions. However, on the basis of the distribution of certain phonemic elements, we shall see that an important sub-dialect, spoken only in a few Baḥārna villages, needed to be distinguished from the main village dialect; similarly, an urban sub-dialect was discovered which could be distinguished from the major Baḥārna town dialect both phonemically and morphophonemically. Analysis of the data of literate speakers from these particular areas threw new light on the general question of the relative status of "sectarian" varieties of BA.

The data analysis presented in the following chapters covers only a small but an important part of the BA language system. Two major groups of variables are dealt with - "phonemic" and "morphophonemic". Phonemic variables apparently involve a choice in the surface phonetic form of lexical items; morphophonemic variables, on the face of it, involve the operation of alternative sets of phonological rules on shared underlying morphological skeletons. In both cases, our aim is to show how variability is linguistically conditioned and socially motivated.

For maximum clarity of exposition, the data-analysis chapters which deal with each type of variable (Chapters 5 and 7) are preceded by background chapters (Chapters 4 and 6). These background chapters describe the "dialectal baselines" or "stereotypes" for each community which were established in the manner described above and compare them with the norms of MSA.

4 The social distribution of some BA phonemes

4.1 The linguistic background

Before 1980, studies of Baḥraini Arabic treated it within an areal dialectal context. Johnstone's (1963) and (1965) articles, for instance, focussed respectively on two phonological changes which have affected a large group of Eastern Arabian dialects – the backing of the alveolar affricate /j/ to a palatal frictionless continuant /y/ and the fronting and affriction of the velar stops /g/ and /k/ to alveolar affricates /j/ and /č/. His lengthier (1967) study provided the first thorough description of the phonology and morphology of the Gulf dialects as a whole. Given the practical difficulties which still hinder the collection of data in socially conservative Muslim countries (and Johnstone's data was collected in the late 50s) it is not surprising to find that Johnstone's treatment of individual country dialects within this group is incomplete. In the Baḥraini case, many of the features attributed to all Eastern Arabian dialects (1967: 1-17) do not in fact apply to the Baḥārna dialects. More recent studies (Prochazka 1981: Al-Tajir 1982; Holes 1981, 1983a) have filled in many of the gaps and provided a much fuller contrastive treatment of BA dialects. In broad typological terms, the 'Arab dialects of Baḥrain follow the classic 'nomadic' pattern in key points of phonology and morphology, whereas the Baḥārna dialects share many features with long-established non-nomadic coastal populations (Holes 1983a: 35-7). The following are, perhaps, the most obvious 'nomadic' ('Arab) versus 'semi-sedentary' (Baḥārna) contrasting features:

OA		'Arab dialect	Baḥārna dialects
1. q	→	g (voiced)	ḳ (voiceless)
2. ṯ ḏ ḏ̣	→	preserved	f d ḍ
3. non final CaG (G = guttural)	→	CGa (e.g. ghawa)	CaG (e.g. ḳahwa)
4. CvCvCvC		CCvCvC (e.g. šrubat, wlidah)	CaCaCaC/CiCCaC (e.g. šarabat or

OA	'Arab dialect	Baḥārna dialects
		širbat, waladah)
5. Theme V and VI preformatives	yti - type	yit - type
6. 3rd person pronouns	əhuwwa əhiyya əhumma	hu hi hum

A number of other features link the Baḥārna dialects with the sedentary coastal dialects of Southern Arabia and Oman, e.g. the 2nd person feminine suffix -š (versus 'Arab -č); the obligatory -in- infix in structures involving a suffixed active participle, in such phrases as /ka:tbinnah/ 'he's written it' (versus 'Arab /ka:tbah/); the interrogative suffix /əh/, e.g. /ša:fkum əh/? 'Did he see you?' The picture is confused, however, by the preservation in some village Baḥārna dialects of a number of features which are normally thought of in other dialectal contexts (c.f. Ingham 1982: 33ff) as more typical of conservative, nomadic speech norms. In the speech of many elderly village Baḥārna, for example, internal passives (instead of the analogically reduced -/in/ and /ta/- formations) are common, as is the use of the indefinite marker in noun phrases. The lack of reliable demographic data for the area as a whole, as well as of data on speech forms in use at earlier periods of Baḥrain's recent history make it extremely difficult to piece together a coherent picture of how the present distribution of dialectal forms came about. What is important from the point of view of this study, however, is that in the face of the reductional changes which are affecting all Gulf dialects, and the increasing linguistic effects, both syntactic and lexical, of MSA, some dialectal features have for some reason remained more impervious than others to the tide of linguistic change. Some twenty-one linguistic features, eight phonological, thirteen morphophonological form the focus of investigation of this work. The questions we have to ask are:

1. Why are some of these features relatively more resistant to replacement than others?

2. Where variation between a 'new' and an 'old' form is occurring, which kinds of words, in what contexts, are most liable to exhibit variant forms?

3. What are the source(s) of the 'new' forms?

4. What kinds of co-occurrence restriction operate on the combination of 'old' and 'new' forms?

This chapter describes some of the more important phonological differences between the 'Arab and Baḥārna dialects, as represented in the speech of older, illiterate speakers talking informally. Questions 1-4 above, which relate to how the forms described here are changing, are addressed in the next chapter. For ease of reference and comparison between these dialects, we follow

Blanc (1964: 6) in using the term Old Arabic (OA) to designate the "putative ancestor of the present-day colloquials; it is a non-committal, blanket term which does not refer to any single, concrete dialect and does not purport to solve questions of reconstruction". Thus a symbolization such as OA /q/ should be construed, in the context of this and the subsequent chapter, as a convenient way of referring to the ancestor of the initial consonant of the 'Arab /ga:l/ 'he said' and "village Baḥārna" /ḳa:l/. What OA /q/ might have sounded like, or whether indeed it was uniform throughout "OA" is a matter for diachronic reconstruction with which this work is not concerned. It will be apparent that the phonological symbols used, e.g. OA /q/, /k/, etc. in such formulas as /g/ < OA /q/, /č/ < OA /k/ etc. are identical with those normally used to represent MSA phonemes. However, we reject such designations as "/g/ < MSA /q/" as illogical since colloquial reflexes cannot be derived from Modern Standard Arabic equivalents (though they may be derived from OA forms which are the ancestors of MSA equivalents; where a dialectal form is replaced by a standard form, MSA, not OA is clearly the source).

I have no doubt, from the large amount of data collected, that the variants referred to as 'Arab (henceforth "A") or Baḥārna (henceforth "B") are seen by native Baḥrainis themselves as markers of sectarian origin when used by Baḥrainis in a Baḥrain context, and I reject the objections of Maṭar (1976: 25ff) to describing, for example, /f/ < OA /ṯ/ as "B", simply because the same reflex happens to turn up in other dialectal phonological systems elsewhere in the Arab world. The point is to discover how linguistic elements are used and evaluated within a specific sociolinguistic context - one in which sect-dialect correlation is an important and locally recognised fact. /f/ < OA /ṯ/ is indubitably seen as typical of B by Baḥrainis, and we recognise this fact by labelling it as such.

The variables with which we are concerned are the dialectal synchronic reflexes of OA /q/, /k/, /gh/ of the velar or post-velar consonants, /j/ of the alveolars, and /ṯ/, /ḏ/,/ḍ/ and /d/ of the interdentals. These variables satisfy Labov's (1966a: 49) criteria for selection in that they are "high in frequency, have a certain immunity from conscious suppression, are integral units of larger structures (lexical items) and may be easily quantified on a linear scale".

4.2 The dialect of the 'Arab

Some A speakers claim to be able to distinguish a Muḥarraqi from a Manāma 'Arab accent. Our data indicated that, while it is probably true that a few A phonetic features - notably the backing and rounding of /a:/ in non-emphatic consonantal environments, and the raising of final /a/ - are more obvious or extreme in Muḥarraqi speech, there do not seem to be the same kind of systematic, clear-cut distinctions in the phonological or morphophonemic systems of the 'Arab dialects which permit divisions to be made comparable to those which, we discovered, exist in the B community (4.3). All the linguistic features described here as A (and many others which do not form part of the analysis) can be found in all Baḥraini 'Arab communities: they are neither 'urban' nor 'rural'. On the other hand B features may be specified as general to all B speech, or as specifically 'rural' or 'urban'.

4.2.1 OA /q/ and /k/

In the A dialect, the synchronic reflexes of OA /q/ are a voiced velar stop /g/, which may be nearer [G] in the contiguity of "emphatic" consonants (or labials and liquids in certain lexical items) and a voiced alveolar affricate /j/ which occurs only in front-vowel environments (especially before or after /i/). In neologisms which have no dialectal equivalents, MSA /q/ is realised as [q], [G] (or occasionally [gh]) in apparent free variation (see 4.2.2 below).

The reflexes of OA /k/ are a voiceless velar stop /k/ and, again in some words only, in front-vowel environments, a voiceless alveolar affricate /č/.

The exact details of how the historical process of fronting and affrication was phonetically conditioned (Johnstone 1963) have been obscured by centuries of lexical borrowing from other languages (notably Persian), or from other varieties of Arabic in which affrication of OA /q/ and /k/ did not occur. Also in recent times, many words containing the affricate phonemes /j/ and /č/ have dropped out of common use as the objects or activities they denote have ceased to be part of everyday cultural life, e.g. /9aččа:f/ 'bride's hairdresser', /ṭa:baj/ 'to come alongside each other (of dhows)'. Nonetheless, there are still quite a large number of words in the A dialect in which /j/ and /č/ occur as fossilized reflexes of OA /q/ and /k/. Here are some examples of dialectal-OA/MSA lexical analogues in which OA (and MSA) /q/ and /k/ correspond to A /g/, /j/, /č/ and /k/.

OA/MSA item		
		A /g/
/qa9ada/	'he sat'	/ga9ad/
/9aql/	'mind'	/9aGiḷ/
/baqiya/	'he remained'	/buga/
		A /j/
/qari:b/	'near'	/jiri:b/
/qala9a/	'he uprooted'	/jala9/
/9ati:q/	'old'	/9ati:j/
		A /k/
/kari:m/	'noble, man's name'	/kari:m/
/ḍaḥika/	'he laughed'	/daḥak/
/kabura/	'he grew'	/kubar/

OA/MSA item		A /č/
/kabi:r/	'big, old'	/čibi:r/
/birka/	'pool'	/birča/
/raki:k/	'fine, thin'	/riči:č/

4.2.2 OA /gh/

While OA /q/ was fronted and in some items affricated in the A dialect, OA /gh/ lost its spirant release and was generally replaced by a voice-indifferent uvular stop, either [G] or [q], which we symbolise phonemically as /q/. In MSA neologisms, e.g. /mugha:dara/ 'departure', /gh/ is commonly treated in this way. Hence the synchronic A equivalent of OA/MSA /taštaghilu/ 'you work' is typically realised [tiš taqil] or [tištaGəl], (more rarely by educated speakers [tiš taghil]), phonemically /tištaqil/; the synchronic analogue of OA/MSA /ghayru/ 'other than' is /qe:r/ (usually [qe:r] or [Ge:r]).

Since MSA /q/ (4.2.1) in neologisms, is realised as a uvular in its modern pan-Arab pronounciation, it is homorganic with the A dialectal reflexes, [G], and[q], which developed from OA /gh/. The recent influx into the dialect of many MSA words containing /q/ for which no BA equivalents exist (e.g. /taqaddum/ 'progress') - 'learned' words in which, as will become clear in Chapter 5, this 'new' MSA /q/ cannot be replaced by either of the A dialectal reflexes /g/ or /j/ of OA /q/ (i.e. */tagaddum/ is not a possible form) - has led to a phonological merger of the dialectal reflexes of OA /gh/ with the A dialectal realisation of MSA words in which this 'new' /q/ occurs. Thus:

in OA words		A dialect	Example	
/gh/	→	/q/ ([G], [q])	[Ga:li] [qa:li]	'dear' (dialectal)
in MSA neologisms		**A dialect**		
/q/	→	/q/ ([G], [q])	[muqa:bala] [muGa:bala]	'meeting' (neologism)

There seem to be no phonetic conditioning factors: both dialectal variants can occur in all positions in apparent free variation as reflexes of OA /gh/ or MSA /q/.

Although MSA neologisms such as /muqa:bala/ are never directly assimilated into the dialectal phonological system by the substitution of /g/ or /j/ for /q/, the reverse process regularly occurs: certain categories of dialectal words may be changed phonologically in dialectal speech to fit MSA norms. For example, A /jiri:b/ 'near' (OA/MSA /qari:b/) can be and frequently is replaced by its MSA equivalent in "literate" conversation. The A realisation of this replacing item /qari:b/ 'near' however, can be either [Gari:b], or [qari:b]. Since OA /ghari:b/ 'strange, alien' also has the A dialectal reflex([Gari:b] or [qari:b]) the result is that these two lexical items are not consistently distinguished in literate speech; illiterates, however would normally preserve the dialectal distinction between /jiri:b/ 'near' and /qari:b/ 'strange'. Diagrammatically:

OA/MSA	A illiterates		A literates
/qari:b/ 'near' →	/jiri:b/		/qari:b/ ([qari:b] or [Gari:b])
/ghari:b/ 'alien' →	/qari:b/	([qari:b] or [Gari:b])	

There are other lexical pairs which also seem to have merged in literate speech e.g. OA/MSA /ghalab/ 'to beat, defeat' and /qalab/ 'to overturn' are both realised as [Galab], etc. Illiterates distinguish this pair, however, normally realising the former as [Galab], or [qalab] and the latter as [galab]. The phonemic merger of /q/ and /gh/ is known by Baḥrainis to be a distinctive marker of A rather than B speech. B speakers frequently commented on it during the course of field-work, citing it as evidence of the "incorrectness" of the A dialect.

4.2.3 OA /j/

OA /j/ corresponds to a frictionless continuant /y/ in all phonetic environments, in a very large number of 'core' lexical items, in the A dialect. There are, however, certain words in everyday use in the modern dialect, most of them clearly recent borrowings from MSA or other languages, in which /j/ is categorical. Some common examples are /je:g/ 'jug' (English) /mikya:j/ 'make-up' (French), and /ja:mi9a/ 'university', /jari:da/ 'newspaper', /jibin/ 'cheese', /ḥijra/ 'room', /barna:maj/ 'programme', /sajjal/ 'to record' (all MSA neologisms). Some older borrowings underwent the /j/ → /y/ change, (e.g. /barastaj/ 'reed-house' and /trinj/ 'type of citrus fruit' are normally /barastiy/ and /triniy/) while for some reason others such as /ja:lbu:t/ 'jollyboat', /ju:ti/ 'shoes', /bijli/ 'lamp' did not, despite the fact that they have been so completely assimilated into the dialect that they have morphologically 'broken' plurals: /jawa:lbi:t/, /jawa:ti/ and /baja:li/ (see Holes 1980: 77-9).

As should be clear from the examples, the recent borrowings from MSA refer to concepts or objects culturally novel in a non-literate society ('university', 'newspaper') or, as in the case of /ḥijra/ and /sajjal/ they are lexical replacements of older dialectal words - in these two cases of BA /da:r/ 'house' and /gayyad/ 'to record'. Other common examples are /zawwaj/ for dialectal /9arras/ 'to marry' and /darra:ja/ 'bicycle' for /se:kal/ (the BA term itself being an older borrowing from English) and /t̲alla:ja/ for /fre:za/ 'refrigerator, freezer'. Nonetheless some of the commonest words in BA which have MSA analogues in which MSA /j/ occurs almost always have /y/ in the A dialect, e.g. /ya/ 'to come', /misyid/ 'mosque', /rayil/ 'man, husband'.

There are also a handful of words in which OA /q/ has apparently first been fronted and affricated to /j/ and then backed to /y/, /yassam/, 'to divide up', (OA /qassam/), /yifra:n/ 'baskets (OA /qufra:n/), /tanyi:l/ 'transportation' (OA /tanqi:l). Such 'old-fashioned' realisations are rare nowadays, however, and only occur with any regularity in the oldest illiterate speakers' speech.

4.2.4 OA /ḍ/ and /ḏ̣/

In common with other 'nomadic' dialects of the area (e.g. Baghdadi, see Al-Toma 1969: 13), the A dialect has a single phoneme /ḏ̣/, a pharyngealised voiced dental fricative, corresponding to the two OA stop and fricative phonemes /ḍ/ and /ḏ̣/. Thus for OA /ḍaraba/ 'he hit' and /ḏ̣uhr/ 'noon', the A dialect has /ḏ̣arab/ and /ḏ̣uhr/. Like /y/ as a reflex of OA /j/ in 'core' dialectal words, the merger of /ḍ/ and /ḏ̣/ is a hallmark of A speech in Baḥrain.

4.3 The dialects of the Baḥārna: the village/urban split

We noted at the conclusion of Chapter 3 that, on the basis of the distribution of certain linguistic features, the B community could be broken down into sub-communities which were not exactly co-terminous with the village/urban sociological split. In fact, it is possible, on the basis of the 'illiterate' B data, to distinguish three separate phonological systems, as follows:

(a) Town-dwellers from Manāma, except those from the quarter in the North-East of the town called Rās-Rummān (henceforth "B I")

(b) All village-dwellers, except for those from Dirāz, Sanābis and Dēh ("B II")

(c) Inhabitants of Rās-Rummān, Dirāz, Sanābis and Dēh ("B III")

This work is not centrally concerned with explaining how these distinctions arose historically, but some brief consideration will be given to this question below.

The village inhabitants, "B II", claim that theirs is the original B dialect of Baḥrain, of which the main town dialect, "B I" is a corruption. There is, it must be said, some linguistic evidence which can be adduced to support the view that the town dialect is an offshoot of the village dialects: all B dialects share many phonological and morphological features, and, where there are differences, the 'novel' forms of the town dialect e.g. /g/< OA /q/ instead of 'village /ḳ/< OA /q/ can generally be explained as the influence of the socially prestigious A dialect with which the town-dwellers, much more than the villagers, have been in contact over a long period. We have already noted how, in the Muḥarraq quarter of Al-Ḥiyāč the Baḥārna sail-makers seem to have completely adopted A forms; we might expect that some lesser degree of assimilation might have occurred elsewhere in the Baḥārna community, particularly where social contact is relatively close, as it is in the town. Chapters 5 and 7 of this study show clearly that borrowing from the A dialect, and the avoidance of distinctively B forms are, in fact, consistent tendencies in literate Baḥārna speech today. It is tempting to surmise that such shifts are the latest manifestations of the process which led to the original urban-village dialect split in the Baḥārna community (i.e. that all Baḥārna speech was originally like that of today's village populations).

However, local anecdotal evidence suggests that synchronic dialect differences may be at least partly the vestiges of the heterogeneous origins of the Baḥārna population rather than the result of recent outside influence. Village mukhtārīn ('headmen'), the repositories of unrecorded demographic history, trace the origin of certain village populations to places as far removed from each other as Yemen (Bani-Jamra - see Al-Tajir 1982: 24), 'Oman ('Āli), and Eastern Saudi Arabia (Sanābis, Dēh and Dirāz). There is a certain amount of comparative linguistic evidence which supports the idea that the minor present-day dialect differences between the villages stem from such disparate geographical origins. The /g/< OA /j/ variant found in 'Āli, as in /igi/ 'he comes', is a peculiarity of this village not found elsewhere in Baḥrain, but found in 'Oman, the putative home of 'Ali villagers in the distant past (Al-Tajir 1982: 20); the /y/< OA /j/ of Sanābis, Dēh and Dirāz, as in /iyi/ 'he comes', which again is not found in any other Baḥārna village as <u>dialectal</u> variant (as distinct from cross-dialectal borrowing of /y/ by literate Baḥārna who wish to imitate A speech) is also found as a <u>dialectal</u> B form in Al-Qaṭīf, Eastern Saudi Arabia (Smeaton 1973: 24; Al-Jishshi 1973: 57) where it is claimed, these villagers' forebears lived. It is also therefore plausible that the present-day urban/village distinctions might similarly have been there <u>ab initio</u>: today's Baḥārna town population may simply be continuing a dialect which was different from that of other groups of Baḥārna at the time when their respective ancestors came to Baḥrain. However, there is such a degree of agreement between <u>all</u> B dialects on a large number of phonological and morphological and lexical variables that common provenance, if not from a single geographical area, then from a single dialect group spread over a wide area in which communication networks were strong, is indicated for all Baḥārna.

The three-way sub-dialectal split we have adopted to describe the B dialects in this study is demanded by synchronic linguistic data, rather than by sociological or other non-linguistic considerations. In particular, our B III group comprises the inhabitants of three villages and a quarter of Manāma which, on <u>phonological</u> criteria alone, form a separate group from the two main Baḥārna groups (where sociological and linguistic criteria, do, in fact, largely coincide). It is, however, probably no accident that the local traditions of these four areas link them to an area of Eastern Saudi Arabia where a dialect phonologically similar to theirs (Al-Jishshi 1973) is spoken.

However, we shall see in Chapters 6 and 7 that there is less justification in regarding the B III dialects as a homogeneous group where certain <u>morphophonemic</u> variables are concerned. The "dialectal baselines" in Sanābis, Dēh, and Dirāz on these variables are the same as all other village dialects - they are therefore subsumed in the B II data. The dialect of Rās-Rummān, on the other hand, is morphophonemically different from both the village <u>and</u> the main urban dialect and is accordingly designated B III:

	<u>I</u>	<u>II</u>	<u>III</u>
Phonological Variables	Manāma	villages [ex. Sanābis, Dēh, Dirāz]	Sanābis Dēh, Dirāz, Ras Rummān
Morphophonemic Variables	Manāma	villages [inc. Sanābis, Dēh, Dirāz]	Ras-Rummān

4.3.1 <u>OA /q/ and /k/</u>

<u>B II (villagers)</u>

In the main village group, the old dialectal reflex of OA /q/, to judge by the speech of present-day illiterates, was /ḳ/, a voiceless, somewhat retracted velar stop e.g. /ḳa:l/ 'he said', /baḳḳa:l/ 'grocer'. The phoneme /g/ does occur in dialectal words, but only apparently in borrowings such as /ga:ri/ (Hindi) 'cart', /je:g/ (English) 'jug'. In the speech of literates and to some extent illiterates' speech, /ḳ/ is being replaced by /g/ and /q/ (see Chapter 5): thus /ga:l/ or /qa:l/ 'he said', at least in conversational contexts such as those in which our data were recorded, are becoming much commoner in literate village speech than /ḳa:l/.

OA /k/ as in the A dialect, underwent fronting and affrication in front-vowel environments to /č/. The details of this process have again been obscured by subsequent borrowing, but broadly speaking, it seems to have affected many more lexical items in the B village dialects than in the B urban, or A dialects. For example, while all BA dialects have /čam/ 'how much?; a little, some' and /ča:n/ 'if' (OA analogues /kam/, /ka:n/) only the village dialects have /č/ in such common-core words as /ačbar/ 'bigger', /ya:čil/ 'he eats', /miča:n/ 'place'.

In such examples as the above, /č/ < OA /k/ and /ḳ/ < OA /q/ are hallmarks of village speech, stigmatised as such by town-dwellers of both sects.

<u>B I (town-dwellers)</u>

In Manāma, the B dialect has /g/ < OA /q/, but <u>never</u> /j/ < OA /q/: thus /gaḷḅ/ 'heart', /ga:m/ 'he got up' are forms common to both

Baḥarna town-dwellers and 'Arab, but A /j/ in e.g. /jiri:b/ 'near', /ba:ji/ 'remainder' contrasts with urban B /gari:b/, /ba:gi/. The typically B II reflex /ḳ/ < OA /q/ occasionally occurred in the speech of some elderly illiterate town-dwellers, which tends to support the idea that /g/ may be a recent replacement of an originally "common B" /ḳ/, as a result of 'Arab influence. As far as the reflexes of OA /k/ is concerned, the distribution of dialectal /k/ and /č/ is similar to that found in the A dialect, rather than to that in the village B dialect.

B III

In Sanābis, Dēh, Dirāz and Rās-Rummān, /g/ is the normal reflex of OA /q/, but /j/ does occur as a genuine dialectal reflex in illiterate speech in these areas, though in far fewer lexical items than in the A dialect. For example, /yitja:balu:n/ 'they meet each other', /saji/ 'high-tide' occurred in our data. Al-Jishshi (1973: 57) notes /j/ < OA /q/ as a dialectal feature of Al-Qaṭīf, Eastern Saudi Arabia, an area with which the B III group is alleged, as we noted above, to have close demographic links. /ḳ/ < OA /q/ the "village" reflex, never occurs in these dialects.

The distribution of /k/ and /č/ < OA /k/ is similar to that found in the urban, not the rural B dialect. Details of the lexical distribution of /k/ and /č/ in all dialects are found in Chapter 5.

4.3.2 OA /j/

B I and II

The reflex of OA /j/ in all lexical items in these dialects is /j/, an alveolar affricate, the voiced counterpart of /č/, e.g. /ja/ 'he came', /jazwa/ 'ship's crew'.

B III

Like the A dialect, and exceptionally for the B dialects as a whole, the B III dialects have /y/, a frictionless continuant, for all occurrences of OA /j/, e.g. /ya/ 'he came', /yazwa/ 'ship's crew'. The remarks made in 4.2.3 about the preservation of /j/ in recent borrowings in the A dialect apply with equal force to the B III.

4.3.3 OA /ṯ/, /ḏ/, /ḏ̣/

One of the most striking features of all the B dialects is their treatment of the OA interdental fricatives. In all phonetic environments /ṯ/ became /f/ (sometimes pharyngealised /f̣/) /ḏ/ became /d/ and /ḏ̣/ became /ḍ/, in each case falling in with the /f/, /d/ and /ḍ/ phonemes which remained as in OA. Thus:

OA	all B dialects	
/ṯala:ṯa/	/fala:fa/	'three'
/ha:ḏa/	/ha:da/	'this'
/ḏ̣uhr/	/ḍuhr/	'noon'

4.4 Summary of consonantal correspondences

The consonantal correspondences between OA and the dialectal variants are summarised in Table 4 below. Where a dialectal variant such as /č/, which is shared by all dialects, has a different lexical distribution depending on which dialect is being considered, examples of each "lexical category" are given. The raison d'etre for these categories, and a full list of the 'member' items is provided in Chapter 5. It cannot be too strongly emphasised that Table 4 is a table of "dialectal baselines" derived from the analysis of illiterate speakers' speech: in both the group and individual cases discussed in

OA/ MSA	Example		A	B I	B II	B III
/q/	/qa9ad/	'to sit'	/ga9ad/	/ga9ad/	/ḳa9ad/	/ga9ad/
	/qali:l/	'few'	/jili:l/	/gali:l/	/ḳali:l/	/gali:l/
/k/(1)	/kabi:r/	'old, big'	/čibi:r/	/kabi:r/	/kabi:r/	/kabi:r/
(2)	/kam/	'how much'	/čam/	/čam/	/čam/	/čam/
(3)	/akbar/	'bigger'	/akbar/	/akbar/	/ačbar/	/akbar/
/gh/	/gharaq/	'to drown'	/qarag/	/gharag/	/gharaḳ/	/gharag/
/j/	/naḍaj/	'to ripen'	/naḍay/or /naḏ̣a/	/naḍaj/	/naḍaj/	/naḍay/
	/majalla/	'magazine'	/mujalla/	/mujalla/	/mujalla/	/mujalla/
/ṯ/	/ṯa:ni/	'second'	/ṯa:ni/	/fa:ni/	/fa:ni/	/fa:ni/
/ḏ/	/ha:ḏi/	'this'(f)	/(ha:)ḏi/	/(ha:)di/	/(ha:)di/	/(ha:)di/
/ḏ̣/	/ḏ̣uhr/	'noon'	/ḏ̣uhr/	/ḍuhr/	/ḍuhr/	/ḍuhr/
/ḍ/	/ḍarab/	'to hit'	/ḏ̣arab/	/ḍarab/	/ḍarab/	/ḍarab/

Table 4: Some phonological correspondences in Bahraini dialects

Chapter 5, there is some degree of variation between these baseline variants and other replacing variants. The degree of variation/ replacement of any particular dialectal variant – and this is a crucial point in our subsequent analysis – relates both to its local sociolinguistic status – whether or not it is a 'marker' of a socially inferior or superior group in Bahrain (and the surrounding area) - and also to whether or not it occurs in a lexical item which has a direct analogue in MSA - that is, whether or not it occurs in an item which is potentially convertible into an MSA word by the simple substitution of one phoneme for another. Thus, the replaceability of the initial consonant in /ga9ad/ or /ḳa9ad/ 'to sit' in Table 4 by MSA /q/ depends on two separate factors:

(a) the relative status of /g/ and /ḳ/ in Baḥrain as dialectal variants: /g/ is more stable than /ḳ/ because it is associated with a socially more prestigious group, and has a wider areal currency than /ḳ/ (Holes 1987:f'coming) in contexts where not all speakers share the same dialectal norms.

(b) the fact that /ga9ad/ and /ḳa9ad/ have purely dialectal meanings other than 'to sit', which is the area of semantic overlap with MSA. /g/ or /ḳ/ in this item is only directly replaceable by /q/ where the meanings of MSA /qa9ad/ and dialectal /ga9ad/, /ḳa9ad/ coincide. Where this condition is not met, /g/ or /ḳ/ is not replaceable by /q/. Consider the following data:

(1) /le:n ga9adt min iṣ-ṣubḥ..../ 'when I got up in the morning'
(2) /ja:sim ka:n ga:9id yištaghil/ 'Jasmin was working'

The verb /ga9adt/ in (1) is used in a dialectal sense not found in MSA ('to get up') and in (2) the present participle of the same verb, /ga:9id/ is used as an auxiliary denoting continuous action, which is again a non-MSA syntactic usage. In neither case is it possible to 'style-raise' by simply substituting /q/ for /g/ (or /ḳ/) - a different lexical item, or different syntactic structure, must be selected if the speaker wishes, for whatever reason, to 'step outside' the dialect. This type of phonemic substitution of an MSA for a dialectal phoneme can only occur in lexical items in which conditions of morpho-semantic congruity between an MSA item and its dialectal equivalent are met. I shall have more to say about this concept in Chapter 5.

It will be clear from Table 4 that it is by no means the case that the A dialect - that of the 'high status' group - always "agrees" with OA/MSA, the supra-dialectal standard, in its consonant system. Sometimes, for example, in the synchronic reflexes of OA /j/ and /gh/, it is one of the B dialects which coincides with MSA, "isolating" the high-status dialect; in other cases the A dialect does so (/ṯ/ /ḏ/ /ḏ̣/), isolating the 'low' status and, in this case 'non-standard' B variants; in yet other cases, there is a partial agreement between the A and B dialects where shared dialectal reflexes contrast with MSA - for example in certain sets of lexical items in which all dialects have /č/. Baḥrainis are undoubtedly aware of these dialectal differences - a particular combination of dialectal variants is associated with a particular area, sect, etc. Some speakers are, of course, nearer the areal or sectarian stereotype than others. It is to be expected that this knowledge of local dialect 'stereotypes', and for educated speakers, MSA, is the cause of much variation; but the direction of this variation depends on a tacit but communally-held appreciation of the status of one stereotype vis-à-vis another: a kind of dialectal 'pecking-order' exists. If we are correct in assuming that the 'Arab speak the more locally prestigious variety of BA, an educated A speaker is simply faced with the fact that at some points, (e.g. PV5 /y/ below) the dialect spoken in his community differs from MSA, which his education encourages him to regard as having a normative status, the popular conception being that the dialects are 'incorrect' corruptions of the classical language which if only the speaker took more care, he could avoid (Al-Toma 1974: 282). The educated B speaker, on the other hand, is part of a community whose dialect he knows is stigmatised as/hamaji/ ('barbaric, wild') but which he nonetheless feels to be more technically 'correct' in the sense that it coincides with the norms of MSA (e.g. PV5 /j/) at a number of points where the prestige dialect does not. The educated B speaker is thus faced with conflicting sociolinguistic status systems: in the 'local' status system, the 'incorrect' A dialect is superior; but in terms of the supra-dialectal system, the status of some features of his 'inferior' dialect are 'more correct'.

In order to make this clearer, the social distribution of phonologically variant forms (PVs) is tabulated below. A phonological variable is defined as a point in the phonological structure of the BA dialects in which their synchronic reflexes of what may have been an originally shared OA form do not agree. Each variant is marked in terms of whether it is typical (+) or not typical (-) of each of the dialect groupings, and MSA, the supradialectal standard.

There are two instances of "A/B dialect agreement" in opposition to MSA: PV1 /g/ and PV2 /č/; two instances of "A/MSA agreement" in opposition to all B speakers: PV3 /ḏ/ and PV4 /ṯ/; two instances of "B/MSA agreement" in opposition to all A speakers: PV5 /j/ and PV6 /gh/. In other cases, the dialects disagree with each other and with MSA:PV1 /ḳ/ and PV1 /j/; and in one case, PV2 /k/, all agree. PV1 and PV2 are of especial interest because although the A and B dialects share in each case one non-MSA variant, the distribution of those shared variants in the common dialectal lexicon is different.

Dialectal variants deriving from OA emphatics /ḍ/ and /ḏ̣/ have been omitted from further analysis because they occured too rarely in the data for reliable conclusions about their variability to be drawn.

PV1: reflexes of OA /q/

/g/		+ A	+ B (I)	– MSA
/j/		+ A	– B	– MSA
/ḳ/		– A	+ B (II)	– MSA
/q/		– A	– B	+ MSA

PV2: reflexes of OA /k/

/k/		+ A	+ B	+ MSA
/č/	(1)	+ A	– B	– MSA
	(2)	+ A	+ B	– MSA
	(3)	– A	+ B (II)	– MSA

PV3: reflexes of OA /ḏ/

/ḏ/		+ A	– B	+ MSA
/d/		– A	+ B	– MSA

PV4: reflexes of OA /ṯ/

/ṯ/		+ A	– B	+ MSA
/f/		– A	+ B	– MSA

PV5: reflexes of OA /j/

/j/		– A	+ B	+ MSA
/y/		+ A	– B*	– MSA

* except for B III

PV6: reflexes of OA /gh/

/gh/		– A	+ B	+ MSA
/q/		+ A	– B	– MSA

Table 5: Status-marking of phonological variants

The maps on the following pages show the geographical distribution of the variants of PV1, 4 and 5 in the northern part of Baḥrain Island and in the capital Manāma. These areas have been picked out because they strikingly illustrate the juxtaposition of different phonological systems in a small area. The variants on the other variables which are characteristic of "A", "B", "C" and "D"-type dialects can be readily supplied by reference to Table 4. As for the distribution of "A" and "C"-type dialects in the rest of Bahrain ("B" and "D" types are completely covered in the maps overleaf), reference should be made to the map of Baḥrain on page 14 : areas marked on this map ● (Baḥārna villages) are "C"-type and areas marked O ('Arab villages) are "A"-type.

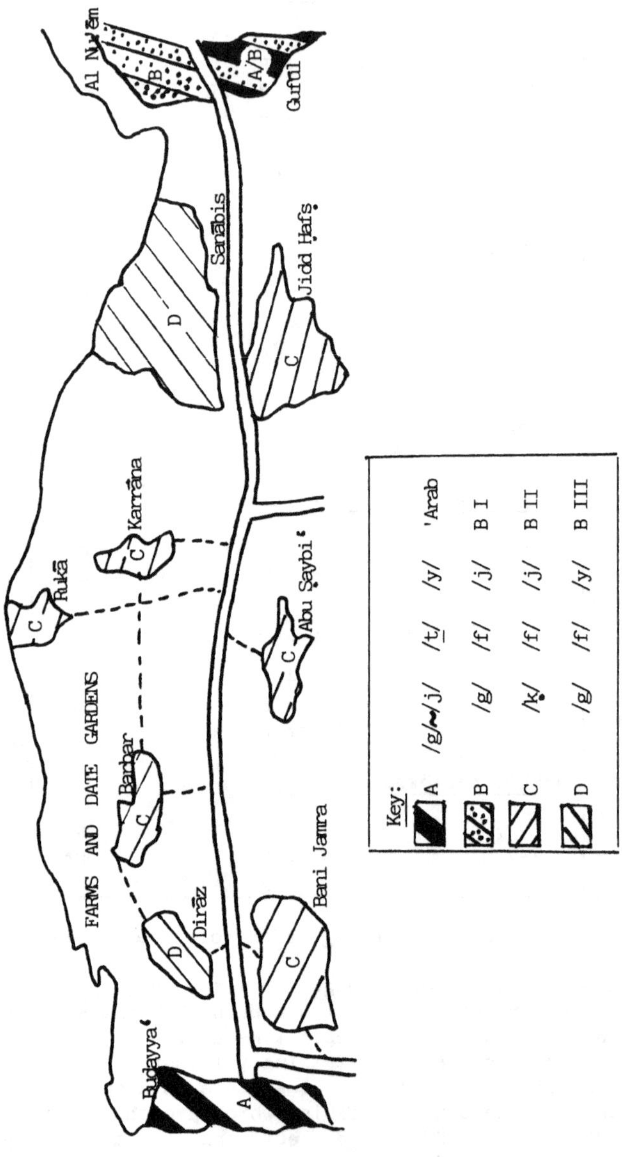

Map 3: Dialectal Consonant Systems in Northern Bahrain

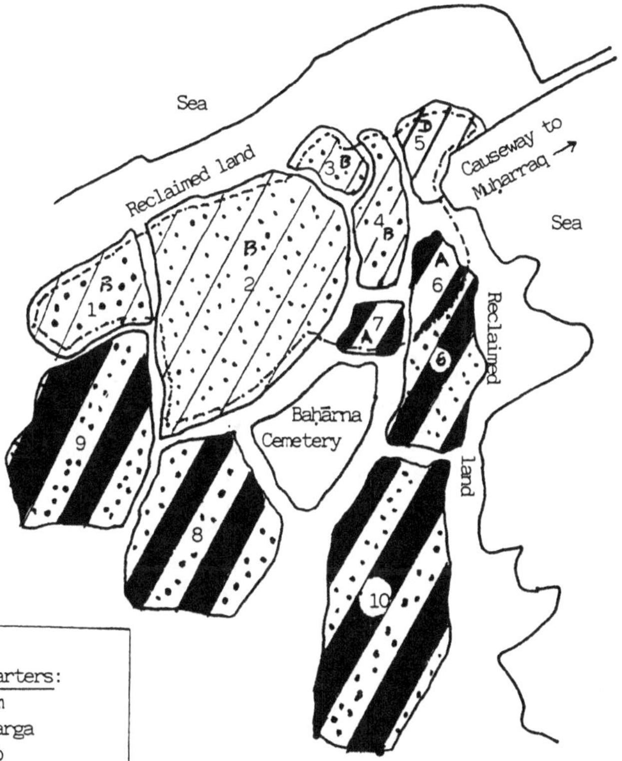

Map 4: Dialectal consonant systems in Manāma

Key:

Baḥārna quarters:

1. Al-Nu'ēm
2. Al-Mukharga
3. Al-Ḥaṭab
4. Al-Ḥammām
5. Rās-Rummān

'Arab quarters:

6. Al-Ḥūra (North)
7. Al-Fāḍil

Mixed areas, recently developed:

6. Al-Ḥūra (South)
8. Salmāniya
9. Gufūl
10. Guḍaybiya

Broken line indicates approximate limit of original town

A	/g/~/j/	/t̲/	/y/	'Arab
B	/g/	/f/	/j/	B I
D	/g/	/f/	/y/	B III

5 Phonemic variation: analysis and interpretation

5.1 Introduction

It was noted in Chapter 4 that at some points in their phonological systems, all Baḥraini communities have dialectal variants which coincide with MSA equivalents, while at others, they have variants which conflict with MSA (Table 5). These conflicts, we noted, could be expected to lead to the replacement of dialectal phonemes by MSA equivalents under certain conditions. We shall show that a condition for this type of "phonemic" substitution, as opposed to other forms of replacement is that there should be both semantic overlap and morphological congruity between the MSA and the dialectal item.

In the first two-thirds of this Chapter, we amplify this principle and also attempt to show the extent to which a speaker's literacy in MSA is related to the likelihood of this phonemic substitution occurring. We also examine how far the local status of dialectal variants, as specified by the markings in Table 5, is a relevant factor in this process: given a variety of 'non-standard' dialectal variants which meet the basic conditions for replaceability (morpho-semantic congruity between the word they occur in and an MSA equivalent), how far does the different local status of these variants, as markers of 'Arab or Baḥārna identity, seem to promote or inhibit their replacement? A further point for consideration on certain variables is what happens when there is a conflict between the demands of the local and supra-dialectal linguistic prestige-systems on the low-prestige dialect.

In the final third of this chapter, we discuss the type of rule which is needed to account for the patterns of variation revealed by the data analysis.

5.2 Measurement of variation

The 'group-scores' which are presented and discussed in

5.7 below were arrived at by calculating the number of times a given dialectal variant was actually used by a given group as a percentage of the number of times it could have been used - that is, speakers were dealt with on a 'group' rather than an individual basis. Scores are expressed as a two-place decimal ranging from 0 to 1. For example, if the 17 "literate 'Arab" of Table 3 produced between them 200 dialectal variants and 100 standard variants for the 300 occurrences in their data in items where there was known to be a choice between the dialectal and standard variant, their 'dialectal' group-score would be $\frac{200}{300} = .66$.

The usefulness of this calculation depends crucially on including in the data base only those items where there is a real choice between a standard and a dialectal variant, and excluding those where either the dialectal or standard variant is obligatory for all speakers. On all variables, it was found that, where there was variation between two equivalent variants A and B, A being dialectal, B standard, there were always distinct groups of words where

(a) A was obligatory
(b) B was obligatory
as well as
(c) A and B were both possible.

Our main focus of interest is on category (c). Only a complete search of the data made it possible to assign lexical items to each of these categories with any degree of certainty, and this was our first task: to focus the investigation of phonological variation on those lexical items in which variation occurred, and to exclude those where it did not.

5.3 Type 1 variables: the data base

Type 1 variables are those where none of the various dialectal variants used in Baḥrain coincided with the MSA equivalent - that is, in which the dialectal variants differed from each other and from MSA. An inspection of Table 5 shows that PV1 and PV2 fall into this category: /j/, /g/ and /ḳ/ are variously found in the dialects where MSA has /q/,and /č/ is found where MSA has /k/, though the distribution of /č/ is different from community to community.

5.3.1 The data base for PV1

There were three clear groups of lexical items revealed by a search of the data:

PV1.1: Words in which the dialectal variants /g/, /j/ and /ḳ/ were never replaced by /q/, the MSA equivalent, by any speaker.

PV1.2: Words in which there was variation between dialectal

variants and /q/

PV1.3: Words in which /q/ always occurred, never a dialectal variant.

It should be noted that we are concerned at this point with the replaceability of dialectal variants as a whole by /q/. We are not claiming that there was no variation between different dialectal variants. (In fact, as we shall see, B II /ḳ/ hardly showed up at all in B II literates' data - it was almost always replaced by /g/ in cases where a dialectal variant was used.)

The PV1.1 words - the 'non-replaceable' set - are listed below. To save duplication, they have been spelt with /g/, though of course in the B II dialect they have /ḳ/ in all items except those marked (F) ("foreign borrowing"). Asterisked items have /j/ in the 'Arab dialect. All items have been given in their A syllabic form, which in some cases differs from the B form in ways which will be specified in Chapters 6 and 7.

The PV1.1 list contains an extremely heterogeneous list of words. The non-susceptibility to replacement of /g/, /j/ and /ḳ/ by /q/ in these words can be attributed to a number of sometimes overlapping factors:

1. Lack of morpho-semantic congruity with MSA - we briefly exemplified this in the last chapter with /ga9ad/ and /ga:9id/. A few of the many examples of words listed which are morphologically similar to MSA words but have different dialectal meanings or syntactic functions are:

/ḥalg/ BA 'mouth' - MSA equivalent /ḥalq/ means 'throat'

/riyu:g/ BA 'breakfast' - MSA equivalent /ruyu:q/ means 'spittle'

/ḥagg/ - MSA equivalent /ḥaqq/ is a noun meaning 'right, due'
The BA word is used as a preposition or a conjunction
e.g. /riḥt ḥagg id daxtar/ (A)
'I went to the doctor's'
/sawwe:ta ḥaḳḳ tistafi:di:n inti:n/ (B II)
'I did it so as you'd benefit!'

Despite their phonological similarity and identical etymology, pairs like /ḥagg/ and /ḥaqq/, /ḥalg/ and /ḥalq/ are in no way surface variants of some identical underlying form: they have different meanings and/or functions and cannot be used interchangeably.

2. Archaisms - there are some dialectal words which could be made by the replacement of /g/, etc., with /q/ but the resulting word, though an MSA "dictionary entry", would have archaic, poetic or other overtones. /ba:g/ for example, which is everyday BA for 'to steal' has an MSA equivalent /ba:qa/ which, however, is very rarely used - /saraqa/ is the normal MSA word.

List PV1.1 Items in which dialectal variants were never replaced by /q/

<u>Prepositions/adverbs</u>

ḥagg	'towards, for, to'
gabil	'before'
gidda:m*	'in front of'
mga:bil*	'opposite'
9agub	'after'
fo:g	'above, over'

<u>Verbs</u>

gidar/yigdar	'to be able'
ga9ad/yig9ad	'to sit; get up'
gala9*/yigla9*	'to uproot, pull out'
giṣab/yagṣub	'to butcher'
wugaf/yo:gaf	'to stand, stop'
rigad/yargid	'to sleep'
laḥag/yilḥag	'to catch up with'
gharag/yaghrig	'to drown'
xalag/yaxlig	'to create'
ḥadag/yaḥdig	'to fish'
falag/yaflig*	'to open an oyster'
fišag/yafšig	'to shatter' (intrans.)
šinag/yašnig	'to hang (someone)'
gaṣṣ/yiguṣṣ	'to cut'
gaṭṭ/yiguṭṭ	'to throw away'
gaḍḍ/yiguḍḍ	'to gnaw, make holes in'
šagg/yišigg	'to rip, tear'
ṭagg/yiṭigg	'to hit'
dagg/yidigg	'to beat, hit'
ga:l/yigu:l	'to say'
ga:m/yigu:m	'to rise, get up'
ga:d/yigu:d	'to lead'
ba:g/yibu:g	'to steal'
sa:g/yisu:g	'to drive'
gala/yagli	'to fry'
buga/yibga	'to remain'
liga/yilga	'to find'
siga/yasgi*	'to water'
gazzar/ yigazzir (F)	'to spend (time)'
gaṣṣas/yigaṣṣis	'to cut into pieces'
garra9/yigarri9	'to frighten'

<u>Nouns/Adjectives</u>

ghawa	'coffee'
gidir*/gdu:r*	'cooking pot'
gafi:r*/ gifra:n*	'basket'
gadu/gda:wa	'hubble-bubble pipe'
rguba/rga:b	'neck'
ga:ri*/ gawa:ri (F)	'cart'
gu:ṭi/ gawa:ṭi (F)	'tin, packet'
gaḷḅ/g̣ḷu:b	'heart'
gumruk/ gama:rik(F)	'customs'
gargu:r/ gara:gi:r*	'bee-hive, fish trap'
gubga:b/ gaba:gib	'wooden clog'
gubgub/ gaba:gi:b*	'crab'
gḥaba/gḥab	'prostitute'
guf̣f̣a/g̣afi:f	'basket'
na:ga/nu:g	'she-camel'
gibli*	'northern'
gumar	'moon'
ga:ṣir	'lacking'
gu:9	'sea-bed'
gadam	'foot (measure)'
galla	'quantity of dates'
ganṣ	'hunting'
gadd	'amount'
guḍb	'cutting, pruning'
ḥalg*/ḥlu;g'	'mouth'
dawšag/ dawa:šig*	'mattress'
9ati:g*/9ta:g	'old'
fari:g*/ firga:n*	'quarter (of a city)'
9irg*/9ru:g*	'vein'
ḥari:ga*/ ḥara:yig	'fire'
bri:g*/ burga:n	'ewer'
rifi:g*/ rifga:n	'friend'

gaššar/yigaššir	'to peel'
gaṣṣar/yigaṣṣir	'to fall short'
gallaf/yigallif*	'to repair a ship'
laggaṭ/yilaggiṭ	'to pick up'
naggal/yinaggil	'to transplant'
nagga/yinaggi*	'to choose, select'
saggam/ yisaggim*	'to pay an ad- vance (to a diver)'
zarrag/yizarrig	'to overtake'
xaffag/yixaffig	'to make (someone lose (something)'
ṭallag/yiṭallig*	'to divorce'
ṣaffag/yiṣaffig*	'to clap'
ṭabbag/yiṭabbig*	'to cover, veil'
ṭa:bag/yiṭa:big*	'to come along- side (boats)'
9allag/yi9allig*	'to hang'
wa:hag/yiwa:hig*	'to bother, give trouble to'
tša:bag/ ytiša:bag	'to quarrel'
trayyag/ ytirayyag	'to have breakfast'
išta:g/yišta:g	'to desire'
istaḥmag/ yistaḥmig istaḥrag/ yistaḥrig	'to get angry'

nigi:la*/ naga:yil	'seedling'
digi:ga/ daga:yig	'minute'
ḥagi:ga	'truth'
rizg*	'sustenance'
ṣidg*	'is that so?'
rang (F)	'colour'
šarg	'east'
nga9	'swamp'
marag	'soup,stew'
9agil	'mind'
9a:gil*	'reasonable rational'
ḍi:ga*	'difficult situation'
su:g/aswa:g	'market'
ghalg*	'obscure, in- comprehensible'
ligma/ligam	'mouthful'
sagf/sgu:f	'roof'
bagil	'green herbs, vegetables'
9agrab/9aga:rib	'scorpion'
sangal/ sana:gil (F)	'chain'
mirgad/mara:gid	'bed'
mitḍayyig*	'upset, depressed'
mugbara	'cemetery'
riyu:g	'breakfast'
mifliga/ mafa:li:g*	'knife for opening clams'

3. Borrowings - words such as /gazzar/ 'to spend time' (Persian?), /ga:ri/ 'cart' (Hindi), /rang/ 'colour' and /sangal/ 'chain' (both Persian) obviously have no MSA morpho-semantic analogues, by virtue of their being borrowings from other languages.

4. Local technical terms - many terms connected with fishing, sailing and agriculture, though ultimately of Arabic origin and in some cases theoretically having direct literary equivalents, have meanings too intimately bound up with the non-literate culture of the area for phonemic substitution to be possible in them, e.g. /gallaf/ 'to repair a ship', /siga/ 'to water, irrigate' (land); to come in (tide)'.

5. Dialectal 'core-items' - a number of very common words such as /ga:l/ 'to say', /ga:m/ 'to get up' are also to be found in the PV1.1 list. Although they do have direct MSA morpho-semantic equivalents, and should therefore on our hypothesis be subject to

replacement, they showed no variation. This seems to be because they are felt by Baḥrainis to be too much a part of the lexical core of the dialect for replacement to occur in anything but the most formal styles of speech. Like /ga9ad/, they have many other uses in the dialect which are lacking, or at least not central, to the meaning of their MSA equivalents. Some examples from the data:

/ani ba:ḳu:m biš/ (B II)
'I'll (f) <u>take care</u> of you (f)'

/...u ga:m yabči/ (A)
'...and he <u>started</u> to weep'

/...9ala ḳo:lat il ḳa:yil.../(B II)
'...as they say...'

The general points made here about why PV1.1 words are invariable apply equally to the other variables examined. In each case a fairly sizeable class of words could be identified consisting of highly specialized, culturally-specific words, old borrowings and a certain number of very common words which despite common etymology and in some cases a degree of morpho-semantic overlap, resisted the influence of "correct" MSA equivalents completely. The strategy of literate speakers in these cases, where phonemic replacement does not seem to be an option was <u>lexical</u> replacement: thus the BA /rang/ 'colour' (Persian borrowing) cannot be "MSA-ized" to */ranq/ but can be replaced by /lo:n/. Similarly, /saraq/, 'to steal' can replace /ba:g/ and /ṣa:d samak/ 'to fish' can replace the BA /ḥadag/. Such lexical replacement is a common strategy adopted by literate speakers wishing to distance themselves, for whatever reason, from dialectal speech forms, in cases where a simple phonemic replacement is not possible.

It may be asked, in cases where there is variation between forms such as /ṣadi:g/ and /ṣadi:q/ 'friend' and (A dialect) /jiri:b/ and /qari:b/ 'near' whether we are correct in assuming that speakers are operating a phonemic rather than a lexical replacement rule: are they simply replacing /g/ with /q/ because the morpho-semantic congruity of the dialectal and MSA words for 'friend' allows them to, or are they replacing "whole" dialectal forms /ṣadi:g/ and /jiri:b/ with equivalent MSA forms /ṣadiq/ and /qari:b/, just as they replace /rang/ with /lo:n/? In other words, do speakers, as they become literate in MSA, simply learn rules which specify equivalences between the dialectal and MSA lexicon, and the co-occurrence rules which govern choice between them, or do they learn morpho-semantically conditioned rules whereby a phoneme from one system can be substituted for an equivalent one in another system? Do we need two lexical entries for /ṣadi:g/~/ṣadi:q/ or one? We shall discuss possible answers to this question in the last third of this chapter after the presentation of all the data. For the moment, for the sake of clarity of presentation, we hold to the "phonemic" replacement explanation.

List PV1.3 contains a list (not exhaustive) of words occurring in the data in which dialectal variants /g/, /j/ and /ḳ/ never occurred, no matter who was speaking. In most cases, it can readily be seen that these are borrowings from MSA denoting new concepts, e.g. /siba:q/ 'race' (as in /siba:q il-xe:l/ 'horse-racing') or they are replacements of BA words e.g. /aṣdiqa:/ 'friends' which can replace BA /ṣidga:n/ or /rifga:n/, (never */ṣidqa:n/, */rifqa:n/) and /minṭaqa/ 'area, location' which replaces BA /balad/ or /di:ra/.

While it is true that the words listed in list PV1.3 tended for obvious reasons to occur with less frequency in the speech of illiterates than literates, they were *not* less likely to have the non-dialectal /q/ variant: */q/ was totally consistent for all speakers of all sects.* It was realised as [G], [q] or [gh] in apparent free variation by 'Arab and as [q] by Baḥārna.

In small number of exceptional cases, it seems that words which form part of the core vocabulary of BA, and have specific local meanings, nonetheless *always* have /q/, e.g. /9aqad/ (noun /9aqd/) 'to conclude a marriage contract', /naqš/ 'a type of engraving', /faqi:r/ 'poor'. From this last root, however, we note the *variable* items /fagr/ ~ /faqr/ 'poverty', /fuga:ra/ ~ /fuqa:ra/ 'poor people'. There is no obvious explanation why /q/ should occur exclusively in such items as /9aqad/ and /faqi:r/, either as a "survival" of original OA /q/ or (less plausibly) as an import from MSA. The case of /qur'a:n/ 'Koran' is simpler. Here the unique pan-Arab religious and literary significance of the scriptures is the reason for the preservation of /q/ in this word in BA (and indeed in all Arabic dialects).

List PV 1.3 Items in which /q/ always occurred in all dialects

Verbs	
qarrar/yiqarrir	'to decide'
qallad/yiqallid	'to imitate'
qanna9/yiqanni9	'to convince'
qa:wam/yiqa:wim	'to resist'
qa:mar/yiqa:mir	'to gamble'
9aqad/ya9qid	'to make a marriage contract'
waqqa9/yiwaqqi9	'to sign'
traqqa/ytiraqqa	'to develop' (intrans.)
tqahhar/ytiqahhar	'to get angry'
tṯaqqaf/ytiṯaqqaf	'to become

Nouns/Adjectives	
ḥadi:qa/ḥada:yiq	'garden, park'
ḥalqa/ḥalaqa:t	'episode'
biṭa:qa/baṭa:yiq	'ration coupon'
fari:q/furuq	'team (sports)'
9uqu:ba	'punishment'
ṯaqa:fa	'culture'
ṯaqa:li:d	'customs'
taqa:9ud	'retirement'
siba:q	'race'
firqa	'pop-group'
naql (il 9a:m)	'public transport'
axla:q	'morals'

	educated'
tna:qaš/ ytina:qaš	'to discuss, quarrel'
tnaqqal/ytinaqqal } intaqal/yintaqil }	'to move to another place'
ittafaq/yittifiq	'to agree'
i9taqad/ya9taqid	'to believe (something)
istaqbal/ yastaqbil	'to greet'

Nouns/Adjectives

qur'a:n	'Koran'
aṣdiqa:	'friends'
qa:nu:n/ qawa:ni:n	'law'
qisim/aqsa:m	'department (of an office)'
qa:9ida/ qawa:9id	'grammatical rule'
qaṣd	'intention'
qudra	'ability, strength'
qarya/qura	'village'
qira:'a	'reading'
baqqa:la	'grocery'
siya:qa	'driving'
9aqi:da	'belief'

minṭaqa/mana:ṭiq	'area'
nuqṣ	'lack, dearth'
wa:qi9	'reality'
sa:biq	'previous'
ra:qiṣa	'dancer (f)'
naqš	'type of engraving'
faqi:r	'poor'
aqall	'less'
taqri:ban	'approximately'
muna:qaša	'discussion, argument'
muqa:rana	'comparison'
muqa:bala	'interview, meeting'
muqa:wala	'contract'
musa:baqa	'competition, contest'
muṣa:daqa	'consent'
mustaqbal	'future'
muqaddas	'sacred'
mustaqill	'independent'
mustaqirr	'established, fixed'

From the point of view of the study of variability in literate as opposed to illiterate speech data, the words listed below in PV1.2 are the most interesting, for three reasons:

(i) they are common to all BA dialects, A and B alike.
(ii) they occur relatively frequently in both 'literate'and 'illiterate' data.
(iii) they do not differ sharply from their MSA analogues either in meaning, morphophonemic shape or syntactic function.

For the literate speaker of any BA dialect, it is in these items, if we adopt the "phonemic substitution" explanation of variation, that the phonological systems of BA and MSA come directly into conflict. This is because in these words there is a maximal overlap of form and function between the dialect and MSA. They consequently form the basis on which the group scores for PV1 were calculated. The words listed in lists PV1.1 and PV1.3 were excluded from the calculations since they failed to show variability between dialectal and non-dialectal variants.

It is, of course, quite valid to examine variability simply between dialectal variants, a phenomenon which does in fact occur in the B II group. This is discussed below as a separate issue. The group scores on PV1 presented in 5.7.2 are simply measures of the preservation of dialectal variants - that is, the strength of the preservation of /g/, /j/ or /ḳ/ (or some combination of these, e.g. A /g/ and /j/, literate B II /ḳ/ and /g/) in the face of MSA /q/. A score of .39 as opposed to .97 on PV1 (B II data, Tables 6 and 7) thus simply indicates a very strongly marked as opposed to a weakly marked tendency to adopt /q/ in items where the conditions for dialect/MSA variation are met.

List PV1.2 Items in which dialectal variants vary with /q/. In the A dialect asterisked items always have /j/ if they are realised with a dialectal variant.

Verbs		Nouns/Adjectives	
gabaḍ/yagbiḍ	'to grasp, seize'	giri:b*	'near'
gabal/yagbil	'to accept'	gili:l*	'little, few'
gatal/yagtil	'to kill'	gidi:m*	'old'
gaṭa9/yigṭa9	'to cut'	gi:ma*	'value, price'
gara/yigra	'to read'	gal9a*	'fort'
gassam*/ yigassim*	'to divide up'	guṭ9a/guṭa9	'piece'
		ṭari:g*	'road'
ga:bal* yiga:bil*	'to meet, be opposite (someone/ something)	ṯigi:l*	'heavy'
		ṣadi:g*	'friend'
		rigi:g*	'delicate'
tga:bal*/ ytiga:bal	'to meet, be opposite (reflexive)'	ṣandu:g/ ṣana:di:g*	'box'
		ba:gi*	'remainder'
tgaddam*/ ytigaddam*	'to go forward, advance'	farg	'difference'
		warag/awra:g	'paper'
wa:fag/yiwa:fig*	'to agree (to something)'	wagt/awga:t	'time, weather'
		fagr	'poverty'
ṣaddag/yiṣaddig	'to believe'	fuga:ra	'poor'

It will be clear from a comparison of Lists PV1.1-3 that, within a single tri-consonantal root, it is possible to identify closely related lexical items which have different probabilities of showing a dialectal or non-dialectal variant according to whether morphophonemic form and syntactic/semantic usage are the same in MSA and the dialects. Consider, for example, the OA/MSA root ṣ-d-q, whose basic meaning contains the notion 'truth, friendship':

	B I	B II	A	
obligatory dialectal variant:	/ṣidg/	/ṣidḳ/	/ṣidj/	'(is) that so (?)'
	/ṣidga:n/	/ṣidḳa:n/	/ṣidga:n/	'friends'

variable dialectal/ non-dialectal variant:	/ṣadi:g/	/ṣadi:k/	/ṣadi:j/	'a friend'
	/ṣaddag/	/ṣaddak/	/ṣaddag/	'to believe'
obligatory non-dialectal variant:		/aṣdiqa:/		'friends'
		/muṣa:daqa/		'consent, sanctioning'

The word /ṣidg/ is used commonly in BA to confirm that a statement is true, or with sharply rising intonation, to question the veracity of a statement, e.g.:

/ma ḍarab il baṣal lijil il milḥ/
/ṣidg/

'The onion didn't take because of the salt (in the soil)'
'That's right.' (or 'Is that so?')

The MSA equivalent of /ṣidg/ is /ṣidqan/, containing the MSA adverbial enclitic morpheme -/an/, a clear marker of MSA not found in the dialectal morphological system. /ṣidg/ is probably too much part of the 'dialectal core' of the lexicon to be classicised to /ṣidq/ or /sidqan/. The case of /ṣidga:n/ and /aṣdiqa:/ is slightly different. Both words mean 'friends' but the MSA word is formed on a morphological plural pattern, aCCiCa:, not found in the dialect, while the dialect word is formed on the pattern CiCCa:n which, though productive in MSA, is rather rarely used in this particular tri-literal root. /muṣa:daqa/ is the most extreme case of MSA/dialect disparity: neither the verb from which the word is derived (/ṣa:daq/) nor the verbal-noun pattern on which it is based (muCa:CaCa) are dialectal.

By contrast with these invariable items, the items /ṣadi:g/~ /ṣadi:q/ and /ṣaddag/~/ṣaddaq/ are morphophonemically and semantically parallel: variation between them is therefore possible. PV1 scores provide a measure of 'dialect preservation' on such pairs for each communal group.

5.3.2 The data base for PV2

We noted in 4.2.1 and 4.3.1 above that OA /k/ appears to have been affected differently in various BA dialects: although there are some lexical items in which all dialects have /č/, there are many in which one or other dialect only has /č/, the others having retained /k/. Accordingly, the data base for comparison between dialects is just that set of lexical items in which all dialects share /č/ as dialectal variant, and which meet the conditions under which /č/ may be replaced by the standard variant /k/ - i.e. they have direct morphophonemic and semantic/syntactic analogues in MSA. PV2 is thus a measure of the replacement of /č/ by /k/ in just those words which are 'common core' to all BA dialects and in which /č/ is potentially replaceable by /k/.

Variation in items in which /č/ is not shared is considered as a separate issue.

Below we give the breakdown of words (excluding obvious borrowings from Persian and Hindi) in which /č/ occurred in the data. List PV2.1 is the data base on which scores on PV2 were based. Words are spelt according to 'Arab dialectal norms e.g. /čaḏḏab/ - the corresponding B forms can be obtained by consulting the table of correspondences (Table 4) above (e.g. in this case /čaddab/).

List PV2.1 Words in which both 'Arab and Baḥārna have /č/ as dialectal variant and which have exact MSA analogues (data base for PV2)

Particles			
in ča:n	'if'	čibri:t	'matches, sulphur'
če:f	'how'	čilma	'word, comment'
čam	'how much, a little'	čala:m	'speech, talking'
		ča:ḏib	'liar'
Verbs		čaḏḏa:b	'liar, cheater, deceiver'
čaḏḏab/yicaḏḏib	'to cheat, lie, deceive'	če:l	'measure, amount'
biča/yabči	'to weep'	či:s/ačya:s	'bag'
čawa/yačwi	'to brand'	samač/asma:č	'fish'
		di:č/dyu:č	'cock'
Nouns		birča/birič	'pond, cistern'
čatf/čtu:f	'shoulder'	sičči:n	'knife'
čalb/čla:b	'dog'	saka:či:n <u>or</u> sača:či:n	'knives'
čibd	'liver, guts (fig)'		

Three different sets of words containing /č/ were excluded from the calculation of PV2. The first set listed in PV2.2 contains words in which all speakers have dialectal /č/ but in which /č/ is not replaceable by /k/ because no exact analogue with the same meaning exists in MSA. The word /ba:čir/ 'tomorrow' is excluded, for instance, because /ba:kir/, by substitution of /k/ for /č/ means 'premature'; if a more "standard" expression for 'tomorrow' is required, either the cognate /bukra/ or /ghadan/ must be used. Similarily, /malač/ means 'to betrothe' in BA, the substitution of /k/ for /č/ makes it into a different word - 'to possess'.

Compared to the words in PV2.1, many of the words in the list PV2.2 below, are associated with the pre-industrial culture of Baḥrain, and have highly specialised meanings, e.g. /čo:čab/, /mačbu:s/, /načča:b/. In other cases, e.g. /smu:č/ and /simča:n/, a morphological pattern, common to the dialect and MSA, has been applied in the dialect to a root to which it is not applied in MSA. Such words cannot therefore be "MSA-ized" by the substitution of /k/ - */smu:k/ and */simka:n/ are non-occurring forms. Compare the <u>variable</u> plurals (list PV2.1) /asma:č/~/asma:k/, where the dialect and MSA <u>share</u> the same morphological pattern. The words listed in PV2.2 were thus excluded from further consideration for the same reasons as those given for the exclusion of the words listed in PV1.1.

List PV2.2 Words in which both 'Arab and Baḥārna have /č/, but which have no exact analogues with the same meaning in MSA

<u>Particles</u>	
čiḏi	'like this, so'
činn (+enclitic)	'as if, like'
<u>Verbs</u>	
čabb/yičibb	'to upset, knock over'
čaffas/yičaffis	'to fold up'
čaffat/yičaffit	'to tie (s'one up)'
čaffan/yičaffin	'to shroud (a corpse)'
čandas/yičandis	'to lean, bend over s'thing'
malač/yamlič	'to betrothe'
načab/yančib	'to ladle'
načal/yančil	'to turn upside down'
ḥa:ča/yiḥa:či	'to address (someone)'
tḥačča/ytiḥačča	'to speak'
inčabb/yinčibb	'to be quiet (vulg)'
fačč/yifičč	'to reveal (bride's face); to release (from contractual obligation)'

<u>Nouns/Adjectives</u>	
čan9ad	'king mackerel'
čiffa	'edge'
čo:cab/čawa:čib	'underwater spring'
bičar	'firstborn'
hala:č	'starvation, death'
rića:b	'riding beasts'
dačča	'stone step'
9ičwa	'tail(of a bird)'
do:č	'type of seaweed'
9ačča:f	'hairdresser (at a wedding)'
načča:b	'ladler (in a ship's crew)'
naččal	'tip-up lorry'
mančab	'ladle'
manču:s	'type of fish'
mačbu:s	'dish of rice and meat or fish (pl)'
smu:č	'fish (pl)'
simča:n	
samma:č/ sama:mi:č	'fisherman'
ḥači/ḥača:wi	'speech, gossip'

The second and third sets of lexical items containing /č/ which have been excluded from the calculation of scores on PV2 are the "non-shared" items. In list PV2.3, the 'Arab dialect has /č/ and all the B dialects have /k/; in List PV2.4, B II speakers only have /č/ and the other dialects 'Arab and urban Baḥārna alike, have /k/. Variation in these items is discussed as a separate issue. Unlike the /č/ in "shared" items, /č/ in these items is a clear marker of one group's speech: literate speakers, as we shall see, avoid /č/ in such words much more markedly than they do in "shared" items.

In the Lists PV2.3 and PV2.4, words with "non-shared" /č/ are spelt according to group-specific morpho-phonemic rules. 'Arab /čibi:r/ 'big' corresponds not to Baḥārna /kibi:r/ but to /kabi:r/; village Baḥārna /čbur/ 'to grow up' corresponds to 'Arab /kubar/, not /kbur/. Morphophonemic differences of this kind between dialects are taken up in greater detail in chapters 6 and 7. But, as we shall see at the conclusion of this chapter, the absence of 'meso-forms' which might be predicted by the simple substitution of one phoneme for another - e.g. the non-occurrence of, let us say, */kbur/ in B II literate speech, but rather the wholesale borrowing of 'Arab morpho-phonemic shape /kubar/ - suggests that a lexical, rather than phonemic interpretation of the variation between forms which just happen to be less morphophonemically distinct (like /ṣadi:g/ and /ṣadi:q/) might also be justified.

List PV2.3 Items in which the 'Arab dialect has /č/, the Baḥārna dialects /k/.

Verbs

čatt/yičitt	'to pour
čammal/yičammil	'to complete'
faččar/yifaččir	'to think'
baččar/yibaččir	'to prepare'
da:bač/yida:bič	'to run'

Nouns/Adjectives

misči:n/ masa:či:n	'poor, wretched'
čiṯir	'amount'
čiṯi:r	'many'
čibi:r	'big, old'
čaba:b	'kebab'
riči:č	'fine, delicate, thin'
ra:čib	'riding, climbing'
warč	'thigh'
ḏičar	'memory commemoration'
tara:či	'pendulous earrings'
mara:čib	'ships'
sibi:ča, čalṯam	'girls' names' (used by 'Arab only)
xičri	'stupid, inconsiderate'
ḏi:č	'this'
sama:bi:č	'sambuks (type of boat)'

List PV2.4 Items in which the B II dialect has /č/, the B I and 'Arab dialect has /k/

Verbs

čbur/yičbur	'to grow up'
čfur/yičfur	'to increase become many'
čadd/yičidd	'to earn'
čarfas/yičarfis	'to knock down, flatten'
čalaf/yičlif	'to turn over (soil)'
čisa/yičsi	'to clothe'
ačal/ya:čil	'to eat'
načaf/yinčif	'to break (a promise)'
rčib/yirčib	'to ride, mount'
ḥazač/yiḥzič	'to get trapped, ensnared'
ḍaḥḥač/yiḍaḥḥič	'to laugh'
ḥarrač/yiḥarrič	'to move (s'thing)'
tčallam/ yitčallam	'to speak'
raččab/yaraččib	'to prepare (e.g. a meal)'
iftačč/yiftačč	'to get free (of something)'

Nouns/Adjectives

čubr	'size'
čba:r (pl)	'big'
čil	'all'
čidda	'job, way of earning a living'
ču:da/čwad	'pile, heap'
čna:r	'fruit of the lotus tree'
čilla, čali:l	'hottest or coldest part of a season'
čarwa, čarawiya	'hire, fare'
čiswa/ časa:wi	'clothes'
čarr	'sling for climbing palm trees'
ču:l	'wormholes (in leaves)'
ačil	'food'
mo:čala:t	'comestibles'
ačbar	'bigger'
ačfar	'more numerous'
ačfariya	'majority'
miča:n	'place'
duḥč	'laughter'
ḥari:ča	'movement (esp. embryo in the womb)'
9ači:sa	'hovel, slum'
binč	'heart, core (of something)'
šo:č	'thorn'
ṣa:ča	'wet, badly drained soil'
dičča:n	'shop'
ba:rič	'kneeling; wretched (fig)'
fa:čih	'insolent'
mčawwad	'numerous, many'
masbu:č	'moulded, inter-woven'
ša:bič bi	'joined, adjacent to'
fačča:či	'openings'

We have grouped PV1 and PV2 together as Type 1 variables, since in both cases we are measuring, across different communities, the replaceability of non-standard dialectal variants by standard variants under the conditions where such replacement is possible. There are, however, differences between PV1 and PV2: PV1 measures the replacement of a variety of non-standard dialectal variants

/g/, /j/ and /ḳ/, whose distribution we have already noted, with /q/; PV2 measures the replacement of a *single shared non-standard variant* /č/ with /k/, a phoneme which is not, like /q/, distinctively "standard" inasmuch as /k/, but not /q/, occurs in a great many dialectal words in all BA dialects. The common denominator of PV1 and PV2, however, is that none of the BA dialectal variants on these variables 'agrees' with the MSA variant and this justifies their classification as the same basic type; contrast this with Type 2 and Type 3 variables below, where either the B or A dialectal variant *does* agree with that of MSA, the supradialectal standard. We shall see that, given that dialectal/MSA morpho-semantic congruity determines whether phonemic replacement can occur at all, it is the local status-marking of the potentially replaceable dialectal variant, as specified in Table 5, which determines the likelihood of literate speakers *actually* replacing it with the standard variant. Morpho-semantic congruity may thus be a *necessary* condition for variation to occur; but it is not *sufficient* as a predictor of which variants are most or least likely to be replaced.

5.4 Type 2 variables: the data bases for PV3 and PV4

Type 2 variables are those where the 'Arab dialectal variant coincides with the MSA variant, "isolating" the Baḥārna variant. If we are correct in assuming that the Baḥārna group is socially inferior to the 'Arab, then the "pull" of the local prestige dialect *and* the supra-dialectal standard on the low-status dialect on Type 2 variables is in the same direction, from the point of view of any literate B speaker. An inspection of Table 5 shows that PV3 and PV4 are Type 2 variables. MSA and the A dialect have /ḏ/ and /ṯ/, the B dialects all have /d/ and /f/, in all lexical items where OA had /ḏ/ and /ṯ/.

The data base for variables PV3 and PV4 was accordingly all items in which /ḏ/~/d/ and /ṯ/~/f/ variation occurs: that is all lexical items in which these variants correspond to OA/MSA /ṯ/ and /ḏ/.

In only one recent borrowing from MSA - /ṯaqa:fa/ 'culture, education' - did /f/ fail to show up in a single B speaker's data. However, it was unclear whether this was because there was genuinely no variation possible between /ṯ/ and /f/ in this word (it is clearly a modern borrowing), or because it only ever occurred in the "literate" data: it is possible (though because of the stylistic constraints given in 1.2 unlikely) that /faqa:fa/ is a possible form for illiterates though it was unrecorded in this research. Tokens of this word were excluded from the data base for PV4 because of its exclusive occurrence in literate data.

5.5 Type 3 variables: the data bases for PV5 and PV6

Type 3 variables are the converse of Type 2: those in which

the B dialectal variants agree with MSA, "isolating" the variants of the 'Arab. Variables PV5 and PV6 are examples of Type 3 variables, except that on PV5 as noted in 4.3.2, a small minority of B speakers, the B III group, also have /y/ as dialectal variant.

5.5.1 The data base for PV5

The variant /y/ in the A and B III dialects corresponds to /j/ in the dialects of the main groups of Baḥārna and MSA. This is true of both BA words which lack an MSA analogue and BA words which also form part of the MSA lexicon. As was pointed out in 4.2.3 however, certain words recently borrowed from MSA or other languages which have no local equivalents always have /j/, never /y/, in all dialects. They were accordingly excluded from the data base for the calculation of variation on PV5. The data base used was the list of words in List PV5.1 which occurred frequently in all dialects, showed variation between /j/ and /y/ and, <u>in most cases</u>, had direct MSA analogues.

Many other words in which the 'Arab and B III speakers had /y/ as opposed to the general B /j/ occurred sporadically in the data but did not appear to be subject to variation at all. These words denoted culture-specific artifacts or activities fast disappearing, and quite outside the sphere of the sedentary, literate culture of educated Baḥrain. Not surprisingly, these words were most often used by illiterate speakers in descriptions of what life was like in the pre-oil era. They comprise List PV5.2 and were not included in the data base since they were invariable items, having categorical /y/ in the 'Arab and B III dialects and /j/ in the others.

List PV5.1 Items in which /j/ ~ /y/ variation occurred in the data (the data base for PV5)

Verbs

ya/iyi	'to come'
ya:b/iyi:b*	'to bring'
ya:z/iyu:z	'to be suitable'
yalas/iylis	'to sit'
yarr/iyurr	'to pull'
yarrab/iyarrib	'to try, test'
yamma9/iyammi9	'to collect'
yawwad/iyawwid*	'to grasp'
naḍay/yinḍay	'to ripen, ready'
9ayaz/ya9yiz	'to be incapable'
9ayyan/ yi9ayyin	'to knead (dough)'
iḥta:y/yiḥta:y	'to need'

Nouns/Adjectives

ya:hil/yuha:l*	'child'
yim9a/yama:9i	'Friday'
yidi:d/yiddad	'new'
ya:r/yi:ra:n	'neighbour'
yibal/yba:l	'mountain'
yadd(a)	'grandfather/ mother'
yizi:ra	'island'
yazar	'carrot, root'
yaḏ9a	'tree-trunk'
yari:d	'palm-branch'
yari:š	'crushed grain'
yu:9	'hunger'
yu:9a:n	'hungry'
yimal/yma:l	'camel'

<u>Nouns/Adjectives</u> (contd.)

yufra/yufar	'hole'	ḥayyi	'Hajji (title)'
yild	'skin'	ta:yir	'merchant'
ya:ff	'dry'	9ayam	'Persians'
yo:z	'almond'	9ayu:z/	'old woman'
yimi:9	'all'	9aya:yi:z	
yima:9a	'assembly of	9ayi:n	'dough'
	people'	šiyar	'trees'
yisir	'causeway, bridge'	ḥayar/ḥya:ra	'stone'
yaras	'bell'	finya:l/	'coffee cup'
rayya:l/	'man'	fana:yi:l	
raya:yi:l*		maynu:n/	'madman'
rayil/	'husband'	maya:ni:n	
raya:yi:l		a9way	'crooked'
ri:l/ryu:l	'foot, leg'	xanyar	'dagger'
yinu:b	'south'	mi:da:f/	'oar'
daray	'steps, stairs'	maya:di:f	
wayba	'meal'	mi:da:r	'fish-hook'
we:h/wyu:h	'face'	wa:yid*	'much, a lot'
dya:y	'chicken'	masyid/masa:yid	'mosque'
		maylis/maya:lis	'sitting-room'

We commented above that <u>in most cases</u> the words in List PV5.1 have MSA analogues. But there are a few commonly occurring items (asterisked) such as /wa:yid/ 'a lot, many' and /ya:b/ 'to bring' which have been included in this list despite the fact that they have no MSA equivalents, or in the case of items such as /rayya:l/ 'man', they have a different morphological shape in MSA though derived from the same root as the MSA equivalent. The reason is that they are such common items in the dialects of a wide area which includes Baḥrain that they seem to have acquired the status of regional standards, and occur freely even in more formal styles of BA speech (in which, for example, MSA lexical influence is strong). Like words which do have MSA analogues, they exhibit /j/ ~ /y/ variation in the speech of educated speakers and so they are included in the data base. However, a detailed investigation into speakers' realisations of the MSA versus non-MSA words in List PV5.1 (Holes 1980) showed that there is evidence to suggest that educated speakers do in fact treat these groups of words differently: "non-MSA items" such as /yawwad/, /ya:b/, /ya:hil/, /wa:yid/, /rayya:l/ <u>do</u> exhibit variation, but are relatively less likely to than items which have MSA analogues (see 5.7.4 below).

List PV5.2 Dialectal items which <u>never</u> exhibited variation between /y/ and /j/: in "/y/-areas" always /y/ and in "/j/-areas" always /j/

<u>Particles</u>

9ayal	'well, so'

<u>Verbs</u>

yazza/iyazzi	'to be sufficient'
yabbab/iyabbib	'to ululate'
tyawwaz/ ytiyawwaz	'to agree'
hayas/yahyis	'to feel (s'thing)'
hayy/yihiyy	'to go, depart'
trayya/yitrayya	'to wait for'

<u>Nouns/Adjectives</u>

yaḥla/yḥa:l	'water-pot'
yiḥḥ	'melon'
yu:niya/yawa:ni	'sack, bag'
yilf/ylu:f	'quantity of dates'
ya:lu:g/ yawa:li:g	'quantity of dates'
yiha:z	'wedding gifts'
yu:d	'water-skin'
yazwa	'crew (pearling dhow)'
hawwa:y	'quack-doctor'
ḥayya:m/ ḥaya:yi:m	'hawker, peddler'
nixxay	'chick-pea'
triny	'type of citrus'
nariny	'type of citrus'
baru:y	'children's game'
daḥru:y	'Stick and Hoop (game)'
barastiy	'reed hut'
mara:yil	'manly virtues'
miyaddif	'stave for holding a boat upright in dry dock'

5.5.2 <u>The data base for PV6</u>

Any instance of OA/MSA /gh/, whether in a dialectal word, e.g. /laghwa/ 'tittle-tattle, talking' or in an obvious recent borrowing from MSA, e.g. /mugha:dara/ 'departure' may be realised in the A dialect with one of the freely varying allophones of /q/: [lɑGwæ] of [lɑqwæ], [muGa:dara] or |muqa:dara| (see 4.2.2). The data base for PV6 consisted consequently of all words in the data containing OA or MSA /gh/.

5.6 <u>Summary</u>

<u>Type 1 Variables:</u> Scores calculated on the basis of items in which <u>no dialect has a variant which coincides with the MSA variant,</u> i.e.

	<u>BA dialects</u>		<u>MSA</u>	
PV1:	/g/, /j/ or /ḳ/	versus	/q/	(List PV1.2)
PV2:	/č/	versus	/k/	(List PV2.1)

Type 2 Variables: Scores calculated on the basis of items in which only the socially superior group's dialectal variant coincides with the MSA variant,i.e.

	A/MSA		B	
PV3:	/t̲/	versus	/f/	(all items)
PV4:	/d̲/	versus	/d/	(all items)

Type 3 Variables: Scores calculated on the basis of items in which only the socially inferior group's dialectal variant coincides with the supra-dialectal variant, i.e.

	B/MSA		B	
PV5:	/j/	versus	/y/	(List PV5.1)
PV6:	/gh/	versus	/q/	(all items)

It will be recalled that on PV5, the variant of one B group, III, coincides with that of the A group.

In section 5.7 we examine and interpret levels of variation on these 6 variables, on a group-score basis.

5.7 Levels of "dialectalness"

The scores in Tables 6 and 7 below are measures of the extent to which a particular group clung to the dialectal variants which we described in Chapter 4 as stereotypically associated with it, calculated in the way described in 5.2. These scores are gross measures of what might be termed the "dialectalness" of different groups defined by sect, area, and literacy. We must be clear, however, precisely what we are comparing is the tendency to preserve dialectal variants - and it can be seen from Table 4 that these variants are not always, or often, shared by different sectarian groups. On PV5, for example, 'Arab and Baḥārna III share /y/ as dialectal variant, while B I and II have /j/. Therefore, the score of .88 for the "literate A" group in Table 6 below means that 88% of this group's realisations of the data base for PV5 (List PV5.1) had /y/ and 12% had /j/; but the score of .82 for the "literate B I" group on the same variable means almost the opposite: 82% of their realisations were dialectal (in this case /j/) and 18% were /y/.

It is quite possible (and as we shall see in 5.8 it is often the case) that individual speakers within the groups defined in Tables 6 or 7 below have 100% /y/ or 100% /j/ - a fact which is inevitably obscured by treating groups as homogeneous wholes. What the group scores do enable us to do is to compare the relative distance that representative groups of speakers, defined by social variables, have "moved away" from dialectal norms in the direction of dialectal convergence.

Variable Type:	1		2		3	
Group:	PV1	PV2	PV3	PV4	PV5	PV6
A	.63	.91	1.0	1.0	.88	.57
B I	.48	.89	.26	.22	.82	.95
B II	.39	.67	.32	.14	.80	.93
B III	.50	.80	.21	.12	.09	1.0

Table 6: "Dialectalness" scores on 6 phonological variables: literates

Variable Type:		1		2		3	
Group:		PV1	PV2	PV3	PV4	PV5	PV6
A	(N = 17)	163	212	511	189	239	367
B I	(N = 7)	89	86	373	145	189	251
B II	(N = 11)	110	121	326	127	227	261
B III	(N = 7)	63	95	259	86	147	181

Table 6(a): Tokens on 6 phonological variables: literates

Variable Type:	1		2		3	
Group:	PV1	PV2	PV3	PV4	PV5	PV6
A	.89	1.0	1.0	1.0	.96	.79
B I	.77	1.0	.54	.83	.99	1.0
B II	.97	1.0	.84	.97	1.0	1.0
B III	.97	1.0	.88	.94	.83	1.0

Table 7: "Dialectalness" scores on 6 phonological variables: illiterates

Variable Type:		1		2		3	
Group:		PV1	PV2	PV3	PV4	PV5	PV6
A	(N = 17)	142	194	469	173	373	362
B I	(N = 7)	46	83	117	66	61	89
B II	(N = 13)	111	150	397	131	292	321
B III	(N = 8)	72	82	252	122	198	201

Table 7 (a): Tokens on 6 phonological variables: illiterates

5.7.1 General comments

A comparison of Tables 6 and 7 points up the following consistent general tendencies:

5.7.1.1 On every variable, every illiterate group had a dialectalness score equal to or higher than, that of its corresponding literate group.

5.7.1.2 On every variable except PV6, the 'Arab literate group had the highest dialectalness score of any literate group.

5.7.1.3 On every variable except PV6, the size of the difference between the dialectalness scores of corresponding literate and illiterate groups was smallest among the 'Arab.

Interpretation

5.7.1.1 suggests that dialectal variants in general were more often preserved in the speech of illiterates than literates. This would be an unsurprising finding if dialectal variants were always 'non-standard'; however, in the case of PV5 and PV6, where the dialect of the B I and II groups agrees with MSA in having /j/ and /gh/, literates still replace this dialectal/MSA variant with 'non-standard' /y/ and /q/ - that is, they seem to have adopted 'Arab norms on these variables to a measurable degree. This indicates that where the local prestige dialect and the supra-dialectal system are different, the former may exert a stronger pull on the stigmatised dialect than the latter.

5.7.1.2 suggests that 'Arab literates were more true to their dialect than were Baḥārna literates, even in one of the two cases where their dialectal variant is isolated and non-standard (PV5). We would interpret this trend as evidence of the linguistic security of the socially prestigious group.

5.7.1.3 suggests that the 'Arab, as a group, spoke a more

homogeneous dialect than did any single group of Baḥārna. There was a much less obvious difference between the speech of 'Arab literates and illiterates than between the speech of Baḥārna literates and illiterates.

5.7.1.1-3 express general tendencies in the group data. These tendencies are examined in more detail below.

5.7.2 Variation on Type 1 variables

	d variant	Literates	d score	Illiterates	d score	
PV1 (List 1.2)	/g/ & /j/	A	.63	B III	.97	most dialectal
	/g/	B III	.50	B II	.97	↓
	/g/	B I	.48	A	.89	
	/ḳ/or/g/	B II	.39	B I	.77	least dialectal
PV2 (List 2.1)	/č/	A	.91	A & all B	1.0	most dialectal
	/č/	B I	.89			↓
	/č/	B III	.80			
	/č/	B II	.67			least dialectal

Table 8: Type 1 variables: measures of "dialectalness" in the data

Discussion

We noted in Table 5 that the dialectal variants of PV1 are not shared: /jili:l/, /gali:l/ and /ḳali:l/ for example are all possible BA realisations of 'a little', with only partially overlapping sectarian distribution; on the other hand, /čam/ 'how much' is common to all BA dialects. This we believe to be one reason why MSA /qali:l/ is a more frequent replacer of its BA equivalents than MSA /kam/ is of /čam/: the use of /q/ as a replacing phoneme for dialectal variants, where MSA/dialectal congruity allows, is one means by which a Baḥraini may obscure his sectarian/regional origin. But the substitution of /k/ for /č/ does not accomplish the same social end in Baḥrain - at least, in any lexical item where all Baḥrainis share dialectal /č/. As Blanc (1960) illustrated, the replacement of non-standard variants by standard equivalents may be triggered by a desire to present one's speech as "educated" - but the likelihood of any particular non-standard variant being replaced can only be explained within the local sociolinguistic context - that is, in terms of the "local evaluation" of that variant.

This explanation would seem to be confirmed by the relative strength of the resistance of PV1 /g/, as opposed to /j/ and /ḳ/, to replacement by /q/: /g/ is shared in many items by the 'Arab and all urban Baḥārna (i.e. 70% of the Arabic-speaking indigenous population). As such, it represents, like "shared" /č/, commonality and sectarian neutrality. It is not then surprising to find that, on a more detailed breakdown of Tables 6 and 6(a), the B II literates were revealed as almost never using non-shared /ḳ/: only 2 instances in 110 tokens. Some 67 tokens of 'standard' /q/ occurred, and 41 of /g/ - this latter fact showing how a non-shared stigmatised dialectal variant (/ḳ/) can give way to a more generally acceptable non-marked, but still dialectal variant /g/. The literate A speakers preserved their marked variant, /j/, more often, as might be expected of a socially dominant group: of 45 occurrences of items where /j/ could have occurred, 10 were actually realised with /j/, and 35 with 'replacing' /q/; of 118 occurrences items where /g/ could have occurred, 91 actually showed /g/, and only 27 /q/.

In general terms, the phonological systems of literate Baḥrainis, compared to illiterates, appear to be moving to a point where /q/ and /g/ are becoming stable, 'shared' phonemes with little overlap, neither of which is associated with any particular sectarian or locationally defined group. /j/ and /ḳ/, the non-shared variants, appear to be gradually disappearing. It is true that /j/ is still heard as a categorical 'frozen' marker of all 'Arab speech in a few items where there is no MSA/dialectal congruity, e.g. /ḥalj/ 'mouth' (see List PV1.1) but /j/ is tending to be replaced by /q/ in all items where there is congruity. /ḳ/ has given way almost completely in literate B II speech to /g/, which seems to be becoming the dialectal norm for all Baḥraini literates, with /q/ acting as a variable replacement of it in cases of MSA/dialectal syntactic or semantic congruity, and as a categorical marker of MSA borrowings which have no dialectal equivalents. In tabular form the situation can be represented as follows (the symbol ~ means 'in variation with').

Dialectal "core" items in which /q/ cannot occur (List PV1.1)		
A	/g/ and /j/	(no variation - all speakers)
B I & III	/g/	(no variation - all speakers)
B II	/ḳ/~ /g/	(illiterates only)
	/g/	(no variation - literates only)
Variable items: MSA/dialectal congruity (List PV1.2)		
A	/g/~ /q/	(realised as [gh], [G] or [q])
	/j/~ /q/	
B I & III	/g/~ /q/	
B II	/ḳ/~ /g/~ /q/	(illiterates)
	/g/~ /q/	(literates)
Invariable items: MSA borrowings (List PV1.3)		
A	/q/	(realised as [gh], [G] or [q])
All B	/q/	

Table 9: Variation between /q/ and dialectal variants in different word groups

The literates' replacement of the shared non-standard variant on PV2 is relatively weak, as Table 8 clearly indicates. We have argued that this is because /č/, on PV2, is not particularly associated with any group's speech - it simply indicates dialectal rather than highly standardised speech and can occur in a wide variety of styles. Certainly the circumstances in which our 'literate' data were collected gave rise to speech styles in which this /č/ could be expected to show up regularly.

The argument that /č/ in certain lexical items has become more resistant to replacement by /k/ because it is shared by all speakers in just those items is bolstered by the contrasting instability of /č/ in items where /č/ is *not* communally shared. Where the B II dialect is alone in having /č/ (List PV2.4), literate villagers almost invariably replace it: 6 occurrences of /č/ in 160 tokens of words in List PV2.4 for literates compare with 61 out of 147 for illiterates. Similarly, where A dialect alone has /č/ (List PV2.3), analysis showed that the literates had /č/ in 9 out of 30 tokens, and the illiterates in 21 out of 40. The parallels with the literate speakers' treatment of the /ḳ/ and /j/ variants on PV1 - variants which are also *non-standard* and *non-shared* - are obvious, and, we would argue, similarly motivated. Differences in recording context (Chapter 3) might partly explain the different frequencies of non-shared /č/ as between literates and illiterates, but it is unlikely to have been responsible for producing such clear effects by itself.

We would then argue that the general probability of /č/-replacement is determined by two factors: whether a given dialect word has an MSA analogue, and, if so, what the *local status* of /č/ in that word is. Phonological factors, such as whether /č/ occurs in a high or low vowel environment (Johnstone, 1963), seem to have no obvious relationship in themselves with the susceptibility of /č/ to replacement. In tabular form:

Non-MSA items
The set of items which have no direct MSA analogues (List PV2.2)

/č/ is *categorical* for all BA speakers if such an item is used.

Potentially MSA items
The set of items which have morpho-semantic analogues in MSA

(a)	'Shared':	/č/ is *least liable* to replacement by /k/ (List PV2.1)
(b)	'Non-shared':	'Arab /č/ is *more liable to replacement than 'shared' /č/* (List PV2.3)
(c)	'Non-shared':	B II /č/ is *more liable to replacement than shared /č/ or 'Arab /č/* (List PV2.4)

Table 10: *Variation between /č/ and /k/ in different word groups*

Cross-dialectal borrowing of /č/ was extremely rare: only 3 instances of Baḥārna (all urban) using 'Arab /č/ were recorded, and none at all of 'Arab using Baḥārna /č/.

We can summarise the society-language relationship on Type 1 variables in the following terms:

(i) Among literate speakers, 'Arab are the least, and B II speakers the most prone, to opt for the standard variant on variables where dialectal variants differ from each other and none aligns with the standard (PV1). The urban Baḥārna occupy a position intermediate between the two extremes - "less dialectal" than the 'Arab and "more dialectal" than the village Baḥārna. These facts are directly explicable in terms of the social attitudes prevalent in Baḥrain: the 'Arab feel the least need to "correct" their speech in the direction of the literary standard because of their social dominance; the village Baḥārna, universally regarded as country bumpkins, over-compensate for their social inferiority to both the 'Arab and town Baḥārna, by the "over-correctness" of their speech. No similar pattern is noticeable in the data for those less familiar with standard forms, as Table 8 shows.

(ii) In the case where the sectarian dialects coincide with each other and oppose the standard variant (PV2), a similar sociolinguistic stratification is evident, albeit in a less extreme form than on PV1. Literate 'Arab replace the non-standard variant least, literate village Baḥārna most, while the town dwellers again occupy an intermediate position. The relative social standing of the groups would again seem to explain the stratification in the levels of "dialectalness" which each group of literate speakers could afford to exhibit. Again, no similar pattern is evident in the illiterate speech data.

(iii) Among literates, non-shared variants which are also non-standard (PV1 /j/ and /ḳ/, PV2 /č/ in items where any of these variants is specific to one or other sectarian group) resist replacement by standard variants less strongly than do non-standard variants such as /g/ which are communally shared. The tendency to zero-out non-shared non-standard variants is much more pronounced in the Baḥārna than the 'Arab literate data because these are the clearest markers of sectarian and geographical origin, and hence social status.

5.7.3 Variation on Type 2 variables

Table 11 gives the relevant data for PV3 and PV4. If we are correct in arguing that non-communally shared, non-standard variants are more prone to replacement by standard variants than are shared variants, and that this tendency is more acute in the A than the B communities because of their relative social position, we would predict that the B variants on PV3 and PV4 would be very markedly avoided by literate Baḥārna, since on these variables the high-status dialect and MSA coincide. This is precisely what occurred as Table 11 below shows. The B variants, especially /f/, showed up only marginally in the literate data, but occurred with great regularity in the illiterate data.

	d variant	Literates	d score	Illiterates	d score	
PV3	/d̲/	A	1.0	A	1.0	most dialectal
	/d/	B II	.32	B III	.88	↓
	/d/	B I	.26	B II	.84	
	/d/	B III	.21	B I	.54	least dialectal
PV4	/t̲/	A	1.0	A	1.0	most dialectal
	/f̄/	B I	.22	B II	.97	↓
	/f/	B II	.14	B III	.94	
	/f/	B III	.12	B I	.83	least dialectal

Table 11: Type 2 variables: measures of "dialectalness" in the data

Literate Baḥārna seem highly sensitive about the specifically B nature of /f/ < OA /t̲/ and /d/ < OA /d̲/. Some educated Baḥārna deny that these variants are ever used in Baḥraini Arabic, while others accept them as "possible", but describe them as typical of 'uneducated' speakers in general, not of Baḥārna in particular. This sensitivity is understandable. Unlike /ḳ/ and "village B" (B II) /č/, /f/ and /d/ are not confined in their distribution to rural communities - they are part of the town dialect as well. Town-dwellers who poke fun at forms like /ḳa:l/ 'he said' and /ačbar/ 'bigger' because they are "rustic" are conscious that they themselves are the butt of 'Arab humour because of forms like /fala:fa/ 'three', /ha:da/ 'this'. Replacement of /f/ in items where /f/ is not replaceable is evidence of this insecurity: /lo:fari/ 'idler, loafer', an Arabised borrowing of English 'loafer', was occasionally realised in the data as /lo:t̲ari/, "borrowed" /f/ being mistaken for /f/ < OA /t̲/ by Baḥārna anxious to avoid the stereotypically B reflex /f/. Indeed, the degree of difference between the "dialectalness" scores of literates and illiterates was much higher for the B groups on PV3 and PV4 than it was on any other variables, as an inspection of Tables 6 and 7 shows.

PV3 /d/ and PV4 /f/ appear to be on the way to becoming markers of illiterate B speech, though, unlike /ḳ/ and "village B" (B II) /č/, they are community-wide, rather than rural in their distribution. The pressures on literate speakers to avoid them are strong because they are at once non-standard and non-high-status. In any social context other than the purely domestic or intimate they are therefore avoided.

Contextual factors which promote or inhibit /d/- and /f/-use were highlighted by the close but uncontrolled observation, over a period of three months, of the speech behaviour of the agricultural research officer who helped in data collection (Chapter 3). During visits to farms, it became clear that the muršid used /f/ and /d/ to the almost complete exclusion of /ṯ/ and /ḏ/. The reason was obvious: the lengthy conversations with farmers, many of whom were acquaintances of long-standing, were set firmly in a rural B social context, and of course, the farmers were illiterate. But back at the research station, a national scientific establishment whose staff was religiously mixed, the muršid's behaviour was quite different. Here he largely avoided /f/ and /d/ even where, it seemed, conversation was relatively relaxed, non-science-oriented and involved B speakers only. /f/ and /d/ were presumably inappropriate in the public, de-personalised atmosphere of the Agricultural Research Station. What was most striking, however, was that when any of these fellow Baḥārna workers - all well-educated and literate - was invited to lunch in the muršid's home after work had finished for the day, /f/ and /d/ immediately resurfaced in conversation in the muršid's dining-room to the virtual exclusion of /ṯ/ and /ḏ/! The more intimate, domestic aspects of the speakers' relationships had obviously become upper-most in the changed social environment, even though the conversational topic was often the same as that which they had been discussing a few minutes earlier at the Research Station. The changed environment was marked linguistically by the use of unmistakably B forms like /f/ and /d/, instead of "educated", "neutral" /ḏ/ and /ṯ/.

Baḥārna literate behaviour on PV3 and PV4 is thrown into stark relief by 'Arab literate behaviour on the Type 3 variables PV5 and 6 - the variables in which the high prestige variants are "isolated", opposing variants which are both B and standard.

5.7.4 Variation on Type 3 variables

Because the patterns of variation on PV5 and PV6 are quite complex, we deal with them sequentially for the sake of clarity. PV5 is examined first.

	d variant	Literates	d score	Illiterates	d score	
	/y/	A	.88	B II	1.0	most dialectal
PV5	/j/	B I	.82	B I	.99	↓
(List	/j/	B II	.80	A	.96	
5.1)	/y/	B III	.09	B III	.83	least dialectal

Table 12: PV5: measures of "dialectalness" in the data

Examining first the illiterate data, we find that each group largely conforms to its dialectal stereotype: the 'Arab and B III groups have almost categorical /y/ and the majority groups in the B community (I and II) have near-categorical /j/. While literacy appears to make little difference to the likelihood of the 'Arab using the non-standard variant /y/, quite a different pattern, or rather patterns, are revealed if we compare the literate and illiterate Baḥārna.

Most strikingly, the literate Baḥārna from areas where /y/ is the basilectal variant appear to have almost completely re-placed /y/ by /j/ - this despite the fact that /y/ is undoubtedly the 'high-status' variant in Baḥrain. But literate Baḥārna from areas where /j/ is the dialectal variant, appear to have operated the substitution process in the opposite direction, by adopting non-standard but 'high-prestige' /y/, as a replacement for their 'standard-like' /j/, to a small but consistent degree.

The explanation of these conflicting patterns of behaviour lies, it appears, in the conflicting demands of different status systems. To the literate B III group, the /j/ variant is not only the standard variant, but also that of their B co-religionists in the surrounding areas: Rās-Rummān, Dirāz, Sanābis and Dēh are small islands of "/y/-users" in a sea of "/j/-users". Group pressure to conform, as well as the influence of literary standards on a low-status group, would partially explain this minority group's behaviour. However, it is also highly probable that the context in which the literate data were gathered was a relevant factor. In "/y/-pronouncing" B areas, /y/ seems to function in literate speech very much like /f/ and /d/ in the literate B community at large - as a marker of group identity in private as opposed to public speech contexts. The interviews the writer conducted with literate Baḥārna from these areas would be seen very much as "public" contexts in which /y/ would be inappropriate. In more casual contexts, however (though the writer's experience of this particular group of speakers was limited), /y/ was more in evidence in literate speech, just as /f/ and /d/ were in the case of our agricultural research officer.

The public utterances of Baḥārna from "/y/-pronouncing" areas on the subject of /y/ tended to be prescriptive: a typical case was that of a literate from Dirāz who spontaneously pointed out that he was bringing up his children to speak "properly" and pronounce Hajji as /ḥajji/, not /ḥayyi/. Notwithstanding the fact that /y/ is the variant associated with the high-status group, literate Baḥārna from the "/y/-areas" regard /y/ as "wrong" and derive a perverse satisfaction from the fact that, in their view, it shows the 'Arab dialect, like that spoken by the illiterates from the area they come from, to be further removed from the "correct" norms of MSA than the dialect spoken by the majority of Baḥārna.

If the reason that the literate B III speakers showed such a strong tendency to switch to /j/ is pressure from the standard form and the B dialectal norm, how can the opposite phenomenon, the marginal switch of the major groups of Baḥārna to /y/ be explained?

Clearly, this is a case of switching to the high-status form, and the mechanism which apparently controls it, revealed by an item-by-item lexical analysis of the data, gives an insight into the articulation of apparently conflicting principles. When the data were examined item by item, it was found that all the occurrences of switching by "/j/-area" Baḥārna were confined to a few lexical items only, and almost always in those items where no conflict between MSA and BA existed - that is in those items in List PV5.1 where there was no direct MSA morpho-semantic analogue. Five items from this list which have no direct analogues, together with one which is a borderline case, accounted for more than 95% of the total number of occurrences of /y/ in the B I and II data. These items were: /ya:b/ 'to bring', /wa:yid/ 'a lot', /ya:hil/, pl /yuha:l/ 'child', /yawwad/ 'to grasp, hold', /rayya:l/ 'man' plus /ya/ 'to come' which does have a direct analogue in MSA, but which has many non-MSA syntactic and semantic functions, e.g. imperfective /iyi/ 'approximately' in such phrases as /iyi šahre:n/ 'about two months', present participle /ya:y/ with the meaning 'to be about to do something' as in /ana ya:y adišš u.../ 'I was about to enter, when...'.

Most remarkably, it was also found that it was in just these few dialectal 'common-core' items that the literate B III group preserved /y/, in the few cases where they did; and, significantly, there was hardly a single instance of a literate A-speaker switching from /y/ to /j/ in these particular lexical items. Switching from /y/ to /j/ in the 'Arab case occurred only in cases where morpho-semantic congruity between the dialect and MSA was complete, e.g. in items like /maylis/ (MSA /majlis/) 'sitting room', /ta:yir/ (MSA /ta:jir/) 'merchant'.

We can summarise the position by saying that:

(i) Literate Baḥārna whose dialectal variant is standard /j/ strongly preserve it in words where BA/MSA morpho-semantic congruity is complete, switching only marginally to the non-standard, high status dialectal variant in such items. But they switch to /y/ much more strongly in items which are non-MSA, 'common-core' dialectal items.

(ii) Literate Baḥārna whose dialectal variant is non-standard /y/ switch very strongly to standard /j/ in items where there is BA/MSA morpho-semantic congruity, but less strongly in the non-MSA, 'common-core' dialectal items - that is, in precisely that category of words in which the 'Arab preserve /y/ and the other Baḥārna switch most strongly to it.

These patterns of /j/$\sim$/y/ variation seem to us to provide a striking example of how the high-status dialect, in the non-MSA dialectal lexical domain, determines where a non-standard variant may be preserved or adopted in the low-status dialects, and how the influence of MSA is dominant over that of the high-status dialect at points where the BA and MSA lexicons overlap. This is illustrated in Table 13 below, in which the superscript numbers represent the approximate strength of the variable switch by literate speakers from their community dialectal variants. Thus a "2" represents a move twice as strong, a "3" a move three times as strong, as a "1". Angled brackets $\langle\ \rangle$ indicate variability, thus $y \rightarrow \langle j \rangle$ means "y is variably replaced by j".

Social group	Prestige	dialectal variant	Lexical Domain			
			← "Dialectal" →		← "Non-dialectal" →	
			no overlap		overlap	no overlap
			List PV5.2	List PV5.1		
			BA only:	BA only:	BA/MSA	MSA only
			culture specific very localized use	common core/ regional standard	morpho-semantic congruity	
'Arab	high	y	y	y	$y \rightarrow \langle j \rangle^{1}$	j
Baḥārna I, II	low	j	j	$j \rightarrow \langle y \rangle^{2}$	$j \rightarrow \langle y \rangle^{1}$	j
Baḥārna III	low	y	y	$y \rightarrow \langle j \rangle^{3}$	$y \rightarrow \langle j \rangle^{8}$	j
			NO VARIATION	VARIATION ↙	↘	NO VARIATION
				high status influence strong, supra-dialectal influence weak	high status influence weak supra-dialectal influence strong	

Table 13: /j/~/y/ variation: interaction of lexical domain, social status and variant replacement

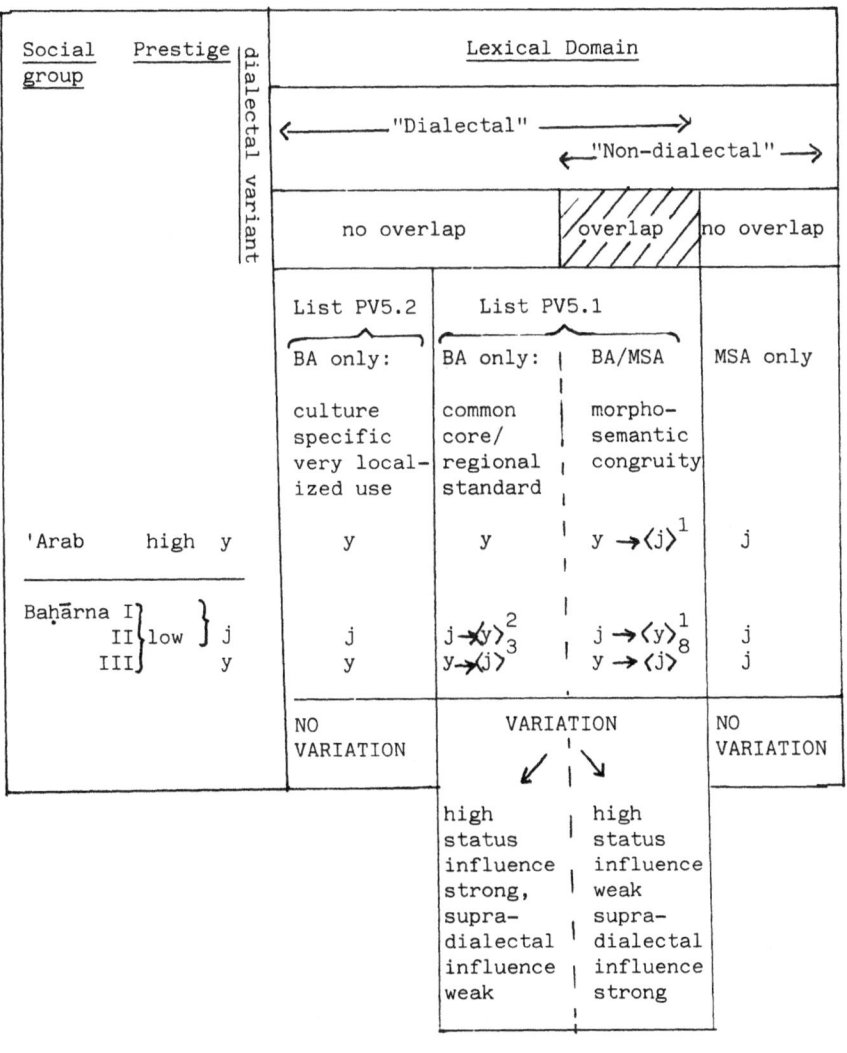

A similar principle explains why the switch of literate village Baḥārna from /ḳ/ to /g/, the dominant dialectal variant, is more pronounced in the words listed in List PV1.1 than it is in the words listed in PV1.2, where they switch more strongly to /q/ than to /g/. The words in List PV1.1 have a specialised dialectal syntactic or semantic function - they are not "possible words" in MSA, so any standardising move has to be towards a "dialectal standard". But the words in List PV1.2 have a sufficient degree of syntactic or semantic overlap with MSA to make them potential candidates for "MSA-ization". In this case Baḥārna village literates tended to opt for the "MSA-izing" variant /q/ more often than they did "standard-dialectal" /g/ (5.7.2). Thus, in the dialectal lexical domain, the switch is towards a dialectal standard, while in the cases of BA/MSA overlap, the supra-dialectal influence is stronger than the influence of the dialectal standard.

We now turn to an examination of the data for PV6, where the low-status variant and the MSA variant also coincide, isolating the high-status variant. The group dialectalness scores are reproduced below in Table 14. The 'Arab scores are a measure of the production of dialectal /q/ ([G] or [q]) in items in which OA/MSA has /gh/, the Baḥārna scores are a measure of the production of dialectal /gh/ ([gh]) in the same items.

	d variant	Literates	d score	Illiterates	d score
PV6	/q/	A	.57	A	.79
	/gh/	B I	.95	B I	1.0
	/gh/	B II	.93	B II	1.0
	/gh/	B III	1.0	B III	1.0

Table 14: PV6: measures of "dialectalness" in the data

Looking first at the B data, we note that the tendency to switch away from the B dialectal, but standard form /gh/ to the non-standard, but 'Arab /q/ parallels the B switch from /j/ to /y/ on PV5. The difference is in the strength of the switch, which is more marginal in the case of PV6. We would, however, explain the Baḥārna adoption of /q/ in the same terms as their adoption of /y/: both the /q/ < OA /gh/ and /y/ < OA /j/ variants are markers of the high-status dialect, and its influence is sufficiently strong to override the influence of MSA and cause variable replacement in Baḥārna speech of what the Baḥārna would no doubt claim are the 'correct' variants. It is interesting to note the consistent size of the difference between the level of literate and illiterate replacement of these standard variants: where the literate switch is relatively strong (PV5), the illiterate switch is weak; where the literate switch is relatively weak (PV6), there is no illiterate switch at all. This seems to be the paradoxical effect of becoming a literate member of the low-status community: the variants one adopts in order to distance oneself from the illiterate speech of one's community, and as it were, authenticate one's status as *literate* may in fact be *non-literary*, while the variants which are replaced may be technically nearer literary standards, but stigmatised locally as low-status.

The interpretation of the 'Arab data is at first sight problematical. Why should the high-status group show such a low level of preservation of /q/ < OA /gh/ compared to /y/ < OA /ǰ/? Both these variants are 'Arab markers, in both cases opposing the main Baḥārna and MSA variant. Why, also, should the literate group in particular have "moved away" so strongly from the dialectal norm (compare their behaviour on PV5)? The probable explanation lies in the need to maintain internal phonological distinctions which would otherwise collapse because of MSA influence.

An inspection of the illiterate group scores shows that, on PV1, the dialectal variants /g/ and /j/ < OA /q/ are near categorical for the group (score .89), while on PV6 the score of .79 shows a relatively strong degree of dialectal /q/ < OA /gh/ preservation. As we shall see in 5.10 below, these group scores obscure the fact that there were some individual illiterates who had categorical /g/ and /j/ on PV1 and categorical /q/ on PV6: that is, there were some speakers for whom there was a categorical distinction between /g/ and /j/ on the one hand, and /q/ on the other. But for many literates, on the other hand, this distinction is becoming blurred because of the influx of neologisms from MSA which contain /q/, and because of the replacement of /g/ and /j/ < OA /q/ by MSA /q/ in items where there is MSA dialectal morpho-semantic congruity. What we are therefore claiming is that there is a link-up between dialectalness scores on PV1 and PV6 in the 'Arab case: any speaker who consistently replaces /g/ and /j/ with /q/ on PV1 risks collapsing the distinction between this "MSA" /q/ and "dialectal" /q/ < OA /gh/ since the allophones of both are the same. The problem is resolved, however, if dialectal /q/ is in turn replaced (and simultaneously 'corrected') by MSA /gh/. Hence, the higher the incidence of PV1 "MSA" /q/, the lower the incidence of PV6 "dialectal" /q/. Our data in fact shows the two groups of 'Arab, illiterates and literates, at different points on a cline between the following two categorical systems:

		System 1	System 2
OA /q/ (PV1)	⟶	/g/ and /j/	/q/ ([G] and [q])
OA /gh/(PV6)	⟶	/q/ ([G] or [q])	/gh/

The illiterate group, with scores on PV1 and PV6 of .89 and .79 are clearly nearer System 1 than the literates, whose corresponding scores of .63 and .57 put them somewhat nearer to System 2, the "MSA" system. The "move away" of the literates from /q/ on PV6 should accordingly be seen in terms of the relationship of the evolving 'Arab dialectal phonological system to MSA rather than as a separate phenomenon which could at first sight be wrongly interpreted as motivated by the need to 'avoid' a non-standard form. That is, the 'Arab "move away" from PV6 /q/ seems to be motivated by *phonological* considerations internal to the 'Arab dialect which are arising as a result of the influence of MSA; it is a different kind of phenomenon from the more marked literate Baḥārna avoidance of /f/ < OA /ṯ/ which has a *local* sociolinguistic origin - the low-status of the group with which /f/ < OA /ṯ/ is associated.

5.8 Summary

So far in this chapter we have described how the replaceability of dialectal phonemes by standard variants depends crucially on the morpho-semantic "match" of dialectal words and MSA equivalents and, *if the conditions for replacement are met*, how the relative sociolinguistic statuses of the replaced phonemes can be gauged by *actual* levels of phoneme replacement as measured by group scores. If the conditions are not met, replacement by supra-dialectal variants cannot take place. Broadly speaking, non-standard dialectal phonemes fall into three categories:

1. Non-standard variants which all or most dialects share		
"communally shared"	/č/ < OA /k/ /g/ < OA /q/	'neutral' variants
2. Non-standard high-status variants		
" 'Arab "	/y/ < OA /j/ /q̣/ < OA /gh/ /č/ < OA /k/ /j/ < OA /q/	high-status variants
3. Non-standard low-status variants		
"Baḥārna"	/f/ < OA /ṯ/ /d/ < OA /d̄/	low-status variants
"village Baḥārna"	/ḳ/ < OA /q/ /č/ < OA /k/	extreme low-status variants

Table 15: *Sociolinguistic status of non-standard phonemic variants within Baḥrain*

We conclude that, in *literate* speech:

5.8.1 Shared or communally neutral non-standard variants are replaced by standard variants considerably less often by the high-status group than they are by the low-status group. We attribute this to the tendency of low-status groups to overcorrect in the somewhat formal circumstances of recording.

5.8.2 The replacement of non-shared high-status variants by the high status group is much less marked than the replacement of non-shared low-status variants by the low-status group. The limiting case is reached with literate village Baḥārna, who zero out the extreme low-status variants associated with rural speech, switching either to a communally neutral variant or the supra-dialectal standard. The strength of these tendencies illustrates the local ranking of dialects: A as the most prestigious, B II as the least, with the urban B occupying an intermediate position.

5.8.3 Marginal switching by low-status speakers to high-status but non-standard variants occurred in the <u>dialectal</u> lexical domain and this again illustrates the 'pull' of the high-status dialect and suggests that sectarian dialectal convergence may not (as 5.8.1 and 5.8.2 might indicate) be simply a question of the sects switching to neutral or standard variants and away from sect-specific ones to varying degrees. In the new sociolinguistic situation which appears to be coming about in Baḥrain, the important contrast will be between 'literate' and 'non-literate' speech, as opposed to the former situation still represented today by illiterate speakers, in which A speech contrasted simply with B speech. The norms of this new literate non-sectarian form of BA would seem to be a kind of standardised but, nonetheless to some degree recognisably A dialect. We substantiate this claim in 5.9 by an examination of the regularity of change in individual grammars.

5.9 Implicational scaling as a data-displaying device

Although comparison between group 'dialectalness' scores can give a useful overview of sociolinguistic relationships <u>across groups</u>, certain important aspects of <u>within-group</u> relationships are either obscured or not brought out by this approach.

Firstly, it depicts each group, or some sociologically defined component part of it, as clustering on a single mean score on each variable: the summing procedure inevitably blurs both <u>different levels of individual variation</u>, and the <u>distribution of variation</u> within the group - one cannot tell whether variation is affecting everybody or just some speakers. (Hudson 1980: 163ff). Each group appears as a monolithic whole, with no internal differences.

Secondly, as pointed out earlier, there is in any case no a priori justification for the assumption that the social variables should be fixed, and the linguistic variables dependent. We may be right in positing some kind of co-relationship between, say, literacy in MSA and the probability of dialectal phonemes being replaced by standard ones, but we could more accurately illustrate it by defining the set of permissible grammars which incorporate the possibility of replacement and by <u>then</u> showing which speakers, with what social characterisitics, tend to 'cluster' on which grammar. The relationship between social characteristics and linguistic behaviour may not necessarily be as direct as assumed.

Thirdly, and most importantly, the 'group-mean' approach does not allow us any insight into the (presumably community-wide) relationships between the application/non-application/variable application of one rule and the application/non-application/ variable application of another. 'Group scores' do not tell us anything of interest about the internal structure and inter-rule relationships of pan-lectal grammars - about which rules, for all speakers, superordinately govern the operation of which other rules, thereby rendering the sociolinguistic information which the subordinate rules carry redundant.

We have recast the numerical data prescribed in Tables 6 and 7 in the form of three-valued implicational scales (Guttman 1944). Because of the relatively small amount of data per speaker on some variables, it was not possible, realistically, to draw up quantitative scales of the kind described in Fasold (1975), so a three-valued model was adopted. Scalograms 1-4 highlight relationships between dialectal/non-dialectal realisations on PV1-6 for our four communities, while Scalogram 5 does the same for variation on 'low-status' and 'extreme low status' variables in the village Baḥārna community. In Scalogram 5 PV1[1] and PV2[1] are respectively measures of the replacement of /ḳ/ by <u>either</u> /g/ or /q/ and 'village Baḥārna'/č/ by /k/.

An implicational scale is "a binary relation between linguistic features...so selected and so arranged in order as to result in a triangular matrix"(De Camp 1971: 33). The ordering of features in such a matrix is determined solely by the criterion of maximum scaleability: that is, the achievement of the best 'fit' of the data into the matrix. The level of scaleability achieved, calculated as the proportion of filled cells which are 'correctly' filled according to the demands of the matrix, is taken to be a measure of the degree to which the features scaled are truly in an 'implicational' or 'hierarchical' relationship.

In Scalograms 1-5, the 'permissible' relationships are as follows:

(i) any + (categorical 'dialectal' variant) implies that <u>all</u> variables to its left will also be +.

(ii) any 0 (variation) implies that the variable to its immediate right may be 0 or - (categorical 'non-dialectal' variant) but not +; and that the variable to its immediate left may be 0 or + but not -.

(iii) any - implies that <u>all</u> variables to its right will also be -, and that the variable to its immediate left may be - or 0 but not +.

(A)	(B)	(C)	(D)	PV:6	5	2	1	4	3	Location	Occupation
98	L	m	20	0	0	0	0	-	-	Al-Mukhārga	student
32	L	m	16	0	0	0	0	-	-	Al-Nu'ēm	schoolboy
82	L	f	20	+	0	0	0	-	-	Al-Ḥoūra	student
94	L	m	19	+	0	0	0	0	-	Salmāniy a	student
84	L	f	20	+	+	+	0	0	0	Al-Mukhārga	student
139	NL	m	34	+	+	+	0	0	0	Al-Nu'ēm	carpenter
138	NL	m	32	+	+	+	0	0	0	Al-Nu'ēm	carpenter
96	L	m	20	+	+	+	0	0	0	Al-Ḥammām	student
30	L	m	17	+	+	+	+	0	0	Al-Nu'ēm	messenger
129	NL	m	37	+	+	+	0	+	0	Al-Nu'ēm	labourer
125	NL	m	55	+	+	+	+	+	0	Al-Mukharga	school-cleaner
126	NL	f	30	+	+	+	+	+	0	Al-Nu'ēm	housewife
31	NL	m	19	+	+	+	+	+	+	Al-Nu'ēm	cleaner
127	NL	f	40	+	+	+	+	+	+	Al-Ḥaṭab	housewife

Scalogram 1: B I (town-dwellers) on 6 phonological variables

Scaleability: 99%

Key:

	PV1	2	3	4	5	6	
+ = categorical	/g/	/č/	/d/	/f/	/j/	/gh/	: 'dialectal' variants
- = categorical	/q/	/k/	/ḏ/	/ṯ/	/y/	/q/	: 'non-dialectal' variants
0 = variation							
Variable type:	Type 1		Type 2		Type 3		

(A) = Speaker No

(B) = Literacy: L = literate, NL = illiterate

(C) = Sex

(D) = Age

(A)	(B)	(C)	(D)	PV:6	5	2	1	4	3	Location	Occupation
83	L	f	20	0	0	0	0	–	–	Dēr	student
26	L	m	30	0	0	0	0	–	–	Samāhīj	mechanic
112	L	m	35	+	0	0	0	–	–	Karzakkān	school-sec'y
111	L	m	32	+	0	0	0	–	–	Jannūsān	govt. clerk
108	L	m	31	+	+	0	0	–	–	Māličiyya	shop-asst.
86	L	f	20	+	+	0	0	0	0	Bani-Jamra	student
135	L	m	18	+	0	0	0	0	0	Dēr	messenger
65	L	m	26	+	0	0	0	0	0	Mā'āmīr	machinist
27	L	m	22	+	0	0	0	0	0	'Arād	mechanic
152	L	f	13	+	+	+	0	0	0	'Ālī*	schoolgirl
143	L	f	25	+	+	+	0	0	0	Jidd Ḥafṣ	teacher
153	NL	f	35	+	+	+	+	0	0	'Ālī*	housewife
78	NL	m	50	+	+	+	+	+	0	Abu Ṣaybi'	farm-labourer
58	NL	m	52	+	+	+	+	+	+	Dumistān	farm-labourer
43	NL	f	40	+	+	+	+	+	+	Nuwēdrāt	cleaner
73	NL	m	45	+	+	+	+	+	+	'Ālī*	farm-labourer
47	NL	m	45	+	+	+	+	+	+	Barbar	farm-labourer
71	NL	m	50	+	+	+	+	+	+	Sitra	farm-labourer
28	NL	f	31	+	+	+	+	+	+	Samāhīj	housewife
51	NL	f	70	+	+	+	+	+	+	Bani-Jamra	housewife
44	NL	f	40	+	+	+	+	+	+	Sanad	cleaner
70	NL	f	45	+	+	+	+	+	+	Sitra	housewife
148	NL	m	70	+	+	+	+	+	+	'Arād	ex-diver
29	NL	f	32	+	+	+	+	+	+	Dēr	housewife

Scalogram 2: <u>B II (villagers) on 6 phonological variables</u>

<u>Scaleability: 97.9%</u>

<u>Key</u>:

	PV1	2	3	4	5	6	
+ = categorical	/ḳ/ or /g/	/č/	/d/	/f/	/j/	/gh/:	'dialectal' variants
– = categorical	/q/	/k/	/ḏ/	/ṯ/	/y/	/q/:	'non-dialectal' variants
0 = variation							
Variable Type:	Type 1 (PV1–2)		Type 2 (PV3–4)		Type 3 (PV5–6)		

Note: in the asterisked village, the dialectal variant on PV5 is /g/ or /ɟ/, and /č/ is realised as |tç| rather than |tʃ|

(A)	(B)	(C)	(D)	PV:6	2	1	5	4	3	Location	Occupation
123	L	m	32	+	0	-	-	-	-	Sanābis	clerk
24	L	f	32	+	0	0	-	-	-	Rās-Rummān	housewife
87	L	f	19	+	0	0	0	-	-	Dirāz	student
90	L	f	21	+	0	0	0	-	-	Sanābis	student
88	L	f	20	+	0	0	0	0	-	Dirāz	student
97	L	m	20	+	0	0	0	0	0	Rās-Rummān	student
92	L	f	21	+	+	0	0	-	0	Sanābis	student
131	NL	f	35	+	+	0	0	0	0	Dirāz	housewife
38	NL	f	41	+	+	+	+	0	0	Sanābis	housewife
35	NL	f	30	+	+	+	+	+	+	Rās-Rummān	cleaner
40	NL	f	45	+	+	+	+	+	+	Sanābis	housewife
34	NL	f	32	+	+	+	+	+	+	Rās-Rummān	cleaner
52	NL	m	55	+	+	+	+	+	+	Dirāz	farm-labourer
128	NL	m	60	+	+	+	+	+	+	Rās-Rummān	watchman
36	NL	f	35	+	+	+	+	+	+	Dirāz	housewife

Scalogram 3: B III on 6 phonological variables

Scaleability: 99%

Key

	PV1	2	3	4	5	6	
+ = categorical	/g/	/č/	/d/	/f/	/y/	/gh/:	'dialectal' variants
- = categorical	/q/	/k/	/d̲/	/t̲/	/j/	/q/:	'non-dialectal' variants
0 = variation							
Variable type:	Type 1		Type 2		Type 3		

(A)	(B)	(C)	(D)	PV:4	3	2	5	1	6	Location	Occupation
144	L	m	26	+	+	0	0	0	0	Muḥarraq	technician
95	L	m	20	+	+	0	0	0	0	Salmāniya	student
101	L	f	19	+	+	0	0	0	0	E Rifā'	student
116	L	m	40	+	+	0	0	0	0	Ḥidd	govt. clerk
122	L	f	26	+	+	0	+	0	0	Al-Ḥūra	social worker
13	L	m	17	+	+	0	0	+	0	Muḥarraq	telephonist
118	L	m	30	+	+	+	0	0	0	Muḥarraq	teacher
104	L	m	20	+	+	+	0	0	0	Al-Ḥūra	student
150	NL	m	45	+	+	+	0	0	0	Al-Ḥūra	watchman
145	NL	f	48	+	+	+	0	+	0	Muḥarraq	housewife
147	NL	f	46	+	+	+	0	+	0	Al-Ḥūra	housewife
103	L	f	21	+	+	+	+	0	0	W Rifā'	student
119	L	m	20	+	+	+	+	0	0	W Rifā'	student
93	L	m	19	+	+	+	+	0	0	Al-Ḥūra	student
100	L	m	18	+	+	+	+	0	0	Muḥarraq	student
19	NL	f	40	+	+	+	+	0	0	Salmāniya	housewife
10	NL	f	40	+	+	+	+	0	0	E Rifā'	cleaner
105	L	m	20	+	+	+	+	+	0	Al-Ḥūra	student
120	L	f	20	+	+	+	+	+	0	Muḥarraq	bank-clerk
85	L	f	19	+	+	+	+	+	0	Ḥidd	student
14	L	f	21	+	+	+	+	+	0	Muḥarraq	bank-clerk
6	NL	m	55	+	+	+	+	+	0	Muḥarraq	ex-diver
7	NL	m	60	+	+	+	+	+	0	Muḥarraq	ex-diver
146	NL	m	70	+	+	+	+	+	0	Al-Ḥūra	ex-diver
21	NL	f	40	+	+	+	+	+	0	Quḍaybiya	housewife
8	NL	m	55	+	+	+	+	+	0	Budayya'	ex-diver
18	NL	f	40	+	+	+	+	+	0	Gufūl	housewife
109	L	f	17	+	+	+	+	+	+	Al-Fāḍil	schoolgirl
1	NL	f	60	+	+	+	+	+	+	Ḥidd	housewife
5	NL	m	60	+	+	+	+	+	+	Muḥarraq	ex-diver
4	NL	m	70	+	+	+	+	+	+	Muḥarraq	ex-diver
134	NL	f	45	+	+	+	+	+	+	Budayya'	school-cleaner
22	NL	f	45	+	+	+	+	+	+	Ḥidd	housewife
2	NL	f	50	+	+	+	+	+	+	Ḥidd	housewife

Scalogram 4: 'Arab on 6 phonological variables

Scaleability: 97.3%

Key

	PV1	2	3	4	5	6	
+ = categorical	/g/ and /j/	/č/	/ḏ/	/ṯ/	/y/	/q/:	'dialectal' variants
– = categorical	/q/	/k/	/d/	/f/	/j/	/gh/:	'non-dialectal' variants
0 = variation							
Variable Type:	Type 1		Type 2		Type 3		

(A)	(B)	(C)	(D)	PV:4	3	1[1]	2[1]	Location	Occupation
83	L	f	20	–	–	–	–	Dēr	student
26	L	m	30	–	–	–	–	Samāhīj	mechanic
112	L	m	35	–	–	–	–	Karzakkān	school-sec'y
111	L	m	32	–	–	–	–	Jannūsān	govt. clerk
108	L	m	31	–	–	–		Māličiyya	shop ass't.
86	L	f	20	0	0	–	–	Bani-Jamra	student
135	L	m	18	0	0	–	–	Dēr	messenger
65	L	m	26	0	0	–	–	Mā'āmīr	machinist
152	L	f	13	0	0	–	–	'Āli*	schoolgirl
143	L	f	25	0	0	–		Jidd Ḥafṣ	teacher
27	L	m	22	0	0	0	–	'Arād'	mechanic
153	NL	f	35	0	0	0	–	'Āli*	housewife
78	NL	m	50	0	0	0		Abu Saybi'	farm-labourer
58	NL	m	52	+	+	[–]	–	Dumistān	farm-labourer
47	NL	m	45	+	+	0	–	Barbar	farm-labourer
43	NL	f	40	+	+	0	0	Nuwēdrāt	cleaner
73	NL	m	45	+	+	0	0	'Āli*	farm-labourer
71	NL	m	50	+	+	0	0	Sitra	farm-labourer
29	NL	f	31	+	+	0	0	Samāhīj	housewife
51	NL	f	70	+	+	+	+	Bani Jamra	housewife
44	NL	f	40	+	+	[0]	+	Sanad	cleaner
70	NL	f	45	+	+	+		Sitra	housewife
148	NL	m	70	+	+	+	+	'Arād	ex-diver
29	NL	f	32	+	+	+	+	Dēr	housewife

Scalogram 5: <u>B II (villagers) on 4 phonological variables</u>

<u>Scaleability: 97%</u>

<u>Key</u>

		PV4	3	2[1]	1[1]	
+	= categorical	/d/	/f/	/č/	/ḳ/	: 'dialectal' variants
–	= categorical	/ḏ/	/ṯ/	/k/	/g/ or /q/:	'non-dialectal' variants
0	= variation					

Variable Type: Type 2 Type 2 ('rural')

Note: in the asterisked village, the dialectal variant /č/ is realised as [tç] rather than [tʃ]

5.10 Interpretation of trends in the scaled data

Turning first to the Baḥārna data in Scalograms 1-3, we note not only a very high degree of scaleability in all three cases, but also that the ordering of the variables with respect to each other which is demanded by the scaling procedure is identical for the B I and II groups (6-5-2-1-4-3), while the B III group differs from this only in the ordering of variable 5. What is even more interesting is that the scaling procedure places the Type 3 variables (PV5 and 6) to the left (the 'most dialectal' end). This suggests confirmation of our general contention: it shows that individual Baḥārna do indeed tend to avoid dialectal variants most regularly if they are 'typically Baḥārna'(because they oppose the MSA/'Arab variant) and cling most strongly to dialectal variants which are 'standard' (because they coincide with MSA and oppose the 'Arab variant). The B III group is the exception which proves the rule: for this group, as we have already argued, dialectal /y/ < OA /j/ is classed with /d/ < OA /d̲/ and /f/ < OA /t̲/ as an 'incorrect', stigmatised variant, and consequently falls further to the 'least dialectal' end of the scalogram with the other, more generally stigmatised variants.

The B scalograms are particularly notable for the way they highlight consistent differences between literate and illiterate speakers and gradations of difference within the literate group. The literates cluster at the top end of the scales, showing varying degrees of distance from the dialectal stereotypes, while the illiterates cluster at the bottom, many of them sharing a combination of features (or 'lect') which is identical with these stereotypes (++++++). In each scalogram, there are only a few lects shared by both literates and illiterates. The six illiterate speakers who *do* have lects incorporating variation, however - Speakers 139, 138, 153, 78, 131, 38 - fit into the hierarchy of rule-relationships established by the *literates.* Significantly, the average age of these six illiterates was, at 37.8, some 5 years younger than the average for the B illiterates as a whole (42.3) and 5 of the 6 were attending adult literacy classes. Consequently, they would almost certainly have had more regular contact with literate speakers than the housewives and farm-labourers who cluster at the bottom of the scalogram and whose speech networks could be expected to be more restricted.

By and large, the process of scaling our Baḥārna data illustrated the high degree of regularity with which literacy as a social variable correlated with dialect type. The illiterates cling to the stereotype dialectal variants of their particular geographical communities, while the literates from whatever area of Baḥrain, form a single, non-geographically defined linguistically homogeneous group.

The 'Arab scalogram for PV1-6 differs in a number of ways from the Baḥarna ones:

(i) Order of variables

Most obviously, the order of the variables is different, the Type 2 variables falling at the left-hand 'most dialectal' end of the scalogram and the Type 3 variables at the right-hand 'least dialectal' end - the exact converse of the Baḥārna case. This mirror-image effect is, of course, exactly what would be predicted if our contention is correct that the major source of variation in BA speech is consciousness of MSA forms: in the 'Arab case, the dialectal variants on the Type 2 variables (/t̲/ and /d̲/) 'agree' with MSA and are hence preserved; those on Type 3 variables (/y/ and /q/) 'disagree' with it and are hence subject to replacement. In the Baḥārna case, it is on the Type 3 variables that the dialectal variants 'agree' with MSA, and on the Type 2 variables that they 'disagree'.

(ii) Level of dialectalness

One of the chief differences between the A and B scalograms is in the proportion of cells showing + and -. 72% of the A cells show + and 0% show -, compared with 57% and 9%, respectively, for the B group as a whole. Scalogram analysis thus confirms our earlier conclusion that the A tendency to avoid dialectal variants is much less marked than the B tendency - a consequence, we would argue of the 'linguistic security' which stems from being the socially superior group.

(iii) Literacy and dialect-type correlation

An A/B difference which the scaling procedure brings out, and which the 'group-score' approach obscures, is the relatively poor correlation between literacy and dialect-type in the A case. An inspection of the A scalogram shows that only one grammar - that 'occupied' by the six speakers at the top of the scale - was the exclusive preserve of literate speakers; on all the others, we find both literates and illiterates. Speaker 109 represents the extreme case of a young, fully literate A speaker who uses a lect identical in the respects examined with that of a 60 year old housewife.

The poor literacy-dialect correlation probably reflects both the fact that the A illiterates are somewhat more open to outside linguistic influences than the conservative B illiterates (see Chapter 2) and that the A literates are less inhibited than the B literates by the need to 'move away' from the dialectal stereotype because of their status as the prestige group. At all events, the change from a dialect which is characteristically 'A' or 'B' to one which incorporates a degree of standardisation has affected the A community in a less consistent, less direct, and less marked manner than is the case in the B community. The 'Arab, as a group, retain a degree of linguistic homogeneity which the Baḥārna no longer have. These communal differences in 'dialectal preservation' by literates are vividly illustrated in Figure 1 below, which shows in graphic form the relative degrees of convergence of the A and each B dialect, towards a non-sectarian 'neutral' form of BA on PV4 and PV5. These two variables were chosen to illustrate the different degree to which high-status, as opposed to low-status speakers 'move away' from non-standard variants - in this case /f/ < OA /t̲/ (all Baḥārna) and /y/ < OA /j/ (all 'Arab).

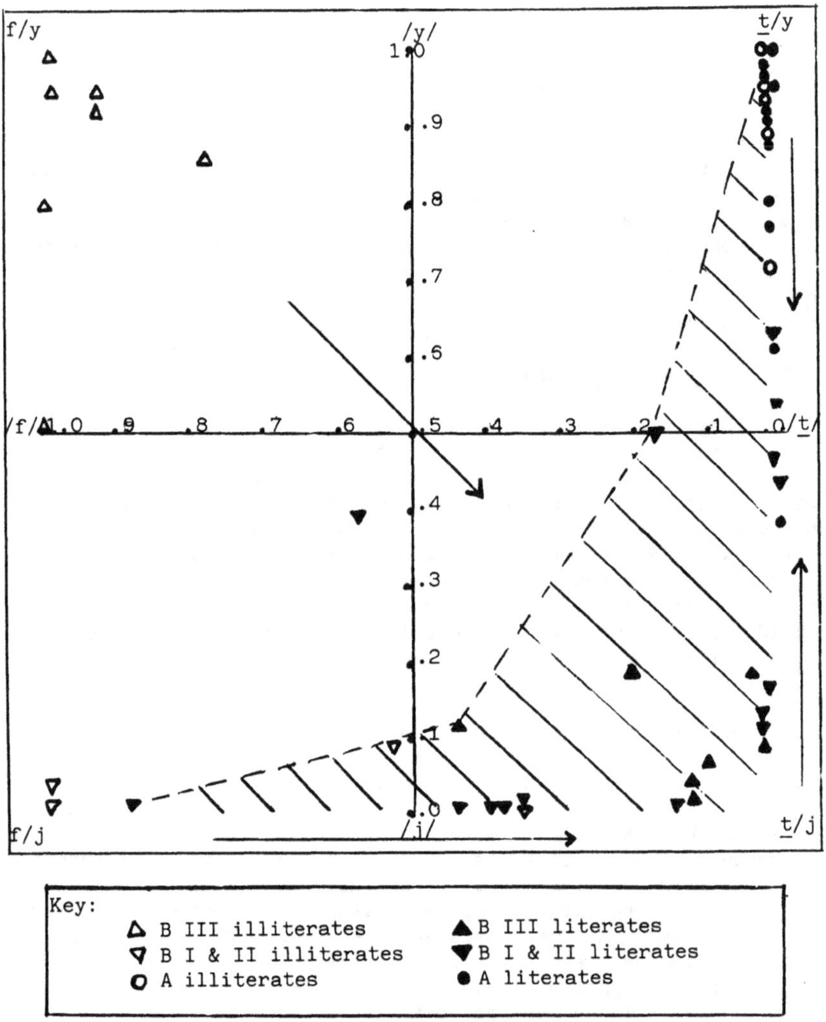

Figure 1: Dialect convergence on two phonological variables

In Figure 1, the vertical axis shows variation between /y/ and /j/ in such a way that categorical /y/=1 is at the top of the axis and /j/=0 is at the bottom. The horizontal axis shows variation between /f/(=1) at the lefthand end of the axis and /ṯ/(=0) at the righthand end. These axes create 4 areas: top lefthand, corresponding to "f/y" dialects (viz B III), bottom left, corresponding to "f/j" dialects (B I and II), and top right, "ṯ/y" dialects (A). The fourth area, the bottom right, is the "ṯ/j" area, which is a combination of variants not found in illiterate speech of any sect, but which is the normal combination in MSA.

The individual triangles and circles represent the positions of individual speakers according to their score on each variable. The stereotypical dialect positions are in the top corners of each of the four squares, and these positions are in fact occupied by a large number of illiterate speakers. (Where two or more speakers, both literate or both illiterate occupy the same position, this has not been indicated.) It is clear that the literate speakers have 'moved away' from their stereotypical position far more than the illiterates have in the case of each group, but that the move in the Baḥārna case is more pronounced than in the 'Arab. More than this, the movement has direction: the 'Arab are distributed *down* the extreme righthand column, moving down from /y/ to /j/, but not deviating from /ṯ/; B I and II have moved right *across* (/f/→ /ṯ/), and those who have done so then begin to move *up*; B III speakers appear to have moved diagonally across (towards both /j/ and /ṯ/). The net result is that nearly all Baḥārna literates have moved into the shaded area, which we might designate as 'basically MSA with some 'Arab influence' - note how the speech of some Baḥārna town dwellers (B I) is in fact indistinguishable from 'Arab speech on these variables, and has in a few cases become 'more 'Arab' than one of the 'Arab literates. The 'Arab appear to have started to move 'down' towards /j/ to 'meet' the Baḥārna coming 'up' towards /y/, but they have not moved 'down' towards MSA with anything like the same strength as the Baḥārna have moved 'up' towards the prestige dialect.

Thus far, the application of implicational scaling to our data has illustrated both the internal regularity of variation in the community and the community-wide hierarchical ordering of the variables which we have picked out for analysis. We have been implicitly assuming that the scalogram is a graphic representation of ordered rule-change across the community. But what kind of 'rule-changes' could encapsulate the type of variation we have observed - which seem to depend on the morpho-semantic status of lexical items - and what is the nature of the inter-rule-relationships which the scalogram seems to capture? We will consider the latter question first.

5.11 Inter-rule relationships

From the synchronic viewpoint, Scalograms 1-5 specify the restrictions on the "real-time" co-variation of the outputs of several linguistic rules in a number of communities. They show, in other words, how the categorical/variable output of one rule predicts, within the limits of a 3-valued scaling procedure, the categorical/variable output of another in a consistent, community-wide manner. What the rules which generate these outputs (or 'variants') actually look like – whether, for example, they should be expressed as phonological or lexical replacement rules, whether they can be accommodated within a 're-write' convention, and whether they are in fact the 'same rules' in each community – these questions are dealt with in 5.12 (see also Holes 1983b). Clearly, however, whatever the eventual form which we decide is most appropriate for the rules which generate the observed outputs, there is no prima facie linguistic reason why variability in one rule should be related to variability in another, given the unrelatedness of the variables involved: there is no reason, for example, phonological or lexical, why a BA speaker who consistently produces forms like /fala:fa/ 'three' should quite predictably also produce forms like /čam/ 'how much?' in the same speech context. That such prediction is possible, we have argued, can be explained if the system of sociolinguistic marking, illustrated in Table 5 is considered to form part of BA speakers' "communicative competence": that is, his knowledge of the 'rules of use' established by the community as a whole, which delimit the theoretically possible choices available.

Some constraints on the co-variation of outputs are strict, others less so. An inspection of Scalogram 5 reveals that in the village Baḥārna community there is an absolute constraint on the appearance of forms like

*/act̲ariya/ 'majority'
*/d̲a:k id diččа:n/ 'that shop'

The rules by which "village B" /č/ is replaced by /k/ (i.e. in items listed in PV2.4) and by which /f/ is replaced by /t̲/ and /d/ by /d̲/ are 'ordered' in such a way that:

(i) if /č/→ /k/ does occur categorically, /f/→/t̲/, /d/→/d̲/ cannot occur even variably

(ii) if /f/→/t̲/, /d/→/d̲/ does occur even variably, /č/→/k/ must occur

Only /ačfariya/, /akfariya/ and /akt̲ariya/ 'majority' and /da:k id diččа:n/, /da:k id dikka:n/ and /d̲a:k id dikka:n/ 'that shop' appear to be permissible form combinations.

The 'ordering' referred to in these cases is not of the kind normally argued about in 'non-social' linguistics, in the sense that rules which capture /k/~/č/, /d̲/~/d/ and /t̲/~/f/ variation, however framed, are phonologically unrelated to each other. The ordering would rather appear to arise from synchronic considerations of stylistic appropriacy or sociolinguistic compatability specific to Baḥrain: the choice of one or another variant automatically triggers the choice of a sociolinguistically compatible, but unrelated variant and blocks the choice of another, over quite long stretches of discourse. In the case cited, /č/ is simply too 'rural', too 'domestic' in its connotations to co-occur with /t̲/ or /d̲/ which, in the Baḥārna community, are 'standardizing' 'external' forms.

These examples are, however, extreme. They illustrate the strongest kind of co-variation constraints on theoretically 'possible' rule outputs. In other cases, the co-variation constraints are less strict. Take, for example, the sentence:

/fala:fi:n ya:ya/ 'Thirty (people) came'

in which /f/<OA /t̲/ and /y/< OA /j/ co-occur. If we inspect the B III data in Scalogram 3, we find that, except for 4 speakers at the top of the scale, this realisation of the sentence is a possible form for all. For the 6 speakers at the bottom of the scale even, it would appear to be categorical. In other words, /fala:fi:n ya:ya/ seems to be the dialectal 'norm' for the B III group. Turning now to the majority Baḥārna groups, I and II, we can see from Scalograms 1 and 2 that only 4 out of a total of 38 speakers had lects which produced /f/~/y/ co-variation at all. Now it is quite clear that all the Baḥārna in the sample could not fail to understand the meaning of /fala:fi:n ya:ya/, and recognise it as a possible BA form. But what the scalograms suggest is that for the B majority it might be a marginal form productively. Apart from the B III group, the only Baḥārna who might produce such forms are literates who are trying to 'speak like 'Arab' - hence the use of /y/ - and not quite managing it, as the variable retention of /f/ suggests! (Some other Baḥārna speakers do apaprently manage this more successfully, e.g. speakers 83 and 26 in Scalogram 2, who have zeroed out/f/ in favour of /t̲/ and whose lect is indistinguishable from that of the 4 speakers at the top of the 'Arab scale. It is highly significant that Speakers 83 and 26 were both young, literate and from the Muḥarraq island villages - a combination of social and geographical factors which could be expected to result in a particularly marked shift to an "'Arab-like" dialect.)

We could summarise the situation by saying that the co-variation of "village B" /č/ with /t̲/ is not permitted because of the stylistic incompatibility of these two variants; on the other hand, the co-variation of /f/ and /y/ is permitted, but is communally restricted: it occurs as the norm only in the minority B III group - otherwise only marginally, apparently as the result of 'Arab influence on the literate Baḥārna majority. In general, the sets of choices which speakers make between the competing members of different pairs of variants can thus be absolutely constrained, where the contravention of permitted choices produces grammatically 'correct' but socially and stylistically uninterpretable utterances, or communally restricted, where strong expectations arise about a speaker's social identity through the combinations of variants he uses. Many combinations of variants, of course, as an examination of individual lects in the scalograms will show, are communally unrestricted. A sentence like

/čam wa:ḥid ga:l lik/ 'How many did he tell you (there were)?'

provides by itself no clue as to the identity of the speaker, beyond the fact that he is speaking a dialect which would fit into any of Scalograms 1-4. The variants /g/ and "shared" /č/ (in words like /čam/)tend to resist replacement by standard forms precisely for the reason that they are communally 'neutral'.

Scalograms give a concrete picture of what we have called the 'rules of use' of a community - rules which, if a speaker is to communicate appropriately, it seems he must obey. It is clear, however, that speakers manage to operate effectively in a wide range of social contexts, involving different kinds of interlocutor, settings and topics. They are not, that is, "single-style". We argued in Chapter 3 that the unavoidably unsystematic way in which part of the data for this study was collected might have led different speakers to different interpretations of the speech context, and hence to the sampling of, say, the 'formal' style of one speaker and the 'informal' style of another. But this unavoidable practical constraint does not seem to have had any kind of adverse effect on the results: the impressive degree of scaleability achieved is, we believe, in itself strong evidence that the rule-hierarchies revealed by our scaled analysis are both non-context-sensitive and community-wide - that is, they inform or underlie all the data. However, the position of any individual speaker with respect to any other down the lefthand side of the scalogram need not, indeed cannot, be fixed. This amounts to a claim that if a speaker were to 'formalize' his speech beyond the level at which it was pitched during the data collection for this research, he would simply move 'up' the same scalogram to a different lect; if, on the other hand, he were to 'colloquialise' it beyond this level, he would move 'down' it. His productive 'communicative competence' would thus consist of a range of linked lects (of which we have sampled a small part), existing within the total permissible range of lects in the community of which we have sampled a part. On this argument, the possibility that we might have sampled different parts of different speakers' ranges would be irrelevant: as competent users of the language system, all speakers' speech would by definition have to conform to the community-wide rules of language use.

The corollary of this argument is that the position of the speakers on Scalograms 1-5 is simply a by-product of the mode of data collection, and, although, we have argued in the Baḥārna case for the discreteness of "literate" and "illiterate" dialects, the relationship between the social characterisitics of age and literacy arranged down the lefthand side of the scalograms, and the lects on the right is probably less clear-cut than it would appear: in reality each speaker could be positioned within an area of any scalogram which represents his/her productive potential. Obviously, not all of this potential can be sampled in a single speech context. Thus, in reply to

/čam wa:ḥid ga:l lik/ 'How many did he tell you (there were)?'

an utterance like

/ga:l fala:fi:n/ 'He said thirty'

would probably fall within the productive range of Speaker 29 (Scalogram 5) and might well occur in a more formal context than that in which she was recorded here, where she always produced /ḳ/ ⟨OA /q/; certainly, the data transcription shows that /ga:l/ was part of her *receptive* range. By contrast, Speaker 83, a literate young woman a few years the junior of Speaker 29, might well utter this reply (or the even more 'rural' /ḳa:l fala:fi:n/) if circumstances demanded - let us say, in conversation with Speaker 29 - notwithstanding the fact that the scalogram shows that in the data she always had /g/ and /t̲/, not /g/ and /f/ or /ḳ/ and /f/. This is unsurprising, but almost certainly attributable to the fact that Speaker 83 was recorded in the semi-formal circumstances of conversation with a foreigner (the writer), while Speaker 29 was recorded talking to a fellow-villager in a domestic context. Only *parts* (different parts) of each speaker's *productive potential* were sampled.

Unfortunately, the practical problems of data collection in a society which is still as conservative as Baḥrain made it impossible to validate this hypothesis by collecting data from each speaker in a variety of different contexts. However, the fact that our 'literate' and 'illiterate' sets of data were collected in such *different* speech contexts and could still be fitted into the same communal rule hierarchies with such a high degree of regularity indicates that the hierarchies we have established may well be non-context-sensitive: they may well represent general synchronic rules of co-variation in Baḥraini Arabic.

5.12 Rule formulation: some issues raised by the data

The standard format for rules which express conditioned variability is:

$$X \longrightarrow \langle Y \rangle \quad \left\langle \begin{matrix} [\text{feat A}] \\ [\text{feat B}] \\ \vdots \end{matrix} \right\rangle \left\langle \begin{matrix} [\text{feat I}] \\ [\text{feat J}] \\ \vdots \end{matrix} \right\rangle \left\langle \begin{matrix} [\text{feat P}] \\ [\text{feat Q}] \\ \vdots \end{matrix} \right\rangle \quad [\text{feat Z}]$$

"where X is replaced by Y in accordance with the quantitative weighting through variable constraints, and each pair of angled brackets contains a list of features (bundles of features or also sub-categories) that can occupy a certain position in the structural description. In analogy to 'more' and 'less' relations ('>' and '<') variable constraints are given between angled brackets, whereas the feature Z, which occurs only between square brackets, stands for an obligatory feature which makes the application of the rule obligatory" (Dittmar 1976: 138).

At first sight, it would appear that the kind of conditioned variability which we have described in this chapter as characterising Baḥraini Arabic might be expressible by a formalism such as the above, e.g.

$$\begin{array}{l} j \longrightarrow \langle y \rangle \ / \ldots\ldots \\ k \longrightarrow \langle \check{c} \rangle \ / \ldots\ldots \ \text{etc.} \end{array}$$

However, there are a number of difficulties entailed in adopting this approach, which relate to the following questions:

(i) how underlying forms are to be identified
(ii) the locus of the variation: is it phonological or lexical?
(iii) the suitability of re-write conventions for expressing the type of variation revealed by our analysis.

These three questions are interlinked and relate, we believe, to a substantive issue in sociolinguistics: the suitability of a *single formalism* such as a re-write rule to express different kinds of linguistic relationships and phenomena: diachronic change versus synchronic variation, and phonological versus lexical alternation, for example.

5.12.1 The identification of underlying forms

Variable rules, whether they operate at the phonological or syntactic level (e.g. Sankoff G: 1973) are always presented in a linear format in which a single input "X" is variably rewritten as a single output "Y", where "Y" may be a *more complex* element than "X" (i.e. "X" plus a feature(s)) or a *less complex* element than "Y" ("X" minus a feature(s)). In the extreme case, "Y" may be Ø. The crucial fact about X→⟨Y⟩ is that "X" is considered to underlie "Y" in all cases where the rule actually goes through; where it does not, "X" itself shows up on the surface. Thus, in the Sankoff article quoted (Sankoff G 1973: 53), the rule of *que*-deletion in Montreal French:

$$\underline{\text{que}} \longrightarrow \langle \emptyset \rangle \quad \left\langle \begin{array}{l} [+\text{ sib}] \\ \begin{bmatrix} +\text{ cons} \\ -\text{ sib} \end{bmatrix} \\ [-\text{ cons}] \end{array} \right\rangle \ \text{——} \ \left\langle \begin{array}{l} [+\text{ sib}] \\ \begin{bmatrix} +\text{ cons} \\ -\text{ sib} \end{bmatrix} \\ [-\text{ cons}] \end{array} \right\rangle$$

gives two possibilities only for every ranked combination of constraints: *que* is either deleted or it shows up on the surface. But either way, it is *underlyingly* there.

Applying this v.r. principle to our BA data, we encounter the first problem. If we assume (where for the moment we will) that alternations like /ke:f/ and /če:f/ 'how?', /qa9ad/ and /ga9ad/ 'he sat' are the outputs of the variable application of phonological rules of the general form

$$X \longrightarrow \langle Y \rangle / \ldots\ldots$$

which of /k/ and /č/, /q/ and /g/ are we to take as the *underlying* input form of the rule?

One answer might be to appeal to the notions of phonological naturalness and diachrony. Diachronically, it has been established by Arabic philologists- see, for example, Cantineau (1960) - that (to confine ourselves to the cases cited) /q/ and /k/ were the OA proto-forms from which /g/ and /č/ subsequently developed in a number of dialects. Johnstone's (1963) and (1965) articles also implicitly assume a direct diachronic line between OA and synchronic dialectal forms. By way of exemplification of this position, we give below some known synchronic reflexes of two OA consonants.

OA /ṯ/ → t (Syrian, Egyptian)
→ ṯ (various Bedouin dialects)
→ f (Shi'i Baḥraini)

OA /q/ → ' (Syrian, Egyptian)
→ q (Algerian sedentary dialects)
→ g (Bedouin dialects in general)
→ ḳ (certain sedentary dialects, e.g. Shi'i Baḥraini)

Phonologically, these changes involve the operation of different sets of natural processes, many of which are attested in other languages. But rules like č→k and g→q look much less plausible as candidates for any kind of natural phonological rule.

It might be argued that /k/, /q/, and the rest of the OA forms (which are identical with MSA forms) should be adopted as the inputs to BA variable rules, showing up in surface realisations when the process of fronting and affrication (k→⟨č⟩); fronting and voicing (q→ ⟨g⟩), and so on, are *not* applied.

There are good reasons, however, for rejecting this diachronic basis for the explanation of synchronic variation. The fact is, there are some speakers, the majority of them illiterate, for whom it would have to be assumed that q→g was a *categorical* rule, not a variable one, since /q/ fails to show up at all in their data. But other speakers, most of them literate, *do* show /q/~/g/ variation and for them a q→⟨g⟩ rule would have to be posited. This puts us in the position of having to argue that the literate speakers manage to somehow make the categorical q→g rule of the illiterates into a variable rule, and that in the extreme case of a literate speaker giving a 'high-style' oration on a public occasion, the q→g rule ceases to operate altogether, and categorical /q/ 'shows through'.

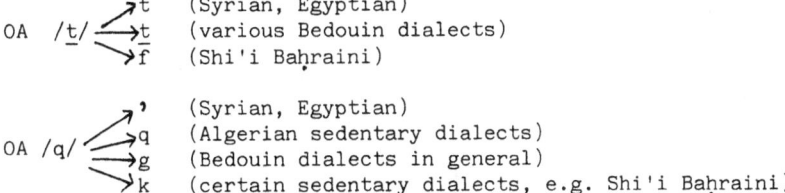

The psychological implausibility of such an explanation is clear. It forces us to depict the underlying phonological forms of all speakers' grammars as identical with those of OA. The illiterate speakers would be depicted as operating rules which obligatorily converted these forms into the observed categorically occurring dialectal forms, while the literates would gradually cease to apply them, recovering the underlying OA forms through some mysterious 'discovery procedure'.

The sociolinguistic facts of how non-dialectal forms are actually 'discovered' are quite different from this. All speakers learn the dialectal system of their community as L1; some of them subsequently learn the MSA system - which we could describe as an L2 closely related to their L1 - through exposure to outside influences, and, in particular through years of formal tuition at school. It is this learning process, this exposure to external influence which leads the speaker to the establishment of L1-L2 correspondence, and to a knowledge of the rules by which the two systems are combined to generate grammatical systems intermediate between 'pure dialect' and 'pure MSA'. On this analysis, it is the dialectal form which is basic and which is variably replaced by the MSA equivalent, not the (identical) OA form which "shows through". Hudson (1980: 46, 182-4) has advanced a similar critique of Labov's attribution of an [h]-deletion rule to speakers who never actually produce [h] - by what right do we assume speakers "know" that words they consistently pronounce without an [h] "really" have one? By what right do we assume that a BA speaker who consistently has /g/ "knows" that /q/ underlies it?

A clear distinction must therefore be drawn between rules which describe diachronic change which is "dead", and rules which account for synchronic variation. Rules of the form:

q → g (g → j in front vowel environments)
q → k
k → č
ḏ → d
ṯ → f
j → y
gh → q

are shorthand ways of expressing diachronic phonological change. They are no longer productive synchronically, and some of them affected some parts of the BA-speaking community and not others. We can exemplify these points by examining /j/~/y/ variation.

The diachronic j → y rule affected the 'Arab community and some parts of the Baḥārna community (our B III group) at some period in the past, but it did not affect what is today the majority B community. For all those speakers who today speak a dialect which was affected by this change it is nonetheless clear that it is no longer a productive rule. We saw in 4.2.3 that recent MSA borrowings such as /ja:mi9a/ 'university', /jibin/ 'cheese' which have become part and parcel of the dialect do not have alternative forms like */ya:mi9a/ etc. even in the speech of illiterates. A more plausible formalism for expressing synchronic variation of the type we have shown would involve the *addition* of a rule which rewrote underlying /y/ as /j/ in certain lexical items, i.e.:

y → ⟨j⟩ /.....

The environment most strongly promoting the operation of this rule would specify that /y/ occurred in an item which was "potentially MSA" and marked as such [+ MSA] in the lexicon; (hence the variability of /yim9a/ ~ /jum9a/ 'Friday'); the environment least strongly promoting the operation of the rule would be lexical items marked [-MSA] (hence the non-variability of /ya:b/ 'to bring'). Wherever variation occurs, we take what we have been referring to as the 'dialectal variant' - i.e. the L1 variant - as the *part of the rule which is operated on*: that is, in this case, /y/ not /j/, would be a constituent of the underlying lexical entry in *variable* items like /yim9a/~/jum9a/ 'Friday', but /j/ not /y/ would be an underlying constituent of *invariable* items like /ja:mi9a/. The y → ⟨j⟩ rule arises as a result of the exposure of speakers (mainly at school, through the media) to standard forms like /jum9a/ which they learn are referentially equivalent to /yim9a/. The overall probability that y→⟨j⟩ will or will not operate depends however, not only on the marking of the lexical item as [+ or - MSA], but on local attitudes to the group for whom /y/ (or /f/ in the case of f→ṯ etc.) is the dialectal variant: in lexical items where y → ⟨j⟩ *is* permissible, it operates much less often if the speaker is 'high-status', than if he is 'low-status' (compare the A and B III operation of the rule).

By the same token, B speakers in communities where diachronic j → y did *not* occur, would have synchronic variation between /j/ and /y/ expressed by a rule which goes in the opposite direction:

j → ⟨y⟩ /....

The lexicon of *their* dialect would list forms like /jum9a/ and /ja:b/ as containing underlying /j/, not /y/. As in the "y"-users case, however, lexical entries would be marked [+ or - MSA]. The differences we noted earlier in the incidence of /j/ ~ /y/ variation for these speakers is again relatable to the same principle of lexical categorisation: in this case, j → ⟨y⟩ is *more likely* to be applied in cases like /ja:b/ and (that is, in what we have described as the dialectal lexical domain) than it is in cases like /jum9a/ (which is marked [+ MSA]). This is quite consonant with the general sociolinguistic forces we observed to be operating in Baḥrain: the learning experience of a speaker who has /j/ as his L1 form is that the supradialectal L2 he learns at school also has /j/ (and is prescriptively 'correct'); but he also learns that, in lexical items where there is no L2 lexical equivalent for his L1 word, the L1 of another, socially high-status group, is /y/ - hence the pattern of high susceptibility of *dialectal* words like /ja:b/ to alternation with /ya:b/, but resistance of words like /jum9a/ to alternation with /yim9a/.

It thus appears that, synchronically, /j/~/y/ variation is

more accurately represented by two communally distributed variable rules, than it is by extending the scope of a single diachronic rule j → y which in any event only affected the dialects spoken by about half of the population. These synchronic rules might look like this:

1. $$y \rightarrow \langle j \rangle \ / \ \left\langle \begin{matrix} [+\ \mathrm{MSA}] \\ [-\ \mathrm{MSA}] \end{matrix} \right\rangle$$ (A and B III)

2. $$j \rightarrow \langle y \rangle \ / \ \left\langle \begin{matrix} [-\ \mathrm{MSA}] \\ [+\ \mathrm{MSA}] \end{matrix} \right\rangle$$ (B I and II)

The placing of one square-bracketed feature above another indicates that the likelihood of the rule operating when the higher feature is present is greater than when the lower one is present, in both cases, and for all speakers.

A similar type of argument would reject synchronically non-productive rules such as k → č as the basis for explaining /k/∼/č/ variation, and q → ḳ (B II) and q → g (A, B I) as a basis for accounting for synchronic variation in these cases. It is truer to the facts to think of the dialectal variant as the underlying form in cases where there is variation, and the "MSA form" as the output. But there are problems here too. For one thing, it is an odd kind of phonological rule which is triggered by the morpho-semantic status of the word in which the input to the rule occurs (as is the case with Rules 1 and 2 above); and for another, rules like g → ⟨q⟩ or č → ⟨k⟩, which are certainly a truer reflection of what happens synchronically than are q → ⟨g⟩ and k → ⟨č⟩ , do have the disadvantage of looking highly unnatural as phonological processes. We must therefore consider the possibility that the variation we have been referring to in this chapter as 'phonemic' is really lexical - that is, the possibility that the replacement of /čam/ by /kam/ is essentially the same linguistic process as that by which BA /lijil/ 'because' gets replaced by MSA /liʾann/. We examine the evidence.

5.12.2 The phonological versus lexical explanation of variation

Thus far, we have assumed that variation between pairs of equivalents like /čam/∼/kam/, /qa9ad/∼/ga9ad/ is phonological, and that it arises because there exist morpho-semantically congruent items in the dialect and MSA. On this analysis, the BA speaker deduces a phonological equivalence between L1 /č/ and L2 /k/, L1 /g/ and L2 /q/, etc. and substitutes the L2 variant for the L1 variant in lexical items where the morphological structure and the semantic content/syntactic function of MSA and dialectal words from the same root match. If the morphological structures match, but the semantic content/syntactic functions do not, phoneme substitution cannot occur, e.g. BA /ga:9id/ in the sentence

/ḥse:n ga:9id yištaghil/
'Hussein is working'

cannot become /qa:9id/ by a g → q rewrite rule because MSA /qa:9id/ means 'sitting' and cannot act as an auxiliary denoting continuous action, as it does in the BA example. Compare this with /qa9ad/~/ga9ad/ 'he sat' where the conditions for /q/~/g/ variation are met and variation occurs. If the semantic content/ syntactic functions match, but the morphological structures do not, then again, variation cannot occur, e.g. BA /ba:čir/ 'tomorrow' in the sentence

/aba:ji ba:čir/ (B II)
'I'll come tomorrow'

can be replaced by the morphologically different /bukra/ 'tomorrow' from the same tri-consonantal root b-k-r, but not by /ba:kir/, through a č → k replacement rule: /ba:kir/ normally means 'premature' in MSA, not 'tomorrow'.

However, a survey of the realisations of some of the commoner lexical items in which /č/~/k/, /g/~/q/, /j/~/y/ etc. alternate leads us to believe that simple rules of synchronic variation of the č →⟨k⟩ type do not convincingly account for the full complexity of the data. Some examples from the 'Arab data will illustrate the point.

The MSA word /jum9a/ 'Friday' has the 'Arab dialectal equivalent /yim9a/ (['yim9a]). The data showed that where 'dialectal' and 'standard' versions of this item alternated, it was not merely the initial consonants which varied, but, concomitantly, the quality of the initial vowel. Speakers either produced |'yɪm9a| with high, front unrounded [ɪ] or ['jʊm9a] with high, back, somewhat rounded [ʊ]. Now, there is no phonetic reason why a switch from y to j (or j to y) should be consistently accompanied by a switch from one vowel quality to another, but the fact is that 'hybrid' forms like *[jɪm9a] or *['yʊm9a] failed to occur. Other examples of alternations were between ['ybæl] and ['jæbæl] (MSA /jabal/ 'mountain'), ['šyar] and ['šæjar] (MSA /šajar/ 'trees') where again, the y → j switch was apparently obligatory accompanied by another phonological change: the insertion of [æ]. The point is that the changes were of an all-or-nothing kind in that they either all occurred or none did: the variant realisations of each lexical item respectively represented bundles of 'dialectal' phonological features, or bundles of 'standard' phonological features: no'medial' forms seemed to occur in which only the /y/ of the dialectal variant was replaced by /j/, or in which some but not all of the concomitant vocalic changes occurred.

The same phenomenon was apparent with our other 'phonological' variables. In sentences of the type

/we:hik činnah gu:ṭi mxaffaṣ/ ('Arab)
FACE-YOU LIKE-IT CAN CRUSHED
'Your face is like a crushed can!

/činn/- 'as if, like' always occurred in this morpho-phonemic form if /č/ was used; the 'literate' equivalent of /činn/ -

clearly a recent MSA innovation, was /ka'ann/ - e.g.

/ka'anni$\check{c}$ ma ti$\check{s}$ta:gi:nah/ ('Arab)
LIKE-YOU NEG YOU DESIRE-IT
'It's as if you didn't want it'

No 'medial' forms such as */$\check{c}$a9ann/-, */$\check{c}$ann/- or */kinn/- occurred: the choice was between the bundle of phonological features represented by /$\check{c}$inn/- and the bundle represented by /ka'ann/-, for all speakers. The sentences above could thus equally be realised as:

/we:hik ka'annah gu:ṭi mxaffaṣ/
/$\check{c}$inni$\check{c}$ ma ti$\check{s}$ta:gi:nah/

Similarily, 'Arab /gital/ (['gɪtəl]) 'he killed' varied with /qatal/ (['qatal]), and not, for example, with *['gatal] or *['qital]. The co-occurrence of features in the particular bundles observed is obviously not random: /$\check{c}$inn/-, /yim9a/ and /gital/ on the one hand, and /ka'ann/-, /jum9a/ and /qatal/ on the other are respectively dialectal and standard versions of the 'same' lexical item, with the same semantic content/syntactic function. If we maintain, in the face of this evidence, a simple phonological analysis of /$\check{c}$/$\sim$/k/, /j/$\sim$/y/ etc. variation, we are in fact maintaining that, at least at the level of word-level phonology, speakers are capable of simultaneously operating or simultaneously not-operating whole sets of unrelated phonological rules, in order to generate the observed forms of individual lexical items.

It is, however, the very "all-or-nothing" aspect of this kind of variation - either /$\check{c}$inn/- or /ka'ann/-, in, apparently, the same syntactic context, but no 'hybrid' form - which suggests that what we are really dealing with is lexical variation. This hypothesis would involve the postulation of a more complex lexicon, but, we believe, is more obviously consonant with the way non-dialectal forms are learnt. On this analysis, the syntactic function performed by the complementiser 'as if' can be realised as one of two equivalent lexical items, depending on (stylistic, sociolinguistic) context, for which two separate lexical entries would be required. No doubt speakers who have learnt MSA are aware that /$\check{c}$/ is "equivalent to" MSA /k/ in many cases, and that /'/ occurs medially in MSA, but not in the dialect. But such phonological facts are not consciously learnt; what is learnt, during the learning of the standard language, is the functional equivalence of BA and MSA items as different as /$\check{s}$inhu/ (BA) and /ma:da:/ (MSA) 'what' and /$\check{s}$a:f/ (BA) and /ra'a/ (MSA) 'he saw'. The functional equivalence of BA /$\check{c}$inn/- and MSA /ka'ann/- is but a special case of the general pattern of BA-MSA lexical correspondences: special because /$\check{c}$inn/- and /ka'ann/- are clearly etymologically related. But just as there can be no hybrid form of functional equivalents such as /$\check{s}$inhu/ and /ma:da:/, so there can be none between /$\check{c}$inn/- and /ka'ann/-, *pace* their surface similarity. The same argument applies with no less force to semantic equivalents which are formally superficially similar - like /yim9a/

and /jum9a/. They 'mean the same' referentially but are kept apart formally because of their social meanings: /yim9a/ is "domestic", "intimate", "dialectal", /jum9a/ is "public", "learned" "standardising" (see Holes 1983b).

While the lexical hypothesis depicts speakers as choosing between closed sets of alternative representations of the same underlying syntactic function or semantic unit, in order to negotiate social meanings, the phonological hypothesis would have them switching between the categorical operation and categorical non-operation of whole sets of ad hoc phonological rules to achieve this end. The phonological hypothesis would clearly involve the speaker in an enormously complex task: in order to correctly arrive at /ka'ann/- on the basis of the input form /činn/-, he would have to somehow learn to simultaneously apply the following rules:

(1)	č → ⟨k⟩		(kinn-)
(2)	i → ⟨a⟩		(kann-)
(3)	∅ → ⟨'⟩	/a – nn	(ka'nn-)
(4)	∅ → ⟨a⟩	/' – nn	(ka'ann-)

Apart from the fact that these rules are highly unnatural looking, ad hoc, and in cases (3) and (4) have no wider applicability in the language than in the correct generation of this one item, they would all have to apply or not apply at the same time. To arrive at /jum9a/ from underlying /yim9a/, the speaker would have to have the following rules:

(1)	y → ⟨j⟩	(jim9a)
(2)	i → ⟨u⟩	(jum9a)

Again, these two variable rules, in this particular combination, would have to be learnt as obligatorily applying together or obligatorily not applying together, to generate a single pair of correct lexical variants. In light of these examples, we reject the purely phonological hypothesis and suggest that variation of the kind we have described in this chapter is basically no different from that between two-member pairs such as /li'ann/ (MSA) and /lijil/ (BA) 'because' - that is, describable in terms of alternative lexical representations which speakers have internalized through exposure to MSA. Consequently, we also reject a rewrite convention as an appropriate formalism for describing it. Neither /činn/- nor /ka'ann/-, /gital/ nor /qatal/ should be described as 'underlying': chronologically, /činn/- and /gital/ (in the 'Arab community) are learnt first, but this is no argument for seeking to derive one from the other by re-write rules. The two exist as separate semantically equivalent items in the lexicon of those speakers who have been exposed to the MSA system.

The only part of the variable data examined in this chapter which might be considered as a candidate for specifically phonological treatment is the cross dialectal borrowing which is a marginal feature of the B I and II data on PV5 and PV6. In PV5, for example, we saw that Baḥārna substitute "'Arab" /y/ for their dialectal variant /j/, but virtually only in non-MSA items such as /ja:hil/ 'child', /rajja:l/ 'man' and /ja:b/ 'to bring'. We attributed this tendency to the dominance of the high-status dialect in the dialectal lexical domain. The interesting point, however, is that unlike the /činn/- and /ka'ann/- BA/MSA variation, only the minimum phonological change is made to the B form in the case of cross-dialectal borrowing. Baḥārna do not, for example, "borrow" 'Arab vowel quality when they "borrow" /y/ in these items. Literate Baḥārna vary between [ræjja:l] 'man' and [ræyya:l], preserving the typically B vowel pattern, and not imitating A [rayyɑ:l]. Similarily, typically B participial constructions like /jaybatinnah/ 'she's brought it' whose morphological constituents are

ja:yib	+ at	+	inn	+	ah
p.part	+ fem. enclitic	+	infix	+	object enclitic

were sometimes realised by literate B speakers as /yaybatinnah/, by the apparently straightforward substitution of /y/ for /j/. However, the "typically B" infix -/inn/- in such construction was never deleted although it never occurs in the parallel A construction, which is /yaybatta/.

In these cases and for these communities only, there seems to be an argument for accounting for variation by an independent variable phonological rule of the form:

$$j \rightarrow \langle y \rangle \;/\; [\overline{-\ MSA}]$$

which may apply only where a lexical item containing /j/ is marked [-MSA], and when it does so, entails no concomitant change in other phonological segments of the word.

5.13 Summary of conclusions: 'phonemic variation'

5.13.1 Level of variation

1. The high-status social group shows a much stronger, and more consistent tendency to stick to its dialectal variants than does the low-status group. There is much clearer correlation between dialectal variant replacement and literacy in the low-status group than there is in the high-status group.

2. The extent to which any particular dialectal item is replaced depends on its status in terms of both the local and non-local linguistic prestige systems. Literate speakers, because of their consciousness of non-local norms, have different perceptions of what the statuses of dialectal items are, compared with illiterate speakers.

5.13.2 Nature of variation

1. Most of the variation discussed in Chapter 5 is probably to

be explained in terms of the acquisition of alternative sets of equivalent lexical entries, rather than by phonological rule, variable or otherwise.

2. There is evidence that one kind of variation, that which we have described as cross-dialectal switching and which is limited to the purely dialectal lexical domain, <u>is</u> plausibly accounted for by phonological replacement rules.

3. In whatever form rules are cast, there seem to be group-specific hierarchical relationships <u>between</u> replacement rules, which correlate with the status of the replaced variants. Implicational scaling reveals community-wide patterns of this kind which other approaches do not.

6 The social distribution of some BA morphophonemic patterns

6.1 Introduction

Thus far, our description and explanation of variation in BA has focused on phoneme pairs such as j/y, k/č, etc. We now turn to variation between alternative morphophonemic patterns in certain common categories of the verb and noun. The literature on Gulf Arabic and the vernaculars of contiguous areas (e.g. Johnstone 1967, Ingham 1973, 1976) describes the co-existence, over a wide geographical area, of alternative syllabic structures such as CvCCv(C) and CCvCv(C) in verbal forms like /ḍirbat/~/ḍrubat/ and nominals like /xišba/~/xšiba/, to name but one type of syllabic alternation. In the terms of historical dialectology, such forms have usually been classified as 'sedentary' and 'nomadic' and the particular arrays of variants displayed on a number of variables in a particular dialect place it on a continuum between an extreme 'nomadic' type and an extreme 'sedentary' type (Ingham 1982). What is clear, however, is that synchronically, like the phoneme pairs, morphonemic alternates are multi-valent: while, in historical terms, a shape like CCvCv(C) in /šrubat/ 'she drank' can be associated with communities which once led a nomadic existence, the present-day sociolinguistic status of such a form - how it is evaluated, what its connotations are, what use of it can tell us about its user(s) - all of this differs somewhat from one Gulf state to another because the demographic history and politico-social structure of each is different. In Baḥrain, a wealth of alternative forms are found, but analysis reveals a clear patterning (or rather some clear patternings) in the liability of certain morphophonemic forms to variation. Once again the sometimes conflicting and sometimes conspiring influences of MSA and the local dialectal prestige system seem to be at the root of variability.

In this chapter, an outline of the different dialectal developments within Baḥrain of what are presumed to have been historically shared forms is given. Nothing of substance in the synchronic analysis of variation which follows in Chapter 7, however, hangs on the accuracy of this historical explanation: as I hope to show, the rules which historically gave rise to the present-day syllabic structure types, which are entirely the result of purely phonological changes, cannot plausibly be invoked as a means of explaining current patterns of variation. Variation between forms seems rather to involve choices between "syllabic templates" which are more or less likely to be applied to different types of consonantal skeletons. This, as we shall see in Chapter 8, involves the positing of some novel formalisms, but such formalisms are necessary if we are to adhere to what Hooper (1976:13) has labelled the 'true generalization condition': all rules express generalizations true for all surface forms (see also Hudson G., 1986).

The forms described for each community in this chapter are, then, basilectal norms: they are the forms which, for each of the verb and noun categories given, are typical of the speech of non-literate speakers speaking in informal circumstances. Chapter 7 describes the extent, and motivation of variation and change in each variable in each community, and draws some general conclusions about the social motivations of morphophonemic change; Chapter 8 tackles the problem of how such variation might be described in terms of formal linguistic rules.

6.2 Socially distributed morpho-phonemic differences: some examples

Most Arabic words, in whatever dialect they occur can be broken down morphologically into a consonantal skeleton (the 'root'), a discontinuous vowel-pattern which is interwoven with the skeleton, and affix morphemes of various types: pre-formatives, post-formatives and infixes (c.f. McCarthy 1981 for an autosegmental analysis of Arabic morphonology and Hudson's 1986 rebuttal). Dialect differences can exist at all or any of these levels of analysis. Consider A and B II forms which translate 'you (f.s.) have grown up'. These are respectively /kbare:ti/ and /čuburti:n/, and they can be broken down as follows:

	A	B II
Consonant skeleton (root meaning: 'to be/ grow big')	k b r	č b r
Vowel pattern (syntactic function: 'past tense')	kubar	čubur
Affix (2nd feminine singular)	kubar+e:ti	čubur+ti:n
Phonological rules (non-final short high-vowel deletion)	kbare:ti	n/a
Surface form	[kḅa're:tei]	[čəbər'ti:n]

At each point in the analysis, the linguistic items typically associated with the A and B II communities differ, and the surface realisations can be depicted as the 'aggregate' of these differences. The example chosen is extreme, in that differences occur in every morphological and phonological component; in the main, differences occur at only one or two of the levels distinguished. Following this scheme, some of the more important distinctive forms which are clear markers of sectarian or geographical origin are listed below. It should be emphasised once again that the treatment of dialectal differences in this way simply serves the purpose of presentational clarity. It does not represent a claim that actual variation is to be conceived of as operating on one, all, or any of these levels. As will become clear later in the exposition, an explanation which posits variation in a holistic way between what we have described as 'syllabic templates' seems truer to the facts of variation, and provides greater economy in description.

Vowel patterns: stems

The stem vowel patterns for the A, B I and B II dialects follow quite different principles in both the past and the non-past verb. The three-way division of the B dialects adopted in the last chapter does not correspond exactly to the division which one would make on the basis of morpho-phonological data. A detailed treatment is found in 6.4.2 below.

Affixes

(i) Lexical enclitics in the 2nd person of the past verb

	2 m.s.	2.f.s.	2 common pl.
all A	-t	-ti	-taw
all B	-t	-ti:n(a)	-tu:n(a)

The 'Arab optionally insert an -/e:/- infix between the perfect stem of strong and hollow verbs (all themes) and consonant-initial lexical enclitics, e.g. /dirse:t/ 'I studied', /ga:le:na/ 'we said', /istaghribe:t/ 'I was amazed'. The Baḥārna do not do this, except, apparently, in the Muḥarraq island village of Dēr, where forms such as /ista:nase:ti:n/ 'you (f.s.) were happy' were recorded regularly in the speech of unsophisticated illiterates (especially women).

(ii) Object and possessive enclitics: 2nd person

	2 m.s.	2. f.s.	2 common pl.
A	-ik	-ič	-kum
B I	-(i)k	-(i)š	-kum
B II	-(i)č	-(i)š	-čim

(iii) Treatment of present participle + object enclitics

The morpho-phonemic shape of the infix which is inserted between singular present participles and object enclitics differs between the sects. The 'Arab have -/a/- or Ø, the Baḥārna have -/in(n)/-:

A	/xa:ṭbaha/ or /xa:ṭibha/	'He's become engaged to her'
B (all)	/xa:ṭbinha/	
A	/xa:ṭbatah/	'She's become engaged to him'
B (all)	/xa:ṭbatinnah/	

Phonological rules: historical developments

In general, in the A dialect (cf Johnstone 1967 : 6-9):

(i) Sequences of more than two short open syllables, or two open syllables plus a final closed syllable were avoided. Thus all nominal and verbal forms which had a CvCvCv(C) structure, arising either as a result of the suffixation of vowel-initial lexical or object enclitics to past verb stems (i.e. CvCvC+vC), or through the suffixation of the feminine ending to noun stems (i.e. CvCvC+v(C)), were resyllabified through the deletion of the vowel of the initial syllable, whatever its height. Examples:

(a)	ṣibagh 'he painted'	+	ah masc.ob.encl.	/ṣbaghah/ not /ṣibaghah/ 'he painted it'
(b)	ṣibagh 'he painted'	+	aw pl.lex.encl.	/ṣbaghaw/ not /ṣibaghaw/ 'they painted'
(c)	ghanam 'sheep' (coll)	+	a(t) fem.noun encl.	/ghnima/ not /ghanama/ 'a sheep'

(ii) All CvCCvC sequences which became CvCCvCv(C) through the suffixation of vowel-initial enclitics were resyllabified to C(v)CvCCv(C). Examples:

(a)	yilbas 'he wears'	+	ah masc.ob.encl.	/yilibsah/ or /ylibsah/ not /yilbasah/ 'he wears it'
(b)	yaktib 'he writes'	+	u:n pl.lex.encl.	/yikitbu:n/ or /ykitbu:n/ not /yaktibu:n/ 'they write'

(iii) Where a 'guttural' consonant (gh, x, ḥ, 9, ', h) occurred as C_2 in a closed syllable an /a/ was inserted after C_2, creating a CvCvCv(C) structure, which was then reduced to CCvCv(C) by the rule of vowel deletion (i) (a)

OA /'axḍar/ became /xaḍar/
/maghrib/became /mgharb/

In the B dialects, by contrast:

Rule (i) (a) only applied where the initial vowel of the stem was /i/ or /u/, but not /a/, e.g. B II /ṣabaghah/ 'he painted it', but /smi9ah/ 'he heard it' (unsuffixed stems /ṣabagh/ and /simi9/

'he heard it').

Rule (i)(b) did not apply. In some B dialects, in some verb categories, the vowel of the second, not the first syllable was deleted, e.g. B I /sama9at/ 'she heard', B II /sim9at/.

Rule (i)(c) did not apply: all Baḥārna /ghanama/ 'a sheep'.

Rule (ii)(a) did not apply where the non-past stem vowel was /a/: all Baḥārna /yilbasah/ 'he wears it'.

Rule (ii)(b) applied in all B dialects, except possibly, that of Rās-Rummān: /yikitbu:n/ or /ykitbu:n/-type forms occur in stems whose vowel is /i/.

Rule (iii) did not apply: all Baḥārna have /aẋdar/, /maghrib/.

In the discussion at the conclusion of Chapter 5, the point was made that what at first sight looked like 'phonological' variation in fact involved concomitant co-variation in morpho-phonology which could best be accounted for if we assumed that variation in individual items of vocabulary had been lexicalised. In Chapters 7 and 8, we investigate the co-variation of variables at the 'vowel pattern' and 'phonological rule' levels shown in the illustrative example given at the beginning of this chapter, in certain complex forms consisting of a stem plus one or more affixes. The point of this is to show how far variation in such forms can be handled in the same way as was suggested at the conclusion of the last chapter, where we claimed that a switch in the composition of the discontinuous 'consonantal skeleton' (e.g. from y-m-9 to j-m-9) was usually associated with changes in 'vowel pattern'.

One point which can be made straight away is that items at the 'affix' level of analysis tend to be least liable to variation, at least between the sects. 'Arab and Baḥārna never seem to borrow each others' lexical or object enclitics, and the infixes -in(n)/- (B) in participial constructions of the type illustrated above, and -/e:/- (A) in forms consisting of a strong verb stem plus consonant-initial lexical enclitic are similarly sect-specific (with the apparent exception of the village of Dēr, as noted above).

Within the B group, the use of the specifically 'rural' object enclitic system (-(i)č, -(i)š, -čim) does appear to have largely given way to the 'urban' B system, especially in the speech of literates, in just the same way as /ḳ/ < OA /q/ has given way to /g/. The lack of cross-sect convergence in the affix system is in stark contrast, as will become plain in Chapter 7, to the evident convergence of the morpho-phonological systems when considered at the level of (to use standard terminology) 'vowel patterns' and 'phonological rules' (6.2 above) - or (to use terminology which reflects more plausibly observed variation), 'syllabic templates'. The sectarian affix systems, for both literates and illiterates of both sects, are fully maintained, while verb stem morphophonology shows signs of a convergence in the speech of literates. This is indeed an interesting fact: despite convergence in other areas of morpho-phonology, towards an essentially 'non-sectarian' form of speech, both sects cling on to the sect-specificity of certain morphemes of very high frequency. Thus, to revert to the example given at the beginning of this chapter, literate Baḥārna villagers often used forms of the /kbarti:n/-type instead of the 'illiterate' /čuburti:n/-type. Note, however, that they always retained the typically B -/ti:n/ suffix, even, as far as the writer was able to observe, in cross-sect conversation in shops and public places. This is, perhaps, evidence that however much low- and high-status literates seemed to be converging towards shared norms of speech, it was still important for them to associate themselves symbolically and unequivocally with the sect-group to which they belonged through the use of sect-specific markers. It is also an interesting, if at present unexplained fact, that the part of the language system which carried this sociolinguistic distinction is the system of inflectional morphology (see Hudson 1980: 44-8 for a tentative rationale for the susceptibility of different types of linguistic item to variation).

6.3 Selection of variables for investigation

6.3.1 Definition of 'variable' and 'variant'

A morpho-phonological variable is defined as a set of alternative morpho-phonological variants which have an equivalent semantico-syntactic function. Thus, the forms /sim9at/, /sama9at/ and /sma9at/ are all possible variants which express the idea 'she heard'. They can be analysed as consisting of the common consonantal skeleton (s-m-9), which expresses the basic meaning 'hearing', on which have been imposed different vowel pattern morphemes which all express the syntactic notion 'past tense', and to which a shared suffix -/at/, denoting '3rd person feminine singular' has been added. Different phonological rules operate on these various combinations of morphemes to generate the variants noted. Each surface variant can be (and in standard generative treatments such as Brame 1970 frequently is) treated as an amalgam of different sets of morphemes on which different phonological rules have operated. Each variable is the sum of the surface variants potentially available to a speaker to express a given semantico-syntactic function.

6.3.2 Criteria for the selection of variables

6.3.2.1 Frequency: that the variables selected should occur with a realistically quantifiable degree of frequency in each of our 87 speakers' data.

6.3.2.2 Communal distribution: that the variables selected should reflect a variety of patterns in the communal distribution of the variants which comprise them. The point here is to investigate how different arrays of social markings (±A, ±B, ±MSA) correlate with levels of variation, and to see how far the patterns revealed by the analysis in Chapter 5 are repeated.

6.3.2.3 <u>Internal structuring of the system</u>: that the variables selected should cover a number of morphological categories. Our purpose is to discover whether (and if so why) variants which are morpho-phonologically identical, but which perform different syntactic functions (e.g. nouns and past verbs which both have a 'dialectal' CvCvCv(C) structure) show consistently different levels of variation. How far, in other words are functional differences starting to be reflected by differences in form in grammars in which variation exists (chiefly those of literate speakers)?

6.4 The variables

The variables which satisfied these criteria were in the following areas of morpho-phonology:

(i) Theme 1 strong past verbs with vowel-initial suffixes.

(ii) Theme 1 strong non-past verbs with vowel-initial suffixes.

(iii) Certain nominal forms

The remainder of this chapter comprises a description of the different basilectal systems in each of these areas. <u>The systems described are 'stereotypes' but are not idealised</u>: there were many speakers, usually illiterates, unused to mixing outside the domestic circle, whose data conformed exactly to the descriptions given here.

6.4.1 Theme 1 strong past verbs

6.4.1.1 The A dialect

Unsuffixed past verb stems, which are of the general form CvCvC- in all BA dialects, can be divided into three groups on the basis of the vowel pattern: CaCaC-, CiCaC, or CuCaC-. The major distinction is between stems which have /a/ as initial vowel and those which do not: as a result of a phonological rule which appears to have applied to the A dialect, /i/ (or /u/ in a limited number of environments involving combinations of labials and velars) occurs to the exclusion of /a/ in short-vowelled non-final open syllables, except in the following consonantal environments (cf Johnstone 1967: 6-9, 257-9):

(i) C_1 or C_2 is a 'guttural' (gh, x, ḥ, 9, ', h)

(ii) C_2 is a liquid (l, r)

Compare:

(a)

<u>C_1 or C_2 = 'guttural'</u>		<u>non-'guttural'</u>	
/xaṭab/	'he betrothed'	/riṭan/	'he gabbled'
/šaghal/	'he operated (s'thing)'	/šinag/	'he hanged (s'one)'

(b) C_2 = liquid / non-liquid

C_2 = liquid	non-liquid
/šarax/ 'he set sail'	/biṭaḥ/ 'he knocked down'
/ṭala9/ 'he went out'	/kubar/ 'he grew big'

The OA/MSA system of past-stem vowelling operates along quite different principles. There are three types of stem, but they are morphological correlates of different semantico-syntactic categories, and are not related to phonological factors: CaCaC- stems, by far the commonest group, consist mainly of transitive verbs; CaCiC- stems are usually intransitive and express non-permanent states; CaCuC- are invariably intransitive and express permanent states. Thus although both the A dialect and OA/MSA have three types of past-stem, the two systems are structured differently.

In the A dialect, the suffixation of lexical or object enclitics which begin with a vowel to past-stems results in the deletion of the initial vowel of the resulting form, and the conditioning of the second vowel (which because of the deletion now becomes the initial vowel) in line with the vowel-conditioning rule described above:

/xṭubat/	'she betrothed'	(xaṭab + at)
/rṭinat/	'she gabbled'	(riṭan + at)
/kbaraw/	'they grew big'	(kubar + aw)

The same applies if the suffix is an object enclitic:

/xṭubič/ 'he betrothed you (f.s.)'	(xaṭab + ič)
/šghalah/ 'he operated it (m.s.)'	(šaghal+ ah)

6.4.1.2 The B dialects

The B dialects, to a greater or lesser degree have retained the semantico-syntactic division of stems found in OA (which is identical with that of MSA):

B II (the 'village' dialect)

In the village dialects, there are two types of past-stem: high-vowelled and low-vowelled. All OA/MSA CaCaC- stems occur as CaCaC- in the villages, and all OA/MSA CaCiC- and CaCuC- stems occur as either CiCiC- or CuCuC-: CuCuC- if C_2 is a bi-labial, otherwise CiCiC-. The basis for the stem categorisation is hence basically semantico-syntactic, as in OA/MSA. However, some transitive verbs, which exceptionally have a CaCiC- stem in OA/MSA are high-vowelled in the village dialects.

Examples:

OA/MSA stem-type	root	village stem-type
CaCaC- (trans)	k-š-f 'discover'	kašaf-
CaCiC- (trans)	s-m-9 'hear'	simi9-
CaCiC- (intrans)	z-9 -l 'get angry'	zi9il-
CaCuC- (intrans)	č-b-r 'grow big'	čubur-

B III (the Rās-Rummān dialect)

The position in Rās-Rummān is similar to that in the village dialects, except that instead of CiCiC- and CuCuC- stems, Rās-Rummānis have CiCaC- and CuCaC- stems. Otherwise the distribution of stem-vowel-patternings (that is, high-vowelled versus low-vowelled stems) is the same. The B III forms which correspond to the examples above are thus:
kašaf-, sima9-, zi9al-, kubar-.

B I (the main 'urban' dialect)

In the main town dialect, the stem system reflects exactly the transitivity marking system: all verbs have a CaCaC-stem if they are transitive, and a CiCaC- or CuCaC- stem if they are intransitive, regardless of OA/MSA vowel-patternings in the same verbs. Hence the urban B equivalents of our four examples are:
kašaf-, sama9-, zi9al-, kubar-.

Notwithstanding these small sub-dialectal differences in stem-vowel pattern system, the morpho-phonemic shape of suffixed forms can be accounted for by three simple rules which, with the exception of Rās-Rummān, apply to all B dialects:

(i) (a) When vowel-initial lexical enclitics are suffixed to any stem which has a CaCaC- shape, no vowel deletion takes place.
(b) If the stem is high-vowelled (CiCiC-, CuCuC-, CiCaC- or CuCaC-), the second vowel of the stem is deleted, never the first.

(ii) If a vowel-initial object enclitic is suffixed directly to a past-stem, no deletion of the second vowel takes place, but in any stem, in any dialect, if the initial vowel is /i/ or /u/, it is deleted.

The B III dialect of Rās-Rummān is exceptional in that all forms which consist of stem plus vowel initial enclitic undergo second vowel deletion and the raising of the initial vowel to /i/ or /u/ - regardless of the vowelling of the underlying stem, and regardless of whether the enclitic is lexical or object.

6.4.1.3 Summary

Table 16 below provides an illustrative summary of the distribution of past-stem vowellings in suffixed and unsuffixed forms in BA. We would emphasise the point that this Table, like Table 4, represents the basilectal distribution of forms.

The form-type chosen for detailed analysis was the "stem + vowel-initial lexical enclitic" on the grounds of the criteria outlined in 6.3.2:

Frequency: Forms of this type were about twice as frequent in the

OA/MSA stem		stem	stem + lex.encl.	stem + ob.encl.
	A	/ḍarab/	/ḍrubat/	/ḍrubah/
ḍarab-	B I	/ḍ̄arab/	/ḍ̄arabat/	/ḍ̄arabah/
'to beat'	B II	/ḍarab/	/ḍarabat/	/ḍarabah/
(trans)	B III	/ḍarab/	/ḍirbat/	/ḍirbah/
	A	/šarab/	/šrubat/	/šrubah/
šarib-	B I	/šarab/	/šarabat/	/šarabah/
'to drink'	B II	/širib/	/širbat/	/š(i)ribah/
(trans)	B III	/širab/	/širbat/	/širbah/
za9il-	A	/za9al/	/z9alat/	-
'to get	B I	/zi9al/	/zi9lat/	-
angry'	B II	/zi9il/	/zi9lat/	-
(intrans)	B III	/zi9al/	/zi9lat/	-
kabur-	A	/kubar/	/kbarat/	-
'to get	B I	/kubar/	/kubrat/	-
big'	B II	/čubur/	/čubrat/	-
(intrans)	B III	/kubar/	/kubrat/	-

Table 16: Distribution of past-stem vowellings in suffixed and unsuffixed forms

data as "stem" alone or "stem + vowel initial object enclitic" forms. All 3rd person feminine singular, and 3rd person common plural forms were countable as examples of "stem + vowel-initial lexical enclitic" in the sense that they all have a similar underlying morpho-phonological structure: CvCvC + $\begin{Bmatrix} \bar{v}(C) \\ vC \end{Bmatrix}$ which shows up in surface structure as CCvC $\begin{Bmatrix} \bar{v}(C) \\ vC \end{Bmatrix}$, CvCvC $\begin{Bmatrix} \bar{v}(C) \\ vC \end{Bmatrix}$ or CvCC $\begin{Bmatrix} \bar{v}(C) \\ vC \end{Bmatrix}$ and can be accounted for by positing the operation of different sets of phonological rules (though whether or not this is the correct analysis will be discussed in the next chapter). All the following forms from the verb root h-j-m 'to attack', for example, would be counted as examples of "stem plus vowel-initial lexical enclitic":

3 f.s.	h-j-m + at	⟶	PHONOLOGICAL RULES	⟶ hjimat, hajamat, hijmat
3 c.pl.	h-j-m + aw	⟶		⟶ hjimaw, hajamaw, hijmaw
3 c.pl.+ ob.encl.	h-j-m + aw + ah	⟶		⟶ hjimo:, hajamo:, hijmo:
	+ ha	⟶		⟶ hjimo:ha, etc.
	+ik/k	⟶		⟶ hjimo:k, etc.
	⋮			⋮

Communal distribution: In the stereotypical forms of dialectal Arabic used by many illiterate speakers, the system by which the syllabic structure of suffixed variant forms is related to the category of the verb-stem is highly community-specific. The maintenance (or lack of it) of various syllabic structure/stem category correspondences in *literate*, as opposed to illiterate speech data, provides a large amount of additional evidence as to the relative statuses of communal dialects, and the extent to which they are converging.

Internal restructuring: The relative susceptibility of *nouns* and *verbs*, which both have an underlying CvCvC + v(C) morpho-phonological structure, to syllabic restructuring in literate, as opposed to illiterate speech is of particular interest. Significant differences in the treatment of noun and verb forms, in terms of the likelihood and level of variation between the dialectal stereotype and some novel form, would indicate that such variation cannot be accounted for in purely phonological terms, but must take account of the morphological status (and hence syntactic function) of the variable item.

A study of the "stem plus lexical enclitic forms" can thus provide evidence about the inter-connected issues of the sociolinguistic structure of Baḥrain and the internal evolution of its dialects.

6.4.2 Theme 1 strong non-past verbs

6.4.2.1 The A dialect

Unsuffixed non-past stems are of the general form $\begin{Bmatrix} y \\ t \end{Bmatrix}$ vCCvC in all forms of Arabic. In the A dialect, there is a rule of vowel-dissimilation in all unsuffixed forms: if the vowel of the pre-formative is high, the stem-vowel is low, and vice versa. It is, however, clearly the height of the stem-vowel which determines that of the pre-formative, and not vice-versa. Stem-vowel height is conditioned by the presence of certain contiguous consonants - the 'gutturals' - and in the non-'guttural' stems, it follows the OA/MSA system of stem-vowel patterning. The following categories of stem can thus be identified:

(i) If C_2 or C_3 is a guttural, the stem-vowel is low, and the pre-formative vowel is high.

(ii) If C_1 is a guttural, the stem-vowel is high and the pre-formative is low. However, since such forms would result in a guttural occurring as the closing consonant of a non-final closed syllable whose vowel is /a/, there is virtually obligatory re-syllabication of the resulting form (phonological rule (iii) in 6.2 above). Compare:

(a) C_2 or C_3 = a guttural

Root	imperfect stem	
ṭ-ḥ-n	/yiṭḥan/	'he grinds'

b-ṭ-ḥ	/yibṭaḥ/	'he knocks (s'one) over'
s-m-9	/yisma9/	'he hears'
n-x-l	/yinxal/	'he sieves'

(b) C_1 = guttural

(I) If C_2 = a liquid

9-r-f	/y9arf/ (not /ya9rif)	'he knows'
h-l-k	/yhalk/ (not /yahlik/)	'he perishes'

(II) If C_2 = any other consonant

x-ṭ-b	/yxaṭub/ (not /yaxṭub/)	'he betrothes'
ḥ-d-g	/yḥadig/ (not/yaḥdig/)	'he fishes'

(iii) If there is no guttural consonant in the root, the stem-vowel may be high or low, and follows the OA/MSA pattern: the low vowel /a/ occurs where the OA/MSA stem-vowel is /a/, and a high vowel occurs in all other cases. The frontness/backness of this high vowel is determined by consonantal environment (basically /u/ occurs where /b/ or /m/ is an effective factor) and does not follow the OA/MSA pattern. Compare:

(I) If OA/MSA stem-vowel = /a/

A root	imperfect stem	OA/MSA equivalent	
l-b-s	/yilbas/	/yalbas/-	'he wears'
n-ḍ-y	/yinḍay/	/yanḍaj/-	'it ripens'
š-r-b	/yišrab/	/yašrab/-	'he drinks'

(II) If OA/MSA stem-vowel = /i/ or /u/

ṣ-b-r	/yaṣbur/	/yaṣbur/-	'he is patient'
ḏ-k-r	/yaḏkir/	/yaḏkur/-	'he remembers'
b-r-z	/yabriz/	/yabruz/-	'he is ready'
m-l-č	/yamlič/	/yamlik/-	'he gets engaged to (a woman)'

In unsuffixed forms, then, non-past stem-vowels can be predicted by two factors:

1. the conditioning power of guttural consonants on contiguous vowels, which is all powerful

2. the historical OA high-low vowel contrast, in non-guttural stems only.

The height of the pre-formative vowel, which is always opposite to that of the stem, follows automatically.

The suffixation of vowel-initial enclitics (lexical or object) to any of the above stem-types results in the resyllabication of the resulting form. All occurrences of:

$$\begin{Bmatrix} y \\ t \end{Bmatrix} \text{vCCvC + v .....}$$

become:

$$\begin{Bmatrix} y \\ t \end{Bmatrix} \text{(v)CvCCv .....}$$

the deletion of the pre-formative vowel being optional. The important point to bear in mind is that the kernel pattern of suffixed non-past forms in the A dialect is stereotypically -CvCC-, not -CCvC-, regardless of the quality of the stem vowel in the corresponding unsuffixed form. Thus we have (pre-formative deleted examples):

(i) stem-vowel = /a/

Unsuffixed form		Suffixed form	
/yišxal/	'he sieves'	/yšaxlu:n/	'they sieve'
/tilbas/	'you (m.s.) wear'	/tlibsi:n/	'you (f.s.) wear'
/yisma9/	'he hears'	/ysim9ah/	'he hears it'

(ii) stem-vowel = /i/ or /u/

/taḍrib/	'you (m.s.)/she hits'	/tḍirbu:n/	'you (c.pl) hit'
/yaḅriz/	'he gets ready'	/tḅirzi:n/	'you (f.s.) get ready'
/taktib/	'you (m.s.)/she writes'	/tkitbah/	'you (m.s.) write it'

The stem-vowel of the resulting suffixed form is conditioned in the same way as noted for suffixed forms in 6.4.1.1., except that /a/ occurs only if a guttural is in contiguity; the liquids are associated with /i/, not /a/ in non-past stems. If the pre-formative vowel shows up in a suffixed form, which it optionally may, it is always /i/ ([I], [ə]) not /a/.

One way of accounting for resyllabicated non-past suffixed forms in general, is by sets of deletion and epenthesis rules; but whether this is the correct formalism for accounting for synchronic variation (as well as diachronic development) is an issue which is taken up in Chapter 8. For the moment, we confine ourselves to the point that resyllabicated forms of the type illustrated here occur categorically in all non-past Theme I stems in the speech of many illiterate (and some literate) 'Arab. In OA/MSA, all suffixed non-past forms are of the other, unresyllabicated type.

6.4.2.2 The B dialects

There is no phonologically conditioned categorisation of stems to be made in an account of the B dialects, as there is in the A. A comparison of the OA/MSA vowel patterns with those occurring in the data for illiterate Baḥārna from a wide variety of localities, in a large number of verbs, showed that the dialectal patterns stereotypically follow those of OA/MSA very closely. In all verbs where OA/MSA has /a/ as stem vowel, the B dialects also have it; in all verbs where OA/MSA has /i/ or /u/, the B dialects have a high vowel, whose frontness/backness and roundness is determined by consonantal environment. Vowel dissimilation only occurs, as it were, coincidentally in the B dialects in verbs which have imperfect stem vowel /a/, since the B pre-formative vowel is always /i/ or /u/. The table below gives an illustrative summary in which representative B and A non-past stems are compared with their OA/MSA equivalents. It will be seen that as far as formal similarities are concerned, the stereotypical B forms are closer to OA/MSA in syllabication and stem-vowel quality (category (a)) and in stem-vowel quality (categories (b) and (c)) than are the A forms. In this area of morpho-phonology, just as in the past verb, the low-prestige B dialects are more formally similar to the supra-dialectal standard than is the local prestige dialect.

(a)	C_1 = guttural			
	OA/MSA root		B equivalent	A equivalent
	/ya9rif/-	'he knows'	/yi9ruf/	/y9arf/
	/yaxṭub/-	'he betrothes'	/yixṭub/	/yxaṭub/
	/taḥbal/-	'she conceives (a child)'	/tiḥbal/	/tḥamil/
(b)	C_2 or C_3 = guttural			
	/yanxul/-	'he sieves'	/yinxil/	/yinxal/
	/yadxul/-	'he enters'	/yidxil/	/yidxal/
	/yaq9ud/-	'he sits'	/yuḳ9ud/ or /yiḳ9id/	/yig9ad/
	/yaṭbux/-	'he cooks'	/yiṭbux/	/yiṭbax/
(c)	non-guttural stems			
	/yaktub/-	'he writes'	/yiktib/	/yaktib/
	/yašrab/-	'he drinks'	/yišrab/	/yišrab/
	/yaḍrub/-	'he hits'	/yiḍrub/	/yaḍrib/
	/yabriz/-	'he is ready'	/yibriz/	/yabriz/

Table 17: A-B differences in the vowel-patterns of unsuffixed non-past stems

In suffixed non-past stems, the B dialects as a whole pattern together as a group (with the exception of the dialect of Rās-Rummān). The village and the main urban dialects show resyllabicated forms only in verbs whose non-past stem vowel is /i/ or /u/; where the stem vowel is /a/, there is no resyllabication. In stems where resyllabication does occur, the stem-vowel in the resulting form is always /i/ or /u/, never /a/.

Although the evidence is rather scanty, it appears that in the dialect of Rās-Rummān (B III), resyllabication of suffixed non-past forms only occurs in G-C-C roots. The paucity of data, however, does not justify any firm conclusion on this score.

We are now in a position to provide a tabular summary of stereotypical suffixed forms for the A and B dialects in all non-past verb categories.

Stem-type	ex	stem-v. (unsuffixed) OA/MSA	B	A	ex. of suffixed forms B I & II	III	A
	ḥ-f-ḍ	a	a	i	yiḥfaḍu:n	(all)	yiḥafḍu:n
C_1 = G	x-ṭ-b	u	u	u	tixiṭbu:n	(all)	tixaṭbu:n
	gh-ṣ-l	i	i	i	tighiṣlah	(all)	tighaṣlah
C_2 or C_3 = G	z-9-l	a	a	a	tiz9ali:n	(all)	tiza9li:n
	d-x-l	u	i	a	yidixlu:n	yidxilu:n	yidaxlu:n
non-G roots	š-r-b	a	a	a	yišrabu:n	(all)	yiširbu:n
	k-t-b	u	i	i	yikitbu:n	yiktibu:n	yikitbu:n
	n-z-l	i	i	i	yinizlu:n	yinzilu:n	yinizlu:n

Summary: 'Arab: all suffixed forms are resyllabicated
Baḥārna I and II: if unsuffixed stem-vowel is high, suffixed forms are resyllabicated; if low, they are not
Baḥārna III: no suffixed forms are resyllabicated
OA/MSA: no suffixed forms are resyllabicated

Table 18: A-B differences in the syllabication of suffixed non-past forms

On the basis of the criteria of frequency, communal distribution and internal restructuring (6.3.2), suffixed non-past forms were selected as a variable for detailed analysis:

Frequency: Suffixed forms occurred in the data between two and three times as often as unsuffixed forms, for obvious reasons: all 2 f.s., 2 c.pl, and 3 c.pl forms, as well as any stem plus vowel-initial object enclitic forms, automatically count as "suffixed non-past forms".

Communal distribution of forms and internal restructuring of dialectal systems: The illiterate data suggested that, as in the case of the suffixed past stem, there are definable, community-specific systems of vowelling and syllabication in non-past forms which remain categorical for some speakers in each of the communities. However, other speakers have introduced a degree of variability into their grammars, so that the rules needed to generate observed forms must have become less than categorical. A comparative study of data across communities should reveal the main trends in how this variability is being introduced: in which stem-categories, in which communities, the stereotypical dialectal forms are most often preserved and in which they are being replaced (and which forms are replacing them). This is an interesting question because the B illiterate systems seem again to be "closer" in surface form to the norms of MSA. Once again, the local and non-local linguistic prestige systems are pulling in opposite directions, and could be expected to bring about some kind of re-structuring in the grammars of literate speakers aware of this tension.

6.4.3 Certain noun categories

The third area of BA morpho-phonology which we shall examine is that of the syllabic shape of certain nominal forms which correspond to OA/MSA nouns having the following syllable structure:

(i) CaGCv(C) (where "G" stands for "guttural consonant")

(ii) CvCvCv(C)

CaGCv(C) includes a category of adjectives e.g. OA/MSA /'a9ma:/ 'blind', nouns such as /maghrib/ 'sunset' and a group of feminine nouns such as /gahwa/ 'coffee'.

CvCvCv(C) is the general pattern for a large group of feminine nouns such as /baraka/ 'blessing' and for 'unitary' nouns derived from collectives, e.g. /ghanam/ 'sheep (coll)', /ghanama/ 'a sheep'.

6.4.3.1 The A dialect

We have already seen that the A equivalent of OA/MSA non-past verb stems like /ya9rif/ 'he knows' is /y9arf/. In the same way, nominal forms which have the same OA/MSA syllabic structure, e.g. /maghrib/, have equivalents in the A dialect of the general form CGaCC, e.g. /mgharb/. It seems that, diachronically, all instances of closed CaG syllables in non-final syllables in whatever morphological category they occurred, became in the A dialect CGa-. Many illiterate 'Arab still use only these resyllabicated forms. (See Johnstone 1967 and Ingham 1973, 1976 for studies of other dialects in the Gulf area where the same development took place.)

We saw in 6.4.1.1 that past verb-stems of the CvCvC- pattern undergo resyllabication to CCvCv(C) when a vowel-initial enclitic is suffixed to them, through the deletion of the vowel of the initial syllable of the resulting form, e.g. /šarab/ 'he drank', /šrubah/ 'he drank it', /šrubaw/ 'they drank'. In the same way, feminine nouns of the general form CvCvCv(C) in OA/MSA have CCvCv(C) equivalents in the A dialect, through the deletion of the initial vowel, whatever its height, e.g. OA/MSA /barada/ 'hail' and /ruṭaba/ 'a date' have the A equivalents /bridi/ and /rṭuba/. As in the case of the metathesis of non-final closed CaG syllables, we seem to be dealing here with a general phonological development specific to the A dialect, which historically affected the initial vowel of all OA CvCvCv(C) forms.

6.4.3.2 The B dialects

In the B dialects as a whole, OA forms like /maghrib/ did not undergo metathesis: non-final closed CaG syllables were not treated differently from any other kind of non-final closed syllable. Thus A /ghawa/ 'coffee', /yḥala/ 'water-pot', /xaḍar/ 'green' contrast with B /gahwa/, /jaḥla/, /axḍar/.

The treatment of CvCvCv(C) nominal forms in the B dialects, as a group, is identical to the treatment of CvCvCv(C) verbal forms which consist morphologically of a stem plus vowel-initial object enclitic. If the initial vowel was high, it was deleted; if it was low, it was not. Examples:

	B II dialect		OA/MSA	
nouns	/rṭaba/	(initial vowel /u/)	cf /ruṭaba/	'a date'
	/baḳara/	(initial vowel /a/)	cf /baqara/	'a cow'
verbs	/smi9ah/	(initial vowel /i/)	cf /sami9ahu/	'he heard'
stem + ob encl	/ḍarabah/	(initial vowel /a/)	cf /ḍarabahu/	'he hit him'

The only apparent exceptions to this schema are a handful of nouns such as /smiča/ 'a fish', /šjara/ 'a tree' and /nsima/ 'a breath' (OA/MSA equivalents /samaka/, /šajara/, /nasama/). It is probably no coincidence that the 'deleted' /a/ of the OA forms occurs in each case in an environment which consists of prepalatal consonants: s-m, š-j, n-s. Such environments are associated in all BA dialects with an extremely fronted and raised /a/, and it may be, historically, that in the items noted OA /a/ was raised to the point where it merged with /i/ and was then deleted by the same high-vowel deletion rule which produced surface /rṭaba/ from ruṭab + a(t) and /smi9ah/ from underlying simi9 + ah. The alternative explanation, that just these three isolated items were selectively borrowed in 'resyllabicated' form from the A dialect, seems improbable.

6.5 Summary

Judging by the criteria set out in 6.3.2, the syllable structure of the dialectal equivalents of OA/MSA CaGCv(C) and CvCvCv(C) forms looked to be another fruitful site for the investigation of types and levels of variation in the BA-speaking communities. Once again, the low-status B dialects align with the supradialectal standard to a considerable degree, creating a tension for the literate speakers between what they know to be "correct" (but locally 'low-prestige') and what they know to be "incorrect" (but associated locally with the speech of the prestige group).

Another, more general reason for examining variation between resyllabicated and non-resyllabicated forms was the light this might throw on the linguistic status of resyllabication as a process: diachronically, though it seems to have affected some Baḥraini communities to different extents, it was clearly phonologically motivated, in that items having a similar phonological structure but a different morphological status were similarly affected. Synchronically, however, it seems that an account of variation in syllable structure has to take account of non-phonological factors. Contrast, for example, the present-day A verb form /ḥrisah/ 'he guarded it'(presumed underlying ḥaras + ah) with the noun form /ḥarasah/ 'his defence force'(presumed underlying form identical to that of the verb). The verb form is clearly part of the 'core' dialect, and undergoes resyllabication; the noun is a recent neologism which conforms to the syllabic structure patterns of MSA. Just as /k/ and /j/ in borrowed words fail to undergo a /k/→/č/ and /j/→/y/ substitution rule, so, it seems, borrowed forms which might be candidates for resyllabication on the basis of their phonological shape fail to undergo it.

In any Baḥraini community where the speech of literates shows variation between resyllabicated/non-resyllabicated forms, and the speech of (some) illiterates from the same communities does not, the question arises whether:

(a) different morphological categories show different probabilities of resyllabication (e.g. CvCvCv(C) nouns versus verbs, CaGCv(C) nouns versus verbs)

(b) such variation should be accounted for by phonological rules - and if so, what the underlying forms might be, and how the rules should be formulated, in the light of the patterns revealed by data analysis (cf the discussion in 5.12).

These questions are now discussed.

7 Morphophonemic variation: analysis and interpretation

7.1 Introduction

We described in Chapter 6 how in BA there are sets of syllabically different variants which are functionally equivalent but which have a specific social distribution (most clearly in the case of the illiterate population). In this chapter, we aim to explain the choices which literate speakers from various Baḥraini communities make between the members of these equivalent sets of syllabic variants: which variant-types they consistently select, which they avoid, and why. In particular, we shall be addressing the following related questions:

(a) whether a syllabic variant with a given social distribution, e.g. CCvCv(C) among 'Arab, is more prone to become variable where it functions as a noun or a verb

(b) what the source for the 'novel' variants, with which each community's 'dialectal' variant has become variable,could be: e.g. given that there are some 'Arab who have CCvCv(C) categorically, and some who have it variably, which variant(s) have been introduced into the dialect by those with 'variable' grammars?

(c) whether in the light of the answer to (b), there is any evidence of sectarian convergence towards a non-sectarian 'shared' morphophonemic system, and how this system is being formed.

This chapter, then, is an attempt to describe and explain how and why the results of sect-specific historical phonological developments, presented in Chapter 6 in terms of stereotypical syllable structure/verb stem combinations are being preserved or are undergoing change in the speech of educated people. All of the data is presented from a 'group' point of view in this chapter, while in Chapter 8, some of the variables are selected for implicational analysis.

7.2 Syllable structure and stem-type

In this chapter we will be using the dialectal systems exemplified in the last chapter as a yardstick against which to examine variation in literate speech. "Literacy", as already noted, implies a considerable degree of familiarity with, and use of MSA; it usually also implies white-collar employment in geographically and religiously "mixed" environments, and hence a higher degree of exposure to the speech of people from social groups other than one's own, than is usual for non-literates. It also implies a different quality of contact: the illiterate Baḥārna villager who sells his farm produce in the public market is certainly exposed to, and understands the speech of 'Arab buyers. But his spoken interaction with them is likely to consist of short, predictable exchanges and cannot be compared with the type of regular and varied conversational interaction which occurs between 'Arab and Baḥārna colleagues in offices, school staffrooms, etc.

Both the possibility of MSA, and 'other dialect' influences needed to be taken into consideration in an account of BA speech variation and this led to refinements in the syllable structure/stem-type framework of analysis. These refinements are described below in 7.2.1 - 7.2.3.

7.2.1 Morphophonemic variable 1 (MV1): the past verb

Three different syllabic patterns, CaCaCaC, CCvCaC occurred in the data. The vowel "v" in the latter two variants is automatically determined according to the principles given in 6.4.1.1, 6.4.1.2.

MV1.1 contains the vast majority of transitive and intransitive Theme 1 strong verbs (List MV1.1 below). These verbs have a CaCaCaC vowelling in OA/MSA. For reasons given below, verbs which have a 'guttural' in C_3 position were excluded from this category. Example of a MV1.1 verb: d-r-s 'to study'

MV1.2 contains a small number of transitive and intransitive verbs (List MV1.2). These verbs have a CaCiCaC vowelling in OA/MSA. Example š-r-b 'to drink'.

MV1.3 contains intransitive verbs (List MV1.3). These verbs have a CaCuCaC vowelling in OA/MSA. Example: k-b-r 'to grow old, big'.

MV1.4: contains a small number of transitive and intransitive verbs which have a CaCaCaC or a CaCiCaC vowelling in MSA, but all have a guttural consonant in C_3 position. (List MV1.4.) Example: ṭ-l-9 'to go out, up'.

The reason for defining the categories of the verb stem in this way was basically to show up any 'restructuring' influence which the MSA system of vowel-patterning might be having on the dialectal systems described in Chapter 6. However, the initial survey of the data suggested that many speakers, who showed no variation at all between syllabic variants in what we have termed "MV1.1" verbs, did show variation in just those verbs which have /x, gh, ḥ, 9, h, '/ in C_3 position (regardless of whether they have a CaCaCaC or CaCiCaC form in OA/MSA). This fact in itself suggested that speakers were treating these verbs as a special category, and justified the refinement of our analytical framework to take account if it. A tentative explanation of the exceptional treatment of "MV1.4" verbs is advanced in 7.3.1.1 below.

With the exception of the CaCaCaC variant in category MV1.3, which never occurred in the data, the examples in Table 19 below are representative of the eleven occurring syllabic variant/stem-type combinations, each of which occurred at least once in the 497 tokens produced by the 87 speaker sample.

	Syllabic variants			MSA
Stem-cat	CaCaCaC	CCvCaC	CvCCaC	CaCvCaC
MV1.1	darasat/w	drisat/w	dirsat/w	darasat
MV1.2	šarabat/w	šrubat/w	širbat/w	šaribat
MV1.3	-	kbarat/w	kubrat/w	kaburat
MV1.4	ṭala9at/w	ṭla9at/w	ṭil9at/w	ṭala9at

Table 19: Occurring variant forms of 3rd person fem.s. & c.pl. past verbs in the data.

Certain of these syllabic structure/verb stem combinations are, as we have seen, typically associated with certain communities; but where a speaker varies between one or more syllabic structures in a given category of verb stems, the question arises: which variants vary with which? Tables 20 and 21 provide the basic answer.

Stem-cat	B I	II	III	'Arab
MV1.1	darasat	darasat	dirsat	drisat
MV1.2	šarabat	širbat	širbat	šrubat
MV1.3	kubrat	kubrat	kubrat	kbarat
MV1.4	ṭala9at	ṭala9at	ṭil9at	ṭla9at

Table 20: Syllable structure/stem category combinations: non-variable grammars

Stem-cat	B I	II	III	'Arab
MV1.1	darasat∼ dirsat	darasat∼ dirsat	dirsat∼ darasat	drisat∼ dirsat
MV1.2	šarabat∼ širbat	širbat	širbat	šrubat∼ širbat
MV1.3	kubrat	kubrat	kubrat	kbarat∼ kubrat
MV1.4	ṭala9at∼ ṭil9at	ṭala9at∼ ṭil9at	ṭil9at∼ ṭala9at	ṭla9at∼ ṭil9at

Table 21: Syllable structure/stem category combinations: variable grammars

When the data of speakers who showed variation was analysed it was found that no individual in any community varied between more than two syllabic variants in any stem category. These variants were: always the variant which the illiterate members of his community typically used in that category, as described in Chapter 6, and one other, as follows:

(a) In any verb category in which CaCaCaC was their dialectal stereotype, there were some B I and II speakers who had CaCaCaC/CvCCaC variation

(b) In any verb category in which CCvCaC was their dialectal stereotype (i.e. all verb categories) there were some 'Arab who had CCvCaC/CvCCaC variation.

(c) In those verb categories in which CvCCaC was their dialectal stereotype, no B I and II speakers showed any variation.

(d) In just those verb categories in which B I and II speakers had CaCaCaC/CvCCaC variation, there were B III speakers who had CvCCaC/CaCaCaC variation.

Interestingly, there were:

(e) No Baḥārna who had even a single instance of CCvCaC in a past verb form.

(f) No 'Arab who had even a single instance of a CaCaCaC past verb form.

It would appear at first sight from this that there is a considerable degree of convergence towards a shared CvCCaC variant in all verb categories in which it is not already a 'dialectal' variant of one Baḥraini community or another: Tables 20 and 21 illustrate this. Table 20 shows the categorical syllable structure/verb stem systems used by some speakers, while Table 21 summarises in a general, unquantified form the points in these systems at which, the data revealed, variation occurs. The symbol "$\sim$" signifies "may vary with".

Following the marking procedures used in Table 5 for phonological variables, and on the basis of the dialectal systems illustrated in Table 20, we could mark the three possible syllabic variants in the following way:

	B	A	MSA
CvCvCaC	+	–	+
CvCCaC	+	–	–
CCvCaC	–	+	–

By bringing in the stem category dimension, we could further refine this marking system to distinguish the B sub-dialects (CvCvCaC variant).

	B I	II	III
MV1.1	+	+	–
MV1.2	+	–	–
MV1.3	–	–	–
MV1.4	+	+	–

(CvCCaC would, of course, be oppositely marked)

These arrays of pluses and minuses represent part of native Baḥrainis' knowledge of the sociolinguistic structure of their society: CaCaCaC, which is the dialectal syllabic variant for the vast majority of Baḥārna in categories MV1.1 and 1.4 (which two verb categories together accounted for 72% of all Theme 1 past verb tokens in the B data) is the characteristically "Baḥārna" suffixed past form, just as /j/ < OA /j/ is also, in the Baḥraini context a "B" form; CCvCaC, like /y/ < OA /j/, is equally clearly its "A" analogue. Partly because of the numbers of people who speak dialects where these equivalents are dialectal norms, and partly because of the frequency with which the verb categories in which they are the norm occur in normal speech, these two syllabic variants, CaCaCaC and CCvCaC, have come to be regarded in Baḥrain as clear linguistic markers of socio-religious allegiance.

The status of the third variant, CvCCaC is particularly interesting. Although it is the dialectal variant of the majority B groups in the less frequently occurring categories MV1.2 and 1.3, it appears from Table 21 that it has been/is being introduced by Baḥrainis of both sects as an alternative to the socially marked CaCaCaC/CCvCaC variants in all categories where it was not already the established dialectal norm. In some sense, it seems to offer the literate speaker a 'neutral' alternative to CaCaCaC and CCvCaC; we shall be exploring this possibility more fully when we come to consider quantified levels of variation and the influence of MSA. Suffice it to say at this point that synchronic dialectal variability in all groups can be plausibly explained only if the MSA system of past-verb categories is conceived of as a "re-structuring" force on the speech of literate speakers: that is, the MSA system of stem categorisation according to stem-vowel height (basically a phonological one, /a/ versus /i/, /u/), may be mirrored in a different sub-system of linguistic structure - in this case one type of dialectal syllable structure versus another - in the speech of those who are familiar with MSA.

'-m-r	'to order'	ḍ-r-b	'to hit'
ṭ-b-r	'to recede (tide)'	ṭ-r-d	'to expel, discuss'
j-l-s	'to sit'	ḏ̣-9-n	'to emigrate, move house'
ḥ-b-s	'To imprison'	ḏ̣-h-r	'to go out; appear'
ḥ-d-ṯ	'to happen'	9-j-z	'to be unable, impotent'
ḥ-ḍ-r	'to be present, attend'	9-d-l	'to be just, act justly'
ḥ-ḏ̣-f	'to throw'	9-r-f	'to know'
ḥ-f-r	'to dig, plough'	9-z-m	'to invite'
ḥ-k-m	'to control, rule'	9-m-l	'to make'
ḥ-l-f	'to take an oath'	9-g-d	'to make a (marriage) contract'
ḥ-m-l*	'to carry'		
x-t-m	'to finish, conclude'	gh-s-l	'to wash'
x-r-j	'to go out'	gh-ṣ-b	'to coerce, compel'
x-ṭ-b	'to bethrothe'	gh-l-ṭ	'to do wrong'
x-ṭ-f	'to hoist (a sail)'	f-r-š	'to furnish'
x-l-g	'to create'	f-š-l	'to fail'
x-m-d	'to die-down (fire)'	f-h-m	'to understand'
d-x-l	'to enter'	g-b-ḍ	'to grasp, get'
d-r-s	'to study'	g-t-l	'to kill'
d-f-n	'to bury'	g-9-d	'to sit, stay; get up (in the morning)'
d-h-n	'to oil'		
r-s-b	'to fail'	k-t-b	'to write'
r-f-ḍ	'to refuse'	k-s-r	'to break'
r-g-d	'to sleep'	k-š-f	'to investigate'
s-'-l	'to ask'	l-ḥ-g	'to catch up with; afford'
s-j-d	'to prostrate oneself'	m-r-s	'to knead'
s-j-n	'to imprison'	m-l-č	'to betrothe'
s-k-t	'to be quiet'	n-b-r	'to make a movement'
s-l-b	'to rob'	n-č-b	'to ladle out; tip over'
s-m-t	'to tighten'	n-č-ṯ	'to break a promise'
š-t-m	'to insult'	n-ḏ-r	'to make a vow'
š-x-l	'to sieve'	n-z-l	'to go down, step over'
š-r-d	'to flee'	n-f-ḍ	'to shake'
š-r-t	'to stipulate'	n-h-m	'to sing sea songs'
š-gh-l	'to work (s'thing)'	h-j-m	'to attack'
š-n-g	'to hang (s'one)'	w-r-ṯ	'to inherit'
ṣ-d-g	'to tell the truth'	w-ṣ-l	'to arrive'
ṣ-g-b	'to raise (a mast)'	w-g-f	'to stop, stand'

List MV1.1

*Baḥārna use different vowels in ḥ-m-l, depending on what it means: /ḥamalat/ 'she carried' /ḥimlat/ 'she conceived (a child)'. It is accordingly listed both here and in List MV1.2.

b-r-z	'to be ready'	š-r-b	'to drink'
ṭ-9-b	'to be tired'	ḍ-ḥ-k	'to laugh'
j-h-z	'to be ready'	9-d-m	'to be destroyed, non-existent'
ḥ-r-d	'to be angry'		
ḥ-z-n	'to be sad'	9-m-y	'to be blind'
ḥ-f-ḍ	'to preserve, learn by heart'	f-r-ḥ	'to be happy'
		g-b-l	'to accept'
ḥ-m-l	'to conceive (a child)'	g-d-r	'to be able'
x-s-r	'to lose'	l-b-s	'to wear'
r-k-b	'to ride, mount'	m-r-ḍ	'to be ill'
z-9-l	'to be angry, upset'	n-s-y	'to forget'
s-l-m	'to be safe; to set (sun)'		

List MV1.2

ṯ-g-l	'to become heavy'	k-ṯ-r	'to multiply, become many'
ṣ-gh-r	'to become small'	k-m-l	'to be complete'
ṭ-r-b	'to be joyful'	g-r-b	'to be near'
k-b-r	'to grow big, old'		

List MV1.3

b-r-x	'to set sail (ship)'	ṣ-n-9	'to make, create'
b-z-gh	'to sprout (hair)'	ṭ-b-x	'to cook'
b-ṭ-ḥ	'to knock down'	ṭ-b-9	'to capsize, sink (boat)'
j-r-ḥ	'to wound'	ṭ-l-9	'to go out, up'
d-f-9	'to push, pay'	f-t-ḥ	'to open'
ḏ-b-ḥ	'to kill'	g-ṭ-9	'to cut'
r-j-9	'to return'	m-r-x	'to massage, annoint'
r-f-9	'to raise'	m-n-9	'to prevent'
z-r-9	'to sow (seed)'	n-j-ḥ	'to succeed'
s-m-9	'to hear'	h-d-'	'to be quiescent, (tranquil)'
š-r-ḥ	'to explain'		

List MV1.4

7.2.2 Morpho-phonemic variable 2 (MV2): the non-past verb

The second morpho-phonemic variable is the syllabic structure of certain Theme I strong non-past suffixed verb forms. There are two variant types:

1. $\begin{Bmatrix} y \\ t \end{Bmatrix}$ vCCvC $\begin{Bmatrix} v \\ \bar{v} \end{Bmatrix}$ C "non resyllabicated" variant

2. $\begin{Bmatrix} y \\ t \end{Bmatrix}$ (v)CvCC $\begin{Bmatrix} v \\ \bar{v} \end{Bmatrix}$ C "resyllabicated" variant

In the dialects of unsophisticated speakers, the occurrence of one or other of these variant types is predictable on the basis of the height of the stem vowel in unsuffixed forms, and the community to which the speaker belongs (6.4.2, Table 18). Literate behaviour is more complex, and a survey of the data indicated that the following verb-stem categories needed to be distinguished in an account of variation.

Verbs with high-vowelled stems in BA

All BA dialects, except that of Rās-Rummān, have the resyllabicated variant in suffixed verb forms where the stem-vowel of the corresponding unsuffixed form is /i/ or /u/. But the vowelling of the resyllabicated variant is different in verbs whose C_1 is a "guttural": the 'Arab dialect has /a/ (6.4.2.1) and the Baḥārṇa have /i/ or /u/ (6.4.2.2) e.g. A /y9arfu:n/, BI and II /y9irfu:n/ 'they know'. This gives the possibility of three-way variation in G-C-C roots between, for example:

(i)	/y9arfu:n/	"resyllabicated"
(ii)	/y9irfu:n/	
(iii)	/ya9rifu:n/ or /yi9rufu:n/	"non-resyllabicated"

(The quality of the unstressed pre-formative vowel in (iii) is irrelevant to the distinction being made.)

In non-guttural, high-vowelled verb stems, there exists an equivalent choice only between (ii)- and (iii)-type forms e.g.:

(i)	/ykitbu:n/	"resyllabicated"
(ii)	/yaktibu:n/ or /yiktibu:n/	"non-resyllabicated"

Two separate categories of high-vowel stems are therefore built into the framework of analysis to handle this two-way, as opposed to three-way opposition:

MV2.2	G-C-C stems	(List MV2.2)
MV2.3	C-C-C stems	(List MV2.3)

Verbs with low-vowelled stems in BA

Low-vowelled stems are not resyllabicated, when suffixed, in basilectal B speech, whereas they are in A (6.4.2). The literate data, however, indicated that a more delicate division of stems than this simple dichotomy is needed in order to highlight patterns of variation. This more delicate division relates again to variability in the syllable structure of forms containing a 'guttural':

MV2.4	C-C-C stems	(List MV2.4)
MV2.5	C-C-G stems	(List MV2.5)
MV2.6	C-G-C stems	(List MV2.6)

The high-vowel/low-vowel categorisation of verbs reflects distinctions in the vowelling of non-past stems in OA/MSA: MV2.2 and MV2.3 are high vowelled, MV2.4-6 mainly low-vowelled in OA/MSA. Just as in the past verb, we wish to see whether the MSA system is reflected in the speech of literates who are familiar with it, and who might be expected to be aware of differences between it and their own dialectal system: does literate, as opposed to illiterate, speech show evidence of a new system of syllable structure distinctions being adopted to reflect the vowel height distinctions of MSA? The justification for the further sub-categorisation into guttural and non-guttural stems arose internally from the patterns of variation observed in the data. Some explanation of why variation in the non-past verb should be structured in the way it is, is given in 7.3.2 below.

Unsuffixed G-C-C forms

One further pattern of syllabic variation in the non-past stem is analysed below, which, although it does not involve suffixed forms, nevertheless involves resyllabication. This is the form of unsuffixed non-past MV2.2 verbs - that is, those verbs which have a G-C-C consonantal skeleton. These verb forms can have either a yaGCiC shape, similar to the yvCCvC of other verb categories, or a resyllabicated yvCaCvC/yiGaCC shape, depending on the consonantal skeleton (6.4.2.1).

As we saw in Chapter 6, the yvGCvC shape is the B form, and the resyllabicated yvGaCCvC/yiGaCC shapes are the A equivalents. Variation in this type of form is considered separately as MV2.1, though the category of verb stems is the same as MV2.2. One of the chief reasons for analysing variation between these variants is to afford a comparison with variation in the noun of the /maghrib/~/mgharb/ type. Diachronically, both the resyllabicated verb and noun forms can be explained by the same phonological processes (see 6.2. rule (iii)); synchronically, they show different probabilities of being replaced by non-resyllabicated forms.

Tables 22 and 23 summarize respectively the categorical systems of syllabicated/non-resyllabicated forms exemplified in the speech of basilect speakers, and an overview of major trends in variation between these forms in literate speech. Once again the symbol "~" indicates "may vary with".

Stem-cat	B I	II	III	'Arab
MV2.1	yi9ruf	yi9ruf	yi9ruf	y9arf
MV2.2	y9irfu:n	y9irfu:n	y9irfu:n	y9arfu:n
MV2.3	ykitbu:n	ykitbu:n	yiktibu:n	ykitbu:n
MV2.4	yišrabu:n	yišrabu:n	yišrabu:n	yširbu:n
MV2.5	yiṭla9u:n	yiṭla9u:n	yiṭla9u:n	yṭil9u:n
MV2.6	yil9abu:n	yil9abu:n	yil9abu:n	yla9bu:n

Table 22: Syllabic structure/stem-category combinations in the non-past verb: non-variable grammars

<table>
<tr><th></th><th>B I</th><th>II</th><th>III</th><th>'Arab</th></tr>
<tr><td>MV2.1</td><td colspan="3">← yi9ruf~y9arf →</td><td>y9arf</td></tr>
<tr><td>MV2.2</td><td colspan="2">y9irfu:n~y9arfu:n~yi9rufu:n →</td><td>y9irfu:n~y9arfu:n</td><td>y9arfu:n</td></tr>
<tr><td>MV2.3</td><td colspan="2">← ykitbu:n~yiktibu:n →</td><td>yiktibu:n</td><td>ykitbu:n~yaktibu:n</td></tr>
<tr><td>MV2.4</td><td colspan="3">← yišrabu:n →</td><td>yširbu:n~yišrabu:n</td></tr>
<tr><td>MV2.5</td><td colspan="3">← yiṭla9u:n →</td><td>yṭil9u:n~yiṭla9u:n</td></tr>
<tr><td>MV2.6</td><td colspan="2">← yil9abu:n~yli9bu:n →</td><td>yil9abu:n</td><td>yla9bu:n~yil9abu:n</td></tr>
</table>

Table 23: Syllabic structure/stem-category combinations in the non-past verb: variable grammars

It can be seen from Table 22 that, according to our marking conventions, the resyllabicated variant-type has the following array of communal markings in the stereotype dialects spoken by those who show no variation in their speech on three variables

	MV2.1	2.2	2.3	2.4	2.5	2.6
B I&II	-	+	+	-	-	-
B III	-	+	-	-	-	-
A	+	+	+	+	+	+
(MSA)	-	-	-	-	-	-

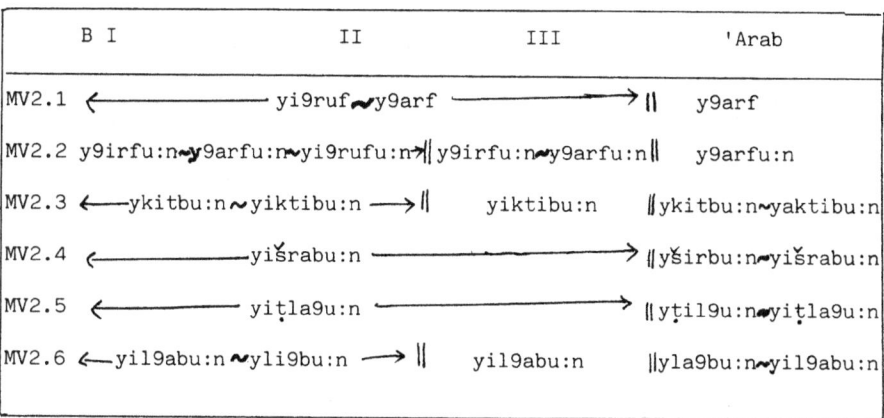

In comparison, the general patterns of variation in Table 23

suggest that:

(a) B speakers appear to have been clearly influenced by the the A dialect on MV2.1, 2.2 and 2.6 (adoption of non-MSA A forms).

(b) A speakers have introduced non-resyllabicated variants on MV2.3, 2.4, 2.5, 2.6 - though whether this is due to B or MSA influence is at first sight unclear, since non-resyllabicated variants are marked "+B + MSA".

(c) B speakers from the major groups also appear to have been influenced by MSA on MV2.2 and 2.3, where non-resyllabicated variants, which are not typical of the A dialect, have also been introduced.

There appears then, to be some degree of convergence between the dialects in the syllabication of the non-past verb forms under study: B speakers on the whole tend to preserve dialectal forms whose syllable structure 'agrees' with that of MSA (e.g. no variation at all in MV2.4 and 2.5), and to introduce other forms (from the A dialect and/or MSA) where their dialectal form is non-standard. Without quantification, it is difficult to see trends in the A data - but it will become clear (7.3 ff) that these are complementary to the B trends: a relatively strong move to "MSA-like" non-resyllabicated forms where the A dialectal stereotype is communally "isolated" (MV2.4-6) and a relatively weak tendency where it shares resyllabicated forms with the main Baḥārna dialectal stereotype (MV2.2-3).

The cross-cutting influences of MSA and the A dialect on the syllabic structure of the non-past verb form used by Baḥraini literates operate in fact in a rather similar way to the way they operate to produce the variable realisations of the sets of lexical items discussed in Chapter 5: where "non-prestige" forms are "non-standard", they tend to be replaced by literates more than is the case with "prestige" forms which are "non-standard"; and there is a clear trend on the part of speakers of the "non-prestige" dialect to borrow "non-standard", but "prestige" forms also (cf Baḥārna adoption of 'Arab /y/ < OA /j/).

Notes on List MV2.1 and 2.2 (below):

1. ḥ-f-d has a guttural in C_1 position and is therefore treated like an MV2.1/2.2 verb root in the A dialect: singular /yḥafiḏ̣/ plural /yḥafḏ̣u:n/. Compare the OA/MSA forms, which group ḥ-f-ḏ̣, š-r-b, l-b-s (and other MV2.4 verbs) in one morphophonemic category.

2. See note to List MV1.1: ḥ-m-l in the meaning 'to carry' has the non-past form /yḥim lu:n/'they carry' in all B dialects (past /ḥamalaw/). But in the meaning 'they conceive' the B forms are /yiḥma lu:n/ (past /ḥimlaw/) i.e. the morphophonemic variant used is, in the B dialect, related to the meaning. Both meanings

are covered in the A dialect by /yḥam lu:n/, /ḥmilaw/.

9-m-r	'to order'	9-r-f	'to know'
ḥ-d-g	'to fish'	9-z-m	'to invite'
ḥ-s-b	'to think'	9-g-d	'to make a (marriage) contract'
ḥ-f-r	'to dig, plough'		
ḥ-f-ḏ[1]	'to preserve, learn by heart'	9-m-r	'to cultivate (land)'
		9-m-l	'to make'
ḥ-k-m	'to control, rule'	gh-r-s	'to plant (seed)'
ḥ-l-b	'to give milk (cow)'	gh-r-f	'to ladle (water)'
ḥ-m-l[2]	'to carry'	gh-r-g	'to drown'
x-b-z	'to bake bread'	gh-s-l	'to wash'
x-t-m	'to conclude, terminate'	gh-ṣ-b	'to coerce, compel'
		gh-l-ṭ	'to do wrong, sin'
x-r-f	'to pluck (dates)'	gh-m-s	'to dip, dunk'
x-s-r	'to lose'	h-j-m	'to attack'
x-ṭ-b	'to betrothe'	h-r-b	'to run away'
x-ṭ-f	'to hoist (a sail)'	h-l-k	'to perish, die'
x-l-ṭ	'to mix'		
9-d-l	'to act justly'		
9-d-m	'to destroy'		

List MV2.1 and 2.2

t-r-s	'to fill'	ḍ-r-b	'to hit'
j-ḏ-b	'to pull, attract'	ṭ-r-d	'to expel, dismiss'
d-b-č	'to run'	ṭ-l-b	'to demand'
d-r-s	'to study'	f-š-g	'to smash'
d-f-n	'to bury'	f-š-l	'to split'
ḏ-k-r	'to mention, remember'	f-l-t	'to throw'
r-b-ṭ	'to tie, attach'	f-l-g/j	'to split open (clam)'
r-s-l	'to send'	g-t-l	'to kill'
r-s-m	'to draw, design'	g-ṣ-b	'to butcher'
r-f-ḍ	'to refuse'	g-ṣ-d	'to intend'
r-g-d	'to sleep	g-l-b	'to overturn'
r-g-ṣ	'to dance'	k-b-r	'to grow old, big'
r-k-ḍ	'to run'	k-t-b	'to write'
s-q-ṭ	'to fail'	k-š-f	'to investigate, discover'
s-k-t	'to keep quiet'	m-r-s	'to knead'
s-k-n	'to inhabit	m-l-č	'to betrothe'
š-r-d	'to flee'	n-č-b	'to ladle'
š-r-ṭ	'to stipulate'	n-č-l	'to overturn'
š-k-r	'to thank'	n-z-f	'to bale out'
ṣ-b-r	'to be patient'	n-s-l	'to coiffe'
ṣ-r-f	'to spend (money)'	n-š-d	'to recite poetry'
ṣ-g-b	'to raise (a mast)'	n-š-r	'to spread, publish'

List MV2.3

b-r-z	'to be ready	š-r-b	'to drink'
ḥ-b-l } ḥ-m-l }	'to conceive (a child)'	g-b-l	'to accept'
		g-d-r	'to be able'
r-k-b	'to ride, mount'	l-b-s	'to wear'
s-l-m	'to be safe'	m-r-ḍ	'to be ill'

List MV2.4

b-r-x	'to lift anchor, set sail'	ṭ-l-9	'to go out, up'
		f-t-ḥ	'to open'
x-ḍ-9	'to be humble'	f-r-ḥ	'to be happy, content'
d-f-9	'to push, pay'	f-ṣ-x	'to take off (clothes)'
ḏ-b-ḥ	'to kill'		
r-b-ḥ	'to profit'	g-d-9	'to have a snack'
r-j-9	'to return'	g-ṭ-9	'to cut'
r-f-9	'to raise'	g-l-9	'to pull up, out (teeth, weeds)'
z-r-9	'to plant, sow'		
s-f-ḥ	'to pour'	k-r-h	'to hate, abominate'
s-m-ḥ	'to allow'	m-n-9	'to prevent'
s-m-9	'to hear'	n-ṣ-ḥ	'to advise'
ṣ-b-gh	'to paint, dye'	n-f-9	'to be useful'
ṣ-n-9	'to manufacture'		
ṭ-b-x	'to cook'		

List MV2.5

t-9-b	'to tire'	ḍ-ḥ-k	'to laugh'
j-9-l	'to put'	ḍ-gh-ṭ	'to apply pressure'
d-x-l[1]	'to enter'	ṭ-ḥ-n	'to grind'
d-h-n[1]	'to oil'	ḍ-9-n	'to move house, emigrate'
r-ḥ-m	'to have mercy'	f-ḥ-ṣ	'to test'
z-9-l	'to be angry, upset'	f-h-m	'to understand'
s-'-l	'to ask'	g-ḥ-b	'to be of loose morals'
s-ḥ-b	'to pull'	g-9-d[1]	'to sit; get up in the morning'
s-ḥ-g	'to crush'		
s-h-r	'to pass the evening'	l-ḥ-g	'to catch up; afford'
š-x-l	'to sieve'	l-9-b	to play'
š-9-r	'to feel'	n-x-l[1]	'to sieve'

List MV2.6

Notes:

1. In the B village dialects these verbs have high vowels (as do their analogues in OA/MSA) in the non-past singular: /yidxil/, /yidhin/ etc. and are treated in these dialects like MV2.1/2.2. verb

roots, i.e. they have the suffixed forms /yidixlu:n/, /yidihnu:n/, etc. (see Tables 17, 18).

7.2.3 Morphophonemic variable 3 (MV3): certain nominal forms

The third set of variables concerns the syllable structure of nominal forms, which, in MSA, have a CaGCv(C) and a CvCvCv(C) form. The categories established were:

MV3.1: CaGCa(C): /maghrib/ versus /mgharb/, /ghawa/ versus /gahwa/-type forms (List MV3.1)

MV3.2: CvCvCv(C): /baraka/ versus /brika/-type forms(list MV3.2)

MV3.3: CvCvCv(C): /samača/ versus /smiča/-type forms(List MV3.3)

The justification for distinguishing MV3.2 and MV3.3 was (as stated in 6.4.3.2) that the Baḥārna dialect distinguishes between the syllable structure of forms which

(a) have a post-palatal consonant in C_1 or C_2 position = CaCaCa(C) structure

(b) do not have a post-palatal in C_1 or C_2 position = CCvCa(C)

The 'Arab dialect has CCvCa(C) for both types of form; MSA has, of course CvCvCv(C) for both types of form. This gives us the following set of forms and communal markings for the basilects:

	Baḥārna	'Arab
MV 3.1	maghrib	mgharb
3.2	baraka	brika
3.3	smiča	smiča

Table 24: Syllabic structure/noun category combinations in certain nominal forms: non-variable grammars

	Baḥārna	'Arab	MSA
CaGCa(C)	+	–	+
$C_1vc_2aCa(C)$ (C_1 or C_2 = post-palatal)	+	–	+
$C_1vC_2aCa(C)$ (C_1 and C_2 = (pre-)palatal)	–	–	+

Analysis showed the following general patterns of variation where variability occurred:

	Baḥārna	'Arab
MV 3.1	maghrib ≈ mgharb	mgharb ≈ maghrib
3.2	baraka	brika ≈ baraka
3.3	s$\begin{Bmatrix}i\\a\end{Bmatrix}ma\begin{Bmatrix}č\\k\end{Bmatrix}$a	smiča ≈ sama$\begin{Bmatrix}č\\k\end{Bmatrix}$a

Table 25: Syllabic structure/noun category combinations in certain nominal forms: variable grammars

In the Baḥārna case, in noun categories where the dialectal variant "agrees" with MSA, there is again (as in MV2) a strong tendency to preserve it, though again we note a marginal degree of borrowing non-standard, but locally prestigious A forms of the re-syllabicated type; but where the B dialect "agrees" with the A dialect in having non-standard forms as the dialectal norm, the switch away from these forms towards the standard equivalents is so strong as to be categorical.

In the 'Arab case, where all the equivalent dialect forms are non-standard, variability occurs in all the noun categories under consideration, though to a lesser degree than in the Baḥārna case.

There is, then, again, some evidence here of linguistic convergence between 'Arab and Baḥārna speakers, towards a form of BA in which the old sect-dialect correspondences are becoming blurred. The extent of the 'move' by 'Arab and Baḥārna is however different, as we shall see in 7.3 below when we consider the degree to which literates/illiterates as groups maintained dialectal forms on each group of variables.

/'aḥsa/	'the Hasa'	/ṭa9ma/	'fertiliser'
/'aḥmar/	'red'	/gaḥba/	'prostitute'
/'axḍar/	'green'	/gaḥma/	'shift (on a pearling dhow)'
/'a9ma/	'blind'	/laḥma/	'blockage, growth (medical)'
/'a9waj/	'crooked'	/ma9ru:f/	'known; good deed'
/'a9war/	'one-eyed'	/maghrib/	'sun-set'
/baghda:d/	'Baghdad'	/naxla/	'female palm tree'
/baghla/	'water-pot'	/na9ja/	'ewe'
/raḥma/	'mercy'	/jaḥla/	'large water vessel'
/šaḥna/	'load'		

List MV3.1 Nouns

/barada/	'hail, sleet'	/maraga/	'soup, stew'
/baraka/	'blessing'	/na9ala/	'sandal'
/ḥaraga/	'eye inflammation'	/waraga/	'paper, leaf'
/ḥaṭaba/	'piece of wood'	/bagara/	'cow'
/xašaba/	'piece of wood'	/ragaba/	'neck'
/xalaga/	'rag, cloth'		

List MV3.2 Nouns

/samača/	'fish'	/nasama/	'breath'
/šajara/	'tree'	/ruṭaba/	'date'

List MV3.3 Nouns

A particularly interesting fact about variation in the form of the word for 'a fish' may be mentioned here, since it gives some insight into the interlinking of variation at different linguistic levels. The occurring variants for this lexical item were /samača/, /simiča/, /simača/, /samaka/ and /smiča/. On the basis of the syllabic pattern and consonantal skeleton combinations occurring in the data, a three way division can be drawn:

	syllable pattern	consonant skeleton
1. /smiča/	CCvCa	s-m-č
2. /simiča/~/simača/~/samača/	CvCvCa	s-m-č
3. /samaka/	CvCvCa	s-m-k

If the relationship between syllable structure variation, and /k/~/č/ variation were purely random, other possible combinations might be expected to occur, e.g. */simika/ */simaka/ */smika/. In fact they did not occur in any community. For all speakers the occurrence of /k/ in this lexeme seems to require that its syllable structure be CvCvCa; the occurrence of /č/ on the other hand implies nothing about syllable structure. Our data also suggest that the possible combinations of syllabic pattern and consonant skeleton for this lexeme are associated broadly with speech styles: /smiča/ is the non-sect-specific 'unmarked' dialectal form, /simača/, /simiča/, /samača/ are found freely varying with each other in somewhat more formal circumstances (e.g. the circumstances in which most of the data for this study were collected), while /samaka/ in extempore speech is highly-marked and seems to betoken a conscious effort to speak in a more 'literary' style.

7.3 Analysis of quantified data

The breakdown of the 87 speakers who produced the data discussed in this Chapter was as follows (cf 3.5, 4.3.1):

Group		Location	Literacy			
			literate	non-literate		
'Arab			17	17	=	34
Baḥārna	I	(town)	7	7	=	14
	II	(all villages)	16	18	=	34
	III	(Rās-Rummān)	2	3	=	5
			42	45	=	87

Table 26: Breakdown of speakers: morphophonemic variables

The "dialectalness scores" of each of these groups on each variable are displayed in rank-order in Tables 27-30. "Dialectalness" is a measure of the extent to which the particular dialectal variant of any group on any variable actually occurred as a proportion, varying between 0 and 1, of the total number of times it could have occurred.

Variable	Illiterates (N= 17)		Literates (N= 17)		Difference	Example		
	Tokens	Score	Tokens	Score	Illiterate-Literate Score	dialectal variant		non-dialectal variant(s)
MV2.2	64	.98	63	.98	0	/yghaslə/	~	/yaghsilə/
MV1.1	85	.98	62	.95	+.03	/drisat/	~	/dirsat/
MV2.1	58	1.00	69	.85	+.15	/y9arf/	~	/ya9rif/
MV2.3	55	.92	47	.83	+.09	/ykitbə/	~	/yaktibə/
MV2.4	12	1.00	6	.75	+.25	/ylibsə/	~	/yalbisə/
MV2.5	29	1.00	23	.65	+.35	/ysim9ə/	~	/yisma9ə/
MV1.3	10	.80	10	.60	+.20	/kbarat/	~	/kubrat/
MV1.2	26	.69	16	.59	+.10	/lbisat/	~	/libsat/
MV3.1	56	.91	21	.50	+.41	/xaḍar/	~	/axḍar/
MV2.6	38	.65	38	.47	+.18	/yila9bu:n/	~	/yil9abu:n/
MV1.4	33	.59	31	.45	+.14	/ṭla9at/	~	/ṭil9at/
MV3.2	18	.77	9	.33	+.44	/brika/	~	/baraka/
MV3.3	10	.80	14	.20	+.60	/smiča/	~	/samača/, /simača/ /simača or/samaka/

Table 27: 'Arab: measures of "dialectalness" on 13 morphophonemic variables

Variable	Illiterates (N=7)		Literates (N=7)		Difference	Example	
	Tokens	Score	Tokens	Score	Illiterate-Literate Score	dialectal variant	non-dialectal variant(s)
MV1.3	6	1.00	5	1.00	0	/kubrat/ ~	non-occurring
MV2.4	6	1.00	7	1.00	0	/yilbasə/ ~	non-occurring
MV2.5	13	1.00	6	1.00	0	/yisma9ə/	non-occurring
MV3.2	7	1.00	5	1.00	0	/baraka/	non-occurring
MV1.2	8	1.00	7	.90	+.10	/labasat/ ~	/libsat/
MV2.6	9	1.00	12	.84	+.16	/yil9abu:n/ ~	/yla9bu:n/
MV3.1	20	.75	10	.80	-.05	/axḍar/ ~	/xaḍar/
MV2.1	26	.88	24	.70	+.18	/yi9ruf/ ~	/y9arf/
MV1.1	16	1.00	15	.60	+.40	/darasat/ ~	/dirsat/
MV2.2	11	.36	20	.30	+.06	/yghislə/ ~	/yghaslə/or/yighsilə/
MV1.4	16	.87	12	.25	+.62	/ṭala9at/ ~	/ṭil9at/
MV2.3	11	.72	18	.16	+.56	/ykitbə/ ~	/yiktibə/
MV3.3	4	1.00	5	00	+1.00	/smiča/ versus	/saṃača/ or /simiča/or /simača/ or /samaka/

Table 28: Baḥārna I: measures of "dialectalness" in 13 morphophonemic variables

Variable	Illiterates (N=18)		Literates (N=16)		Difference	Example		
	Tokens	Score	Tokens	Score	Illiterate-Literate score	dialectal variant		non-dialectal variant(s)
MV1.1	39	1.00	33	1.00	0	/darasat/		non-occurring
MV1.3	9	1.00	6	1.00	0	/kubrat/		non-occurring
MV1.2	5	1.00	8	1.00	0	/libsat/		non-occurring
MV3.2	21	1.00	10	1.00	0	/baraka/		non-occurring
MV2.4	18	.94	12	.91	+.03	/yilbasə/	~	/ylibsə/
MV3.1	28	1.00	14	.85	+.15	/axḍar/	~	/xaḍar/
MV2.5	21	.85	31	.83	+.02	/yisma9ə/	~	/ysim9ə/
MV2.6	26	1.00	16	.81	+.19	/yil9abu:n/	~	/yla9bu:n/
MV2.1	90	.84	54	.74	+.10	/yi9ruf/	~	/y9arf/
MV1.4	12	.83	7	.57	+.26	/ṭala9at/	~	/ṭil9at/
MV2.2	29	.58	40	.42	+.16	/yghislə/	~	/yghaslə/ or /yighsilə/
MV2.3	46	.89	36	.41	+.48	/ykitbə/	~	/yiktibə/
MV3.3	7	.71	5	0	+.71	/smiča/	~	/samača/ or /simiča/or /simača/ or /samaka/

Table 29: Baḥārna II: measures of "dialectalness" on 13 morphophonemic variables

Variable	Illiterates (N=3)		Literates (N=2)		Difference	Example	
	Tokens	Score	Tokens	Score	Illiterate-Literate Score	dialectal variant	non-dialectal variant(s)
MV1.3	3	1.00	2	1.00	0	/kubrat/	non-occurring
MV1.2	3	1.00	3	1.00	0	/libsat/	non-occurring
MV2.6	11	1.00	6	1.00	0	/yil9abu:n/	non-occurring
MV2.4	3	1.00	5	1.00	0	/yilbasu:n/	non-occurring
MV2.5	5	1.00	3	1.00	0	/yisma9ə/	non-occurring
MV2.3	8	.88	11	1.00	-.12	/yiktibə/ ~	/ykitbə/
MV1.4	4	1.00	5	.80	+.20	/ṭil9at/ ~	/ṭala9at/
MV2.1	5	.40	18	.50	-.10	/yi9ruf/ ~	/y9arf/
MV1.1	5	.80	6	.33	+.47	/dirsat/ ~	/darasat/
MV2.2	8	.75	8	0	+.75	/yghislə/ ~	/yghaslə/ or /yighsilə/

Too little data on MV3.1-.3 to be realistically quantifiable

Table 30: Baḥārna III: measures of "dialectalness" on 13 morphophonemic variables

7.3.1 The past verb

Extracting the relevant data from Tables 27-30, we note that the dialectalness scores on MV1.1-4 are as follows for each of our communities.

		MV1.1	1.2	1.3	1.4	Examples of basilectal variants
A	literate	.95	.59	.60	.45	/drisat/ lbisat/ /kbarat/
	illiterate	.98	.69	.80	.59	/ṭla9at/
B I	literate	.60	.90	1.0	.25	/darasat//labasat/
	illiterate	1.0	1.0	1.0	.87	/kubrat/ /ṭala9ạt/
B II	literate	1.0	1.0	1.0	.57	/darasat/ /libsat/
	illiterate	1.0	1.0	1.0	.83	/kubrat/ /ṭala9at/
BIII	literate	.33	1.0	1.0	.80	/dirsat/ /libsat/
	illiterate	.80	1.0	1.0	1.0	/kubrat/ /ṭala9at/

Table 31: Measures of "dialectalness" in four communities in four stem categories of the past verb

For 'Arab and Baḥārna I and II, where the dialectal variant is non-categorical, the replacing variant was always of the type CiCCaC. For B III, the dialectal variant itself is always of the type CiCCaC, and the replacing form was always CaCaCaC - i.e. the same as the B I dialectal variant for MV1.1, 1.2 and 1.4.

What hypotheses could be offered to account for these patterns of variation? Let us look first at the data for the 'Arab group.

7.3.1.1 'Arab variation

The behaviour of the literate and the illiterate 'Arab is strikingly similar from MV1.1 through MV1.4, despite differences in the actual frequencies of occurrence of the dialectal syllabic variant. Both literates and illiterates exhibit the same rank-order of dialectalness:

MV1.4 least dialectal (least CCvCaC)
MV1.2 ↓
MV1.3
MV1.1 most dialectal (most CCvCaC)

In MSA, there is a distinction, as we saw in Chapter 6, between verbs which have a stem vowel /a/ e.g. /darasat/ 'she studied' and those, far fewer in number, which have a high vowel, either /i/ or /u/ e.g. /labisat/ 'she dressed', /kaburat/ 'she grew'. In the 'Arab dialect, there are some illiterate speakers who have CCvCaC forms for *all* these verb categories. A possible explanation for the high degree of difference between the literates' treatment of MV1.1 vis-à-vis MV1.2 or MV1.3 is precisely that literate speakers are aware of the low vowel/high vowel dichotomy of MSA and are 'restructuring' their dialectal system under its influence by taking the 'line of least resistance'. That is, the 'Arab literates make their dialect more isomorphic with the MSA system by changing the syllable structure of the least commonly occurring verb categories. Thus, whereas many illiterate speakers show categorically:

MV1.1 /drisat/
1.2 /lbisat/
1.3 /kbarat/ } CCvCvC (the 'one variant' dialectal system)

Some literates have:

MV1.1 /drisat/ CCvCvC

1.2 /libsat/
1.3 /kubrat/ } CiCCaC } (a new 'two variant' system)

in which a new dialectal *syllable structure* distinction has been created to mirror the MSA *vowel-height* distinction:

MV1.1 /darasat/ low stem vowel

1.2 /labisat/
1.3 /kaburat/ } high stem vowel

The figures in Table 31, which give group average scores, obscure this fact; some 'Arab literates show the 'two-variant' system with virtually categorical CCvCvC-type forms in MV1.1 and CvCCaC in the other verb categories, whereas others are nearer the categorical 'one variant' system, and yet others are between the two.

We are thus conjecturing that purely internal dialectal resources can be utilised to create a new system modelled on that of an external standard without the same elements of linguistic structure being used: MSA vowel-height differences are being expressed in terms of a dialectal syllabic structure distinction. But are we justified in claiming that it is 'internal dialectal resources' - in this case the CiCCaC variant - which are being utilised? Why should the literate 'Arab, if their switch to CiCCaC is motivated by consciousness of verb-category distinctions in MSA, as we claim, not switch rather to CaCaCaC-type forms which, after all, are also an 'internal dialectal resource' (in fact, the commonest form of the B I and II group) and have the added advantage of being formally more similar to MSA forms?

The answer seems to lie in the evaluation of the CaCaCaC and CiCCaC variants in the local sociolinguistic context: specifically, in the feelings that 'Arab apparently have that in normal conversational interaction as opposed to public oration, CaCaCaC forms would be distinctly "Baḥārna", and are hence to be avoided, pace their similarity to MSA forms. But are not CiCCaC forms similarly "tainted"? The answer seems to be no, and we present a tentative answer as to why not. CiCCaC is the normal dialectal form in all verb-categories for only one tiny group of Baḥārna from Rās-Rummān, In the dialects of the two major B groups it is, in absolute terms, a much less commonly heard variant: it figures as normal dialectal variant only in the two least common verb categories: MV1.2 and MV1.3. In Table 32 below, the percentage contribution of each verb category to the total number of past verb tokens in the data illustrates this. The boxed percentages are those in which village and town Baḥārna have CiCCaC as normal dialectal variant. We have no reason to believe either that our sample was wildly unrepresentative of the target populations or that the data collected was unrepresentative of their normal linguistic behaviour.

	MV1.1	1.2	1.3	1.4		
A	50	15	7	28	=	100
B I	38	17	12	33	=	100
B II	63	10	11	16	=	100
B III	35	19	17	29	=	100

Table 32: Percentage of past verb tokens by stem-category

So from the point of view of relative frequency of occurrence, CiCCaC might be felt a "less B" variant than CaCaCaC. But what is perhaps more significant is that CiCCaC is also perhaps the most widely used variant form in the dialects of neighbouring literate urban centres with which literate Baḥrainis are likely to have had contact: in Baghdad, (Erwin 1963: 87) CiCCaC is categorical in all Theme 1 verb categories, and it has been noted by Johnstone (1967: 70) as a commoner form in neighbouring 'Arab-dominated Kuwait than CCvCaC.

So far, we have been considering MV1.1 in relation to the MV1.2 and 1.3. How do we explain the most strongly marked movement of all away from the CCvCaC variant - that of MV1.4? It must be said that the explanation advanced below is tentative, since it turns on fine phonetic differences which are sometimes difficult to distinguish on tape with absolute certainty.

We noted in Chapter 6 that where, in MSA and the Baḥārna dialects, a guttural consonant closes a non-final syllable whose vowel is /a/, e.g. /gahwa/ 'coffee' /maghrib/ 'evening', the 'Arab dialect has forms of the type /ghawa/, /mgharb/. This resyllabication, as we have called it, is normally considered to occur only in non-final closed syllables (Johnstone 1967: 6-7). MV1.4 verbs give rise in the 'Arab dialect to forms such as /ṭla9at/ 'she went out', /rja9at/ 'she returned', /gṭa9aw/ 'they cut' where the nuclear syllable is open, but precedes a guttural consonant. The clearest recorded examples of illiterate 'Arab producing such forms as /ṭla9at/, however, led us to believe that a more accurate narrow transcription would be:

[əṭla9'æt]

That is, there is a marked rise in pitch on the stressed syllable, with the [9] being treated as part of it, followed by a discernible break in voicing and with a glottal onset ['] of the vowel-initial enclitic. These phonetic phenomena were noted only for those verbs in List MV1.4 which had /9/ in C_3 position - that is for some ten of the twenty-one verbs listed. If the description above is correct - and a strictly controlled acoustic experiment would be needed to establish if it were - we might have an explanation of why the switch from CCvCaC forms to CiCCaC forms in MV1.4 verbs is so pronounced:speakers may be interpreting CCaGaC as /CCaGCaC/, and the CaG non-final closed syllable which would result from the insertion of ['] is being avoided by a switch to CiCGaC. This argument, however, does not apply to verbs which have a different guttural consonant in C_3 position. This latter group of verbs do, in fact, show a tendency to have CiCCaC, but it must be said that in MV1.4 groups as a whole, the vast majority of the actual occurrences of CiCCaC are in verbs with /9/ in C_3 position. It might be more accurate, then, to think of just those verbs with/9/ in C_3 position as being treated as a separate group, the other gutturals behaving more like MV1.1 verbs in being only very marginally variable. This is certainly an explanation which the data would bear, but which, considering the relative scarcity in the data of verbs having a guttural in C_3 position, would need to be replicated by a study with a bigger data base.

Let us at this point reiterate the main points of our explanation of 'Arab variation in the syllabic structure of the past verb forms under consideration, before examining the B data:

(a) The motivation for variation and change in the 'one variant' (all verbs CCvCaC) is explicable partly in terms of literates' consciousness of the high vowel/low vowelled verb dichotomy in MSA, and partly as the result of internal dialectal phonological pressure (though we would not over-stress this last point too strongly in the absence of controlled acoustic evidence). 'Restructuring' of the system reflects the MSA high-vowel/low vowel dichotomy, but not through the borrowing or copying of MSA forms. It is the less frequently occurring dialectal verb categories which undergo change, when the 'one-variant' 'Arab system becomes a 'two-variant system'.

(b) The source for the replacing variants is apparently the most socially 'neutral' of those available and is also an areal "dialectal standard". The commonest alternative BA dialectal variant, and the one which is formally closest to the external standards of MSA is also the one most clearly associated with Baḥārna speech, and seems to be avoided for that reason.

(c) Replacement of the CCvCaC variant in different verb categories in non-literate speech shows the same relative strength as in literate speech, though the actual level of replacement in each category is lower.

7.3.1.2 Baḥārna variation

Variation in the B groups can be explained in terms of the twin influence of the MSA supra-dialectal standard and the prestige A dialect. It was noted in 6.4.1.2 that the B village dialectal verb-category system was formally more like the MSA one than the A one: in the village dialects, the categories of verbs which have dialectal CiCCaC are the same as those which in MSA have a high stem vowel. But in the dialect of Manāma, the transitive verbs which have a high stem vowel in MSA appear to have been 're-classified' and treated as CaCaCaC verbs. In Rās-Rummān, by contrast, all Theme 1 verbs have CiCCaC in illiterate speech. The basic systems used by many illiterate urban and village speakers are, as we have seen:

MV1.1	/darasat/	CaCaCaC	the B II (village) system
1.4	/ṭala9at/		
MV1.2	/libsat/	CiCCaC	
1.3	/kubrat/		
MV1.1	/darasat/	CaCaCaC	the B I (town) system
1.2	/labasat/		
1.4	/ṭala9at/		
MV1.3	/kubrat/	CiCCaC	
MV1.1	/dirsat/	CiCCaC	the B III system
1.2	/libsat/		
1.3	/kubrat/		
1.4	/ṭil9at/		

An inspection of Table 31 tells us that variation in the B groups is non-existent in MV1.3 - i.e. in that category in which all groups share dialectal CiCCaC. In MV1.2, variation only occurs in the literate town group, who switch from CaCaCaC to CiCCaC to a small but measurable degree. All other B groups, however defined, stick to CiCCaC for MV1.2 as well as MV1.3. Why should MV1.2 and 1.3 show so little variation? The explanation would seem to be that:

(a) the B village dialectal system coincides with MSA in its classification of verbs: the high-vowel/low-vowel split in MSA is matched by a CaCaCaC/CiCCaC syllable split in this dialect. Literate villagers are conscious of this fact and quite able to articulate it, claiming it as evidence of the "correctness" of their dialect. Given also the fact that the speech of the literate 'Arab is also showing a strong move from CCiCaC to CiCCaC in just these verb categories MV1.2 and 1.3, it is not surprising to find that the literate villagers preserve their dialectal variants in these variables with no evidence of variation. On these variables, the pressure from MSA and the local prestige dialect is in the same direction.

(b) The main urban dialect, which differs from the village one in having dialectal CaCaCaC for MV1.2 verbs, is showing signs of conforming to the trend noted in (a) above: /labasat/-type forms, as far as can be ascertained from the small data base, are starting to be replaced by /libsat/ in literate speech presumably because of literates' consciousness of the MSA system and the concomitant change which seems to be occurring in literate 'Arab speech. Given the relatively prestigious status of the town Baḥārna vis-a-vis the village Baḥārna, and the amused indulgence with which the former regard the peculiarities of the inhabitants of Rās-Rummān, it is unlikely that the reason for the adoption of the /libsat/ forms is B II or B III influence on the B I dialect.

(c) For the same reasons (the MSA system and changes in the A dialect), CiCCaC-type dialectal forms are categorically <u>preserved</u> in the B III literate speech in MV1.2 and MV1.3, where, of course, they are the basic dialectal variants.

We can generalise by saying that in MV1.2 and 1.3 there is in general a strong trend towards the replacement of non-CiCCaC forms (either 'Arab CCiCaC or urban Baḥārna CaCaCaC) by CiCCaC. But what of the B treatment of MV1.1 or 1.4? It is here that A influence is most apparent. The 'Arab treat MV1.4 differently from MV1.1, it has been argued, for phonological reasons: non-final closed CaG syllables are to be avoided. But there is no such constraint on the occurrence of CaG syllables in illiterate B speech which shows CaG syllables occurring frequently, and the resyllabication of CaG is not a feature of any B dialect. But an inspection of the figures in Table 31 suggests strongly that literate Baḥārna (and to a minor extent some illiterates) did indeed treat MV1.4 - or at least verbs with /9/ in C_3 position - as a separate category.

Levels of variation in MV1.1, and MV1.4, across all B groups, including B III, can be explained quite simply as imitatory of prestige group behaviour:

(a) CiCCaC is <u>much more likely</u> to occur as a replacement of B dialectal CaCaCaC in MV1.4 than in MV1.1 (B I and II).

(b) CiCCaC is much less likely to be replaced in MV1.4 than in MV1.1 where it is a B dialectal variant (B III).

We can thus generalise that all literate groups, 'Arab and Baḥārna alike, tend to treat MV1.4 verbs in the same way: either by replacement (A, B I and II), or by preservation (B III), CiCCaC is being adopted as a shared, inter-group variant. Since the phonological constraints on the appearance of gutturals in non-final closed syllables do not obtain in the B dialects, we can only assume that literate Baḥārna's adoption or preservation of CiCCaC is motivated by socilinguistic factors: that is, the desire to identify with the prestige-group.

It is highly interesting to note that the variant by which the B III group replaces dialectal CiCCaC in MV1.1 or 1.4 is CaCaCaC, the "B" variant, not CCvCaC the "A" variant. If identifying with prestige group behaviour seems to mean restructuring one's dialectal system according to the ground rules laid down by the dominant group, it does not mean not actually importing wholesale the linguistic forms by which they do it, especially where this would involve adopting forms which do not conform to the general syllable structure rules of the innovating dialect. On this argument, CCvCvC verb forms are not adopted by Baḥārna, and CaCaCaC forms are not adopted by 'Arab (though see 7.3.3), in part because these forms go contrary to mutually exclusive, dialect-specific constraints on syllabic structure. CiCCaC forms, however, are permissible variants in all BA dialects. In this sense, as in the sociolinguistic sense, CiCCaC is a 'neutral' variant.

On MV1.1 - the largest number of verbs fall into this category - literate Baḥārna stuck more strongly to dialectal CaCaCaC, or changed more strongly to it if they had dialectal CiCCaC than was the case with MV1.4: literate villagers showed 100% /darasat/, 0% /dirsat/; Rās-Rummānis 67% /darasat/, 33% /dirsat/ (CiCCaC → CaCaCaC) and the main urban group 60% /darasat/, 40% /dirsat/ (CaCaCaC → CiCCaC). Literate 'Arab, as we have seen, showed a much less marked tendency to switch away from dialectal CCvCaC on MV1.1 than on MV1.4.

Generalising about the behaviour of our speaker sample on this variable is problematic, but the data suggests that it is here, in the most commonly occurring verb category, that dialectal stereotypes show the strongest resistance to replacement. Paradoxically, the explanation seems again to lie in 'Arab behaviour. If our analysis is correct that the literate 'Arab switch from CCvCaC to CiCCaC in MV1.2 and MV1.3 is a way of restructuring the 'Arab dialectal system to make it congruent with the vowel-height distinctions of MSA, then might it not follow that Baḥārna whose variable or non-variable behaviour on MV1.2 and MV1.3 (and, as we have just seen, MV1.4) is determined by 'Arab behaviour, will also follow 'Arab behaviour in making a strong distinction between MV1.1 and other verb categories? The B II and B III evidence suggests that this is what is happening.

Literate villagers clearly oppose MV1.1 (categorical /darasat/-type forms) to /libsat/, /kubrat/ and /ṭil9at/ (categorical CiCCaC in MV1.2 and 1.3, variable CaCaCaC/CiCCaC in 1.4); Rās-Rummānis switch strongly to /darasat/-type forms in MV1.1 but preserve /dirsat/-type form strongly in all other categories. In both these cases, if one compares these 'restructured' systems to the dialectal systems of the illiterates from the same communities, the tendency to convergence among literate speakers is obvious.

In the B I case, the evidence for this is less conclusive: once again speakers are tending to preserve or switch to CiCCaC forms in MV1.2-4; but there is also quite a strong switch to CiCCaC in MV1.1, though CaCaCaC still accounts for 60% of the tokens in the MV1.1 verb category.

7.3.1.3 Conclusion

Despite the uncertainty in the interpretation of the B I data on MV1.1, the framework within which past verb variation (and it is to be assumed, eventual change) is to be explained seems to be 'Arab-determined: several different Baḥārna dialectal systems are tending towards coalescence through the suppression of the use of certain variants in certain verb categories. The new B system is structuring itself in the same way as the new A one, in that in both cases MV1.1 is becoming opposed to MV1.2-4 in syllabic structure. The systems differ in that the syllabic variants which are becoming standard for each sect in this shared system are formally the same in only one half of the dichotomy, viz:

MV1.1 → CaCaCaC (all B)
MV1.1 → CCvCaC (all A)
MV1.2, MV1.3, MV1.4 → CiCCaC (all speakers)
} the new 'literate' BA system

In conclusion, it appears that compared to the illiterate speakers, Baḥraini literates are beginning to show a degree of dialectal convergence on the past tense variables examined. The detailed analysis presented above illustrates the general principles governing this convergence. We will now turn to the non-past and nominal variables, where convergence is also apparent, and can be accounted for by similar principles.

7.3.2 The non-past verb

Suffixed forms of the Theme I non-past strong verb occur in BA in two syllabic configurations (7.2.2 above): what we termed the "non-resyllabicated" variant form:

$$\begin{Bmatrix} y \\ t \end{Bmatrix} (v)CCvC \begin{Bmatrix} v \\ \bar{v} \end{Bmatrix} C$$

and the "resyllabicated" variant form:

$$\begin{Bmatrix} y \\ t \end{Bmatrix} \text{(v)CvCC} \begin{Bmatrix} \underline{v} \\ v \end{Bmatrix} \text{C}$$

The choice of the terms "resyllabicated" and "non-resyllabicated" is not meant to prejudice the issue of how synchronic variation should be accounted for, but is merely a convenient way of referring to these types of form. We have already doubted the legitimacy of using phonological re-write rules to explain variation between "phonemic" variants, and we shall be broadening the discussion in Chapter 8 to include the characterisation of syllabic variability.

Variation in the non-past verb may be conveniently discussed in two sections. The first concerns variation between forms which are syllabicated and non-resyllabicated e.g. /ysiknu:n/~/yiskinu:n/ 'they inhabit', /yṭil9u:n/~/yiṭla9u:n/. Here the variable feature is simply syllabic structure, and MV2.3-6 may be dealt with purely in these terms. Variation in MV2.1 is similarly also a matter only of syllabic variation, though here it is unsuffixed forms which are affected. But in MV2.2, variation - and it seems, socially significant variation- is found not only in syllable structure but also in the height of the stressed vowel of the resyllabicated variant:

	non-resyllabicated		resyllabicated		
			high vowel		low vowel
MV2.2	/yaghsilə/	~	/yghislə/	~	/yghaslə/

Many individuals show three-way variation between, for example, /yaghsilə/, /yghaslə/ and /yghislə/-type forms in contrast to what occurs in the past verb where, although three syllabic variants are, as it were communally 'available' only two are found in any one individual's data.

7.3.2.1 MV2.3-2.6

We begin our analysis with MV2.3-6, the more straightforward cases, where variation is purely a matter of the syllabication of suffixed forms. Table 33 below extracts from Tables 27-30 the dialectalness scores on these variables for our four communities. In interpreting these figures, we must bear in mind that: the 'Arab have the resyllabicated variant for all four verb categories as their basic form; B III apparently have the opposite - non-resyllabicated variants in all four categories. The two major B groups - the main urban group and all the villagers - agree in having the resyllabicated variant for verbs which have a high stem-vowel in the unsuffixed forms of the verb (e.g. /yiktib/ 'he writes', /ykitbu:n/ 'they write') and the non-resyllabicated variant in /a/-vowelled unsuffixed forms (e.g. /yišxal/ 'he sieves', /yišxalu:n/ 'they sieve') - that is, they have a syllable structure opposition between MV2.3 and MV2.4-6.

		MV2.3	2.4	2.5	2.6	Examples of dialectal variants
'Arab	literate	.83	.75	.65	.47	/ykitbə/ /yširbə/
	illiterate	.92	1.0	1.0	.65	/ysim9ə/ /yla9bu:n/
B I	literate	.16	1.0	1.0	.84	/ykitbə/ /yišrab /
	illiterate	.72	1.0	1.0	1.0	/yisma9ə//yil9abu:n/
B II	literate	.41	.91	.83	.81	/ykitbə/ /yišrabə/
	illiterate	.89	.94	.85	1.0	/yisma9 //yil9abu:n/
B III	literate	1.0	1.0	1.0	1.0	/yiktibə/ /yišrabə/
	illiterate	.88	1.0	1.0	1.0	/yisma9ə//yil9abə/

Table 33: Measures of dialectalness in four communities in four stem categories of the non-past verb

Let us now examine in detail the trends in the data. Two major tendencies are reflected by Table 33:

(a) The A literates chose the non-syllabicated (i.e. MSA-like) forms much more frequently in /a/-stem than /i/-stem verbs, bearing in mind that the basilectal A dialect has the resyllabicated form in all verb categories.

(b) The Baḥārna especially the literates, show a very marked preference for the non-resyllabicated (MSA-like) forms in /i/-stems. But in /a/ stems, where their dialectal variant is the non-resyllabicated one, they show a slight but measurable tendency to adopt the resyllabicated,"'Arab-like", non-Baḥārna, non-MSA forms.

7.3.2.1.1 Interpretation of the 'Arab data: MV2.3–2.5

It is obvious that there are close parallels between 'Arab behaviour on the non-past and past variables. These can be explained by the same argument. Just as MSA morphophonology can be invoked as the guiding principle in the "new" dialectal distribution of syllabic variants in the past verb - witness the CCvCaC/CiCCaC split in literate speech which more or less closely parallels the low/high theme-vowel split in MSA - so a "new" syllable structure split in the non-past verb between MV2.3 verbs on the one hand and MV2.4-6 on the other seems to be coming into being. In non-literate speech, all verbs normally have the dialectal, resyllabicated variant; in literate speech, a resyllabicated/non-resyllabicated distinction is arising between /i/-stemmed and /a/-stemmed non-past verbs, corresponding closely to the distinction in MSA between high-(/i/ or /u/) and low-(/a/) vowelled non-past verbs. The verb-category distinction in MSA, of course, is carried solely by vowel height, not by syllabic structure, just as it is in the past verb. Diagrammatically, the general position can be depicted as below:

	"non-literate" system	MSA influence	"literate" system
past verb	CCvCaC (all categories)	vowel height distinction: /i/ and /u/ versus /a/	→CCvCaC (MSA /a/ stem vowel)
			- - - - - - - - - - - -
			→CiCCaC (MSA /i/ /u/ stem vowel)
non-past	{y, t}(v)CvCC{v̄, v}C (all categories)		→{y, t}(v)CvCC{v̄, v}C (MSA /i/ /u/ stem vowel)
			- - - - - - - - - - - -
			→{y, t}vCCvC{v̄, v}C (MSA /a/ stem vowel)

The broken lines in this diagram indicate that the distinctions are not yet communally categorical: they represent trends which are relatively strongly pronounced in some literates' data, but relatively weak in other literates' and in most illiterates' data.

It must be borne in mind that the somewhat formal context in which the data was collected might have predisposed the literates to increase the frequency with which they replaced certain dialect forms. But the evidence is (and this is a vital point) that if the frequency of some variants did rise, it did not do so randomly. Nor do we believe, on the evidence of systematic observation in which recording did not take place, that dialect "restructuring" was merely an artifact of the mode of data collection. There was no question but that, in the vast majority of the unrecorded observations the writer made in shops, clubs, houses, etc., the illiterate speakers tended overwhelmingly to the 'one-variant' system for the past and non-past variables, while the literates consistently showed the 'two-variant' system. Without a transcribed record, however, it is impossible to say whether the same rank order of variant-replaceability, obtained in Table 33 from recorded conversations, would also have applied to these, by definition, less formal contexts.

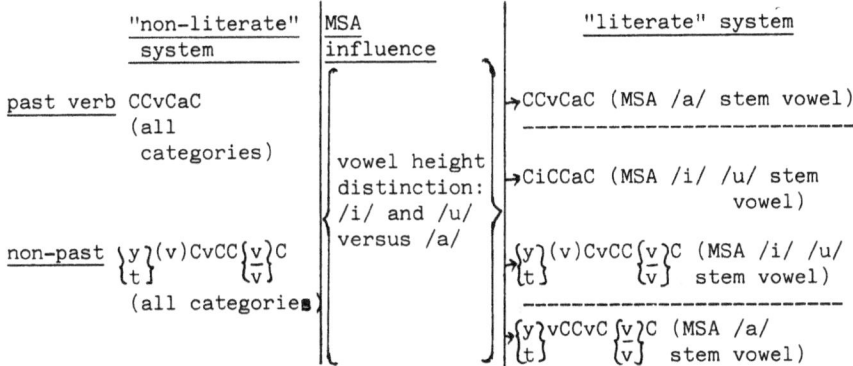

As we shall see in Chapter 8, the ordered patterns of variant-replacement found in data gathered for the thirty-four 'Arab show such a degree of agreement that they could not possibly have arisen by chance. If, as Labov has constantly observed, natural speech data is more homogeneous than speech data collected where there is greater attention being paid to what is said, then we might expect the internal patterning revealed by our data to be more marked in more 'natural' speech, rather than less. The act of recording a speaker may make him more conscious of how he is speaking and make him eschew certain features of his natural speech, or reduce their frequency; but it seems that the variability/replaceability of one element in a linguistic system is related to the variability/ replaceability of other elements in the system. These inter-relationships seem to be communally-held - a speaker may not, even in formal conversation, transgress against them if what he says is to be said in an acceptable manner. Knowledge of the inter-relationships between these variable elements forms part of his communicative competence in the language. We will have more to say on this point when considering the actual scaled grammars which our data gives us.

But to revertto Table 33: how are we to explain, within the MV2.4-2.6 group, the ordering:

MV2.6	<u>least dialectal</u>
MV2.5	↓
MV2.4	<u>most dialectal</u>

in the literate data? It fits the facts too, to consider the illiterate 'Arab data as also conforming to this ordering: MV2.6 the 'least dialectal' category for the literates is also the one category of the three which is variable in the illiterate data.

The apparent susceptibility of $\left\{\begin{matrix}y\\t\end{matrix}\right\}$(v)CvCC$\left\{\begin{matrix}v\\\bar{v}\end{matrix}\right\}$C to replacement by $\left\{\begin{matrix}y\\t\end{matrix}\right\}$vCCvC$\left\{\begin{matrix}v\\\bar{v}\end{matrix}\right\}$C in MV2.6 - that is, in C-G-C roots - is explicable in the same terms as the replacement of CCvCaC by CiCCaC in MV1.4 past verbs. Examples of MV2.6 resyllabicated variants are /yla9bu:n/ 'they play', /ysa'lu:n/ 'they ask', /tḏaḥku:n/ 'you (pl) laugh', all of which, it will be noticed, contain a <u>non-final CaG closed syllable</u>. But such syllables are normally avoided and rearranged into a CGa combination wherever possible in the 'Arab dialect (6.2). Both illiterate and literate speakers are thus faced with a 'rule-contradiction' internal to the dialect: a general dialectal rule of syllabic concatenation prescribes a $\left\{\begin{matrix}y\\t\end{matrix}\right\}$(v)CvCC$\left\{\begin{matrix}v\\v\end{matrix}\right\}$C form for all suffixed non-past strong Theme I verbs; but another rule of <u>syllabic structure</u> disallows the CaG non-final closed syllable which results from the application of this concatenating template to C-G-C roots.

If we are right in supposing that the main motivation for change in literate 'Arab speech on variables MV2.3-2.6, is restructuring according to MSA stem-vowel height distinctions, then literate speakers would be <u>doubly</u> motivated on MV2.6 to avoid such forms as /yla9bu:n/: both the rule proscribing non-final closed CaG and the influence of MSA (equivalent form /yal9abu:na/ - stem vowel /a/) would encourage a switch away from dialectal /yla9bu:n/-type forms. The illiterate speakers, on the other hand, would only be motivated by the dialectal phonological consideration, not by the 're-structuring' one - hence they show variability on MV2.6 but, unlike the literates, not on MV2.4 and MV2.5, where, on our analysis, the proscription of non-final CaG cannot be a factor (since there is no guttural consonant in the root), and consciousness of MSA would be the only factor which could be causing variation.

But this still leaves unanswered the question of why it should be in the /a/-stemmed and not the /i/-stemmed verbs that literates adopt the non-resyllabicated variant, bearing in mind that all verb categories are treated the same by some of the least sophisticated illiterate speakers of the 'Arab dialect. The dialectal phonological constraint which, it was argued in the previous paragraph, would give rise to the adoption of non-resyllabicated variants supplies only part of the answer. It is possible that the literates are taking the 'line of least resistance', in the sense that the /i/-stemmed verbs as a whole occur more frequently than the /a/-stemmed: in our 'Arab data there were 229 tokens for MV2.2 and 2.3 as against 146 for MV2.4-6. It is also more than coincidental that the past verb category MV1.1, in which the 'Arab also clung to the dialectal variant much more frequently than in MV1.2-4, accounted for 147 tokens, compared with 126 for MV1.2-4 put together. We are thus conjecturing that while the twin linguistic motivations for 'dialectal restructuring' in the 'Arab dialect are the influence of the supradialectal standard and rule-conflicts internal to the dialect, an additional factor in deciding which of the elements of the dialectal system are actually replaced in order to effect the restructuring may be the lower frequency of occurrence of some elements (or verb categories or environments) compared to others.

7.3.2.1.2 Interpretation of the Baḥārna data:MV2.3-2.6

The general trends in the Baḥārna data on the non-past variable cannot be explained by a simplistic hypothesis that literate Baḥārna simply "correct" their dialect to conform with the supradialectal standard. In fact, as Table 33 shows, they are in general less likely than their illiterate co-religionists to produce MSA-like non-resyllabicated variants on MV2.4-6, despite the fact that their dialectal variant in these verb categories is certainly non-resyllabicated. That is to say, where the "B" variant agrees with the MSA variant in 'opposing' the "A" variant, and in terms of our marking procedure is marked locally as "+ B + MSA - A" literate Baḥārna nonetheless tend to adopt the A variant to a certain degree. But where the A variant and B variants are the same, and differ from MSA - e.g. on MV2.3 - there is a much stronger movement by the literate Baḥārna to adopt "correct" (MSA-like) variants than by the literate 'Arab. MV2.3 would be marked locally as "+ B + A - MSA" This interpretation of Baḥārna behaviour is supported by the data on MV2.3 for the B III group, whose dialectal variant in this verb stem category, unlike the other B groups, is non-resyllabicated: that is, like MSA. This group of speakers preserves its dialectal non-resyllabicated variant just as strongly as the other B groups switch to it from their dialectal resyllabicated variant.

This type of communal variant is comparable with that already noted for lexical items containing phonological elements which have similar arrays of communal markings. On the /k/~/č/ variable, where all 'Arab and Baḥārna shared a non-standard dialectal reflex of OA/MSA /k/ (that is, marked like MV2.3 as "+ A + B - MSA"), the literate 'Arab on the whole "corrected" to /k/ less often than the Baḥārna; but on the /j/ variable, where the major urban/rural Baḥārna group opposed the 'Arab as to dialectal variant, with the Baḥārna having the same dialectal reflex as OA/MSA, the 'Arab showed little tendency to switch from non-standard /y/ to /j/, while the Baḥārna showed a marginal tendency to adopt /y/ in the same way as they adopt the A resyllabicated variant on MV2.4-6. This latter tendency probably reflects an unconscious identification by the literate Baḥārna group with the speech of the dominant sect: unconscious, since some of them vehemently denied using /y/ or such forms as /yila9bu:n/, describing them as "incorrect". In verb categories where non-standard variants are shared by both sects, they are simply locally marked as "non-standard", (+ A + B - MSA), that is, not particularly associated with one sect or the other. They are therefore subject to the pattern of "correction" according to which the low prestige social groups standardise their speech more noticeably than do dominant groups, who preserve their dialectal system more intact precisely because it is a badge of prestige-group identity.

It is also worth noting that the adoption by the Baḥārna of A forms seems to directly reciprocate 'Arab patterns of variation - at least in the major groups, B I and II. The rank-order of dialectalness is ordered for the B II group exactly as for the 'Arab over the three categories MV2.4-2.6, and the one category where the B I data is variable is in MV2.6 - just where the switch away from dialectal variants is most pronounced for the A group.

7.3.2.1.3 Conclusion

Our data seems, then, to point to a degree of convergence of all literate speakers on /a/-stemmed verbs, but to divergent behaviour on /i/-stemmed. The literate 'Arab data leads us to believe that the dominant group is adopting a restructured dialectal morphophonemic system whereby MSA /i/ and /u/-stemmed non-past verbs show the resyllabicated, and /a/-stemmed verbs the non-resyllabicated variants. If this analysis is correct, in the long run, the interesting marginal shift of the Baḥārna to 'Arab-like resyllabicated variants in /a/-stemmed verbs, may be a temporary phenomenon, since the 'Arab themselves are moving away from the use of this type of variant in these verb categories, and the Baḥārna might be expected to follow the lead of the prestige group. Diagrammatically we can illustrate these dialect developments as follows:

	old'literate system	new 'literate'system
	'Arab	
OA/MSA high-vowel stems	------------------→	resyllabicated variant
	resyllabicated variant only (↗ resyllabicated variant; ↘ non-resyllabicated variant)	
OA/MSA low-vowel stems	------------------→	non-resyllabicated variant
	Baḥārna	
OA/MSA high-vowel stems	resyllabicated variant	} → non-resyllabicated variant
OA/MSA low-vowel stems	non-resyllabicated variant	

At the moment, as we shall see when we come to consider individuals' data in scalar form, examples of invariant usage of what we have termed the 'old' and 'new' systems which relate to each sect can be found; but as literacy and increased social mixing become the norm, we would expect the adoption of the 'new' systems to become more widespread. These 'new' systems, and the variable grammars which form the bridge between them and the 'old' system, are the result of cross-cutting internal and supradialectal sociolinguistic forces.

7.3.2.2 Variation on MV2.1 and 2.2

In 7.3.2.1 we looked at variation in one verb category where the sects share a non-standard dialectal variant (MV2.3), and in three categories where they have different variants, with the non-prestige Baḥārna dialectal variant coinciding with the equivalent forms of MSA (MV2.4-6).

MV2.1 and 2.2 are treated separately for the following reasons:

(a) MV2.2 showed, alone among all the variables chosen, three-way variation. That is to say that most speakers in our sample showed three different types of variant for suffixed non-past verbs with G-C-C verb roots. This is not the same situation as in the past variables MV1.1 - 4 where although the three variant-types CCiCaC, CaCaCaC and CiCCaC occurred in the data, only two ever showed up in any one individual's data.

The factor which distinguishes MV2.2 from other non-past variables, is that, although the Baḥārna and 'Arab both 'oppose' MSA in having a non-standard resyllabicated dialectal variant they differ from each other in the height of the stem-vowel in this variant, thus:

	MSA	Baḥārna	'Arab
MV2.2:	/yaghsilu:na/	/yghislu:n/	/yghaslu:n/
Compare			
MV2.3:	/yaskunu:na/	/ysiknu:n/	

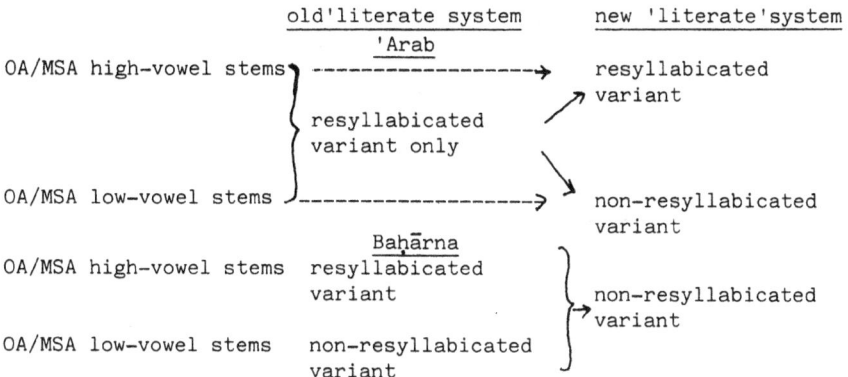

In the context of this study, the interesting point about variation on MV2.2 is that a three-way choice, where each variant is associated respectively with the 'Arab dialect, the Baḥārna dialects and MSA, can more clearly show the articulation of the local and supradialectal linguistic prestige system than variation on two-choice variables, such as MV2.3, can. The difficulty with two-variant variation is that it is impossible to prove conclusively that the observed switch by the dominant sect from a resyllabicated variant such as /yla9bu:n/ to a non-resyllabicated variant (/yil9abu:n/) is motivated by consciousness of MSA forms rather than Baḥārna influence, since both the B dialect and MSA share /yil9abu:n/ as their basic form. Obviously, it would be surprising if a socially dominant group were adopting linguistic features associated with the speech of the group it dominates, and we have been assuming that this is an unlikely explanation of 'Arab variation. MV2.2 provides a ground for testing this assumption against actual data since here, any 'Arab switch to the Baḥārna rather than MSA form would show up unambiguously as such. A three-variant variable such as this can also provide a clearer insight into the relative strength of the literate Baḥārna's "move away" from their dialectal variant towards the MSA and A variants, since in this case, the MSA and A variants are different.

(b) MV2.1 is treated as a separate category although it is really a sub-category of MV2.2. It covers variation in unsuffixed forms in the same set of verb roots (G-C-C). This is to allow for the possibility that suffixation, and the presence of a guttural consonant, which are both associated in the A dialect with resyllabication, operate independently of each other. Thus while any A replacement of /y9arfu:n/ by /ya9rifu:n/ might be inhibited by two factors:

(i) avoidance of CaG non-final closed syllables

(ii) general dialectal preference for the resyllabicated variant in all suffixed forms.

A switch from /y9arf/ to /ya9rif/ would be constrained only by the first of these factors, and hence might be generally more likely to occur than a switch from /y9arfu:n/ to /ya9rifu:n/.

A further interesting comparison, and one which gives an indication of the relative strength of factor (i) above, is between MV2.2 (G-C-C suffixed forms) and MV2.6 (C-C-C suffixed forms). In MV2.2, we would hypothesise that maintenance of the resyllabicated variant is promoted by the fact that the replacing form (e.g. /ya9rifu:n/) contains a CaG syllable of the type normally avoided; conversely, replacement of the same type of variant (e.g. forms such as /yla9bu:n/) is promoted by the fact that a CaG syllable is thrown up through the regular dialectal resyllabication of $\begin{Bmatrix} y \\ t \end{Bmatrix}$ vCCvC $\begin{Bmatrix} v \\ \bar{v} \end{Bmatrix}$ C in C-G-C roots. Such a hypothesis is supported by the data:

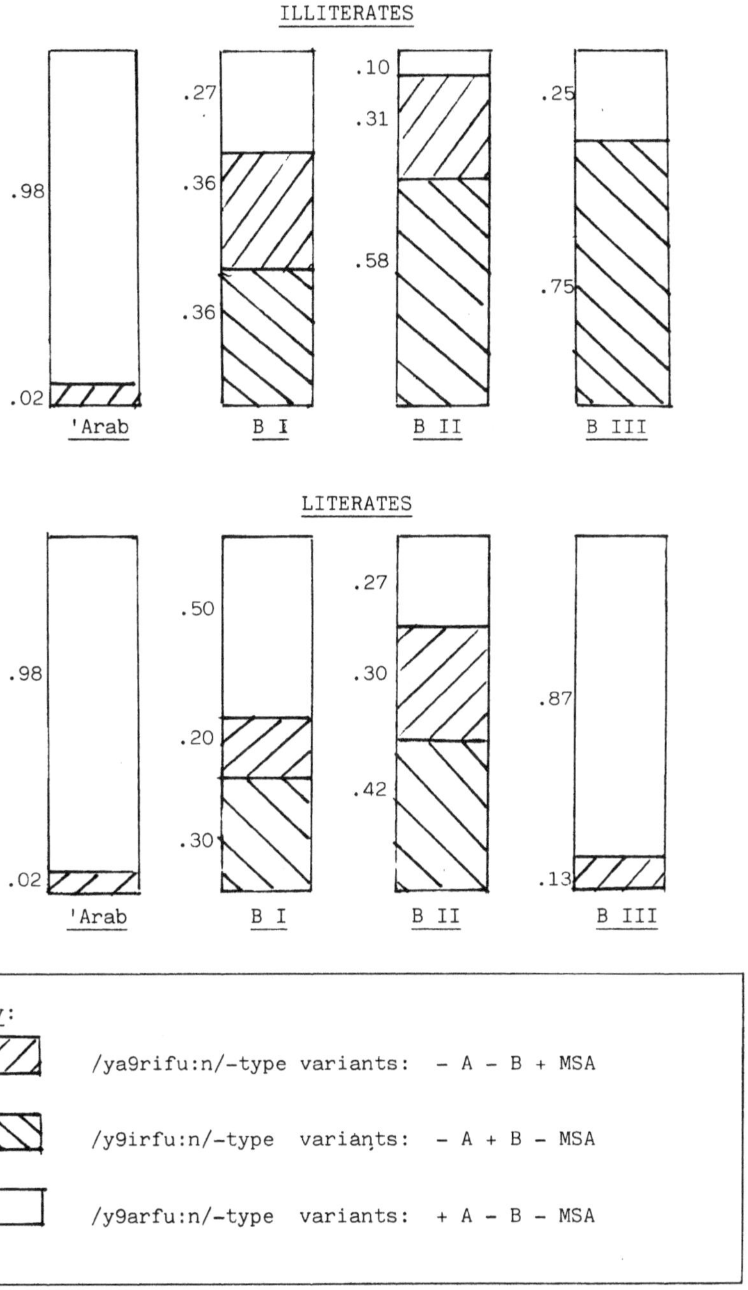

Figure 2: Convergence in the non-past verbs: MV2.2

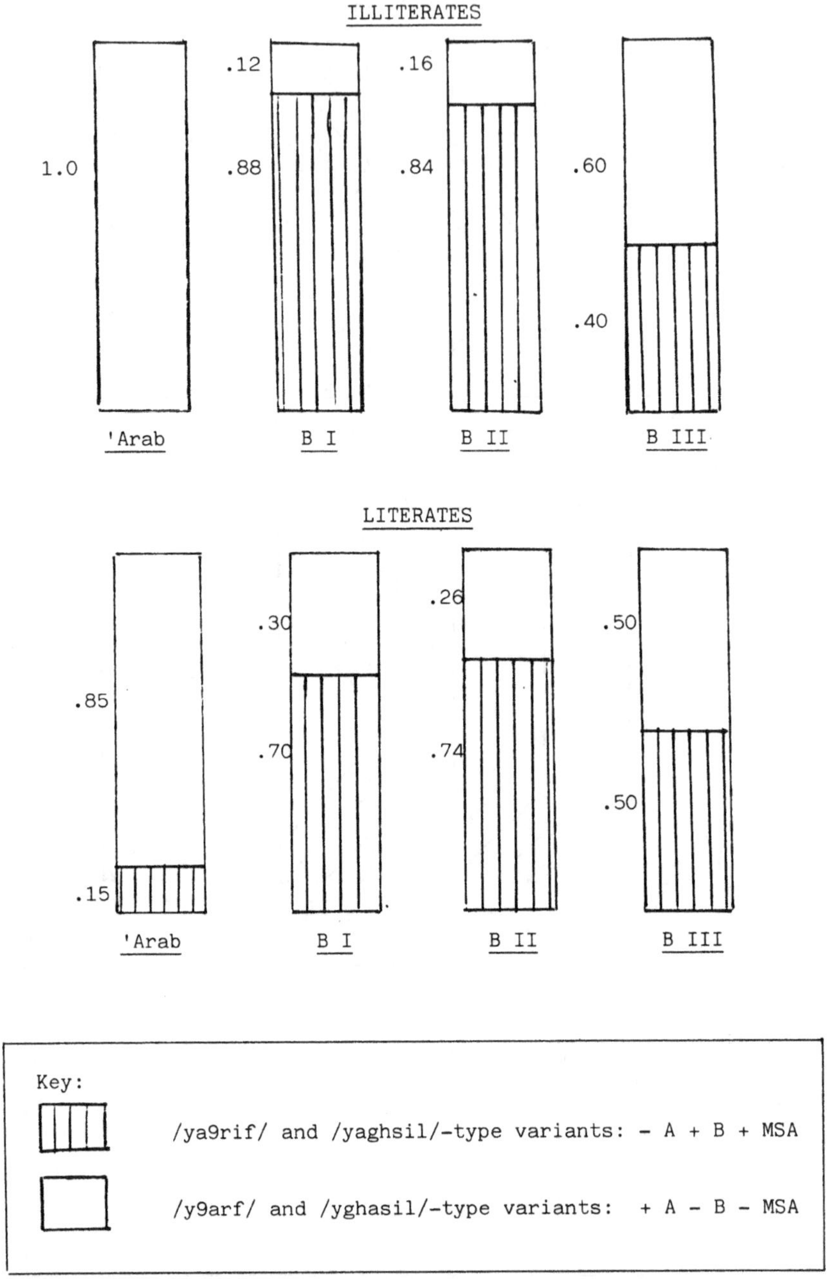

Figure 3 : Convergence in the non-past verb: MV2.1

replacement is virtually non-existent for all 'Arab in MV2.2, but is strongest for all in MV2.6.

Figure 2 illustrates communal variation on MV2.2 in suffixed forms in our four sect/locationally defined communities. It is clear from the figure that:

(i) Variation in the 'Arab community is one-way - between the 'Arab dialectal variant-type /y9arfu:n/ and the MSA equivalent /ya9rifu:n/. There was not a single instance of an 'Arab speaker producing a B variant. What switching there is to MSA variants is extremely marginal, even in literate speech. This is the most clear-cut evidence produced yet of the dominant group's tendency to stick to its dialectal variant and confirms that where variation does occur, in the prestige dialect it is supradialectally motivated

(ii) The Baḥārna groups, literate and illiterate, all tend to switch away from the B variant to both the A and MSA variants: and rather more strongly to the former than the latter. This switch is so marked in the literate B III group, which is in the closet geographical proximity to 'Arab-dominated Muḥarraq of any B group, that the dialectal variant disappears completely and is replaced mainly by the A equivalent. On balance, the urban literates show a stronger tendency to adopt the A variant than do village literates.

Figure 3 shows a similar situation.

(i) Variation in the 'Arab community is again marginal, and here limited to literate speech. The slightly stronger preference for MSA forms in MV2.1 compared to MV2.2 (.15 as against .02) could be explained by the fact that only the "CaG-avoidance" constraint is operating on MV2.1, whereas the general tendency to avoid non-resyllabicated variants in general in suffixed forms (and particularly in /i/-stemmed verbs) is an additional factor which would decrease the likelihood of a switch to the MSA variant on MV2.2..

(ii) The Baḥārna groups' /yi9ruf/-type variant on MV2.1, which this time coincides in syllabic structure with MSA - is again subject to replacement by the A variant to an extent comparable to the extent /y9irfu:n/ is replaced by /y9arfu:n/ on MV2.2. Replacement is again more pronounced in literate than in illiterate speech for the two main B groups. In the B III group, on this variable, there is a somewhat stronger tendency to adopt A forms, though paucity of data makes it difficult to draw any definite conclusions, as does the fact that the tendency is somewhat more pronounced in illiterate than literate speech - the opposite tendency to that observed on almost all other variables for all groups.

7.3.2.3 Variation in verb morphophonemics: main conclusions

'Arab

1. The main force for linguistic change acting on 'Arab verb morphophonology is the influence of MSA. This is reflected in the literate speakers' apparent abandonment of a morphophonemic system which has a single syllabic variant for all past, and all non-past verbs, in favour of a system which has two variants for the past and two for the non-past. The levels of variation observed in particular groups of verb roots lead us to believe that the guiding principle of change is the need to make the 'Arab dialect isomorphic with MSA: the new 'two-variant' system expresses in BA dialectal terms (a syllabic structure opposition), morphophonemic differences which are important in MSA (a stem-vowel height difference in different verb categories).

2. Where this re-structuring occurs, the replacing variants are chosen for their local sociolinguistic neutrality and areal currency. Avoidance of CaCaCaC-type syllabic forms in the past verb, where on purely surface criteria, this form is 'closest' to MSA, indicates how important the local linguistic prestige system is in mediating the effects of externally motivated change.

3. But change is also phonologically constrained: syllabic structure preferences specific to the dialect may be a major factor in promoting or inhibiting the replacement of dialectal forms, e.g. variation in MV1.4, avoidance of surface CaG in non-final closed syllables in MV2.2 (where replacement is inhibited), and in MV2.6 (where replacement is promoted).

Baḥārna

1. In contrast to the 'Arab, the Baḥārna community has a number of basic dialectal morphophonemic systems. These systems appear to be converging under the joint influence of MSA and the 'Arab dialect.

2. Where the 'Arab dialects already show a high degree of congruence with the MSA dialect - in the past verb - there is a cross-over phenomenon whereby the literates marginally adopt non-literary forms in apparent imitation of the prestige group (e.g. MV1.4, 1.1). Where the degree of congruence with MSA is less - in the non-past verb - the marginal cross-over phenomenon is again apparent, but here it is allied to a very strong switch to supra-dialectal syllabic forms. The Baḥārna literates' dialect thus shows the influence of both the 'Arab dialect and MSA - and the latter influence, whenever it occurs, is much more pronounced than it is in the 'Arab case.

7.3.3 Certain nominal forms

The dialectal syllabic structures of the nouns in categories MV3.1

and 3.2 correspond, as noted above in (6.4.3.1), to those of the verb categories MV2.1 and 1.1:

MV2.1		MV3.1	
Baḥārna	'Arab	Baḥārna	'Arab

/yi9ruf/ versus /y9arf/ correspond to /maghrib/ versus /mgharb/

MV1.1		MV3.2
/darasat/ versus /drisat/	corresponds to	/baraka versus /brika/

As far as syllabic structure is concerned, the Baḥārna nominal variant forms are identical to those of MSA, but, in the social context of Baḥrain, are nonetheless "low-status" in the same way as past-verb variants.

MV3.3 is a different case. On this variable the sects share CCvCa-type forms as dialectal variants, in contrast with MSA CaCaCa, e.g. A/B /smiča/ versus MSA /samaka/. From the point of view of the communal distribution of syllabic variants, therefore, MV3.3 is identical with the non-past verb variable MV2.3, where it will be recalled, the sects share a resyllabicated /ykitbu:n/-type dialectal variant in contrast with MSA non-resyllabicated /yaktubu:na/.

Extracting the relevant figures from Tables 27-30, we obtain:

Group		MV3.1	3.2	3.3
A	illiterate	.91	.77	.80
	literate	.50	.33	.20
B I	illiterate	.75	1.0	1.0
	literate	.80	1.0	1.0
B II	illiterate	1.0	1.0	.71
	literate	.85	1.0	0
B III		too little data		

Table 34: Measures of "dialectalness" on 3 noun categories

In general, the B literates show a remarkable degree of consistency on MV3.2 and 3.3: where their dialectal variant is CaCaCa, they categorically preserve it; where it is CCvCa they categorically replace it by an MSA-like CvCvCa in which the vowel-pattern may be i-a, a-a, or i-i. The 'Arab literates also show a high level of replacement of dialectal CCvCa by CvCvCa on both 3.2 and 3.3. Leaving aside MV3.1 for the moment, how do the patterns of communal variation in MV3.2 and MV3.3 match up with those on MV1.1 and MV2.3 respectively?

The point of making these comparisons is that:

(i) In the case of MV3.2 and MV1.1, nominal and verbal variants are syllabically the same: 'Arab /brika/ and /drisat/ oppose Baḥārna /baraka/ and /darasat/. But the data for the 'Arab literates in Table 27 above shows clearly that nouns and verbs are treated differently: /brika/-type forms are very likely to be replaced by /baraka/-type forms, but /drisat/-type forms are never replaced by /darasat/-type forms and only very marginally by /drisat/-type forms. To what factors should we attribute this difference in the incidence of variation between nouns and verbs?

(ii) In the case of MV3.3 and 2.3, on the other hand, there is clearly no similarity of syllabic structure. The point of the comparison is that MV3.3 and 2.3 are the only morphophonemic categories examined in this study in which all dialects share a non-standard syllabic variant: that is, in which a non-standard variant has the same communal distribution. But Tables 27-29 above show that literate 'Arab and literate Baḥārna treat these categories quite differently. The literate 'Arab strongly retain the dialectal form in the verb category (.83), but replace the dialectal form in the noun (.20): the literate Baḥārna strongly replace both, to the point where, in the noun, zeroing out of /smicā/-type forms takes place. Why should there be this communal difference in the treatment of nouns and verbs by literates, where all speakers, regardless of sect, share the same dialectal variant?

7.3.3.1 Variation in nouns versus verbs with the same dialectal syllabic structure

Let us take the case of MV3.2 versus 3.1 first. A crucial factor in variation in the past verb, as opposed to the noun, is that there is no alternative nominal variant which has a communally 'neutral' status, equivalent to the CiCCat-type verbal variant. We saw above that literate 'Arab replaced CCvCat, and literate Baḥārna CaCaCat, by 'neutral' CiCCat, and that these switches could be explained by a combination of sociolinguistic factors and (in the 'Arab case) internal dialectal phonological factors. Between-sect convergence in verb categories MV1.1 and 1.4 takes place not through any one-sided, or reciprocal, adoption by the groups of each other's dialectal variant, but through a switch to a third variant.

In the noun, no 'neutral' third variant such as */wirga/ (instead of 'Arab /wriga/, Baḥārna /waraga/ 'leaf') exists. It might appear from the data in Table 27 that the literate 'Arab, on MV3.1 and 3.2 are adopting a B form in contradiction of the general principle already elaborated whereby literates of the low-prestige group switch marginally to the non-standard variant of the high-prestige group. The contradiction is in fact only apparent as we shall now see.

Variation in the past verb can be represented in its general form in BA as follows:

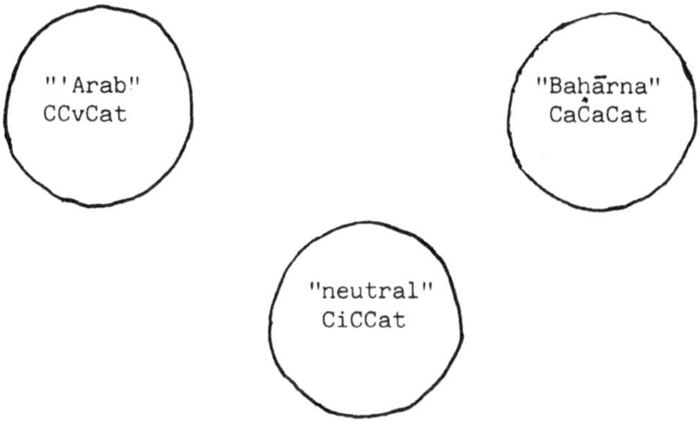

Figure 4: Non-reciprocal variation in the past verb

Variation of this type gives us an interpretive framework within which we can place variation on the "two-variant" nominal variables MV3.1-3.3: if, on "three-variant" variables such as MV1.1 the literate 'Arab are clearly not choosing to replace their dialectal variant by the distinctively Baḥārna variant but by a 'neutral' variant, then on "two-variant" noun variables such as MV3.1-3.3 we can be confident in interpreting the 'Arab switch to CaCaCa as being motivated, just as it is in the verb, by consciousness of the MSA morphophonemic system rather than by borrowing from the Baḥārna system. The fact that the verb forms adopted are syllabically identical with the B dialectal variants is on this analysis simply coincidental - it is not 'Arab consciousness of B dialectal forms but of MSA forms which motivates 'Arab variation. Evidence to support this explanation is also the A switch to the MSA, rather than the B variant on MV2.2 discussed above. Accordingly, the correct diagrammatic representation of variation in the noun is:

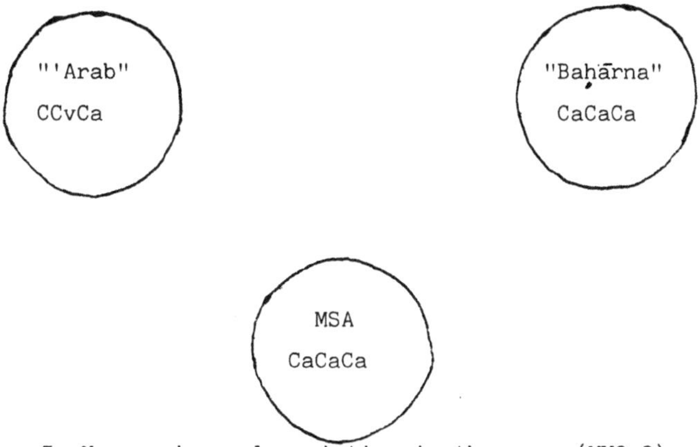

Figure 5: Non-reciprocal variation in the noun (MV3.2)

All apparent switches by 'Arab literates to B nominal forms (on MV3.1 and MV3.2) can be explained in the same way: the B forms just happen to be syllabically similar to MSA equivalents.

We explained variation in the past verb in the A literate data as mainly due to the influence of the MSA morphophonemic system (7.3.1.1): a new dialectal syllabic distinction reflects stem-vowel differences in MSA. This involved dialectal CCvCaC-type forms becoming commoner in the MV1.1 category (/a/-stemmed verbs in MSA), while CiCCaC-type dialectal forms are tending to be adopted in verb categories whose MSA equivalents have a high stem-vowel.

Variation in noun forms whose dialectal syllabic structure is CCvCa(C) can be explained as a part of the same development - the syllabic particularization in the dialect, and by dialectal means, of distinctions which are relevant in MSA. In the case of nouns, the syllabic variant which literates adopt is just that variant - CaCaCa(C) - which is never found in verbs. Literates seem, in other words, to be treating nouns and verbs whose dialectal syllabic structures are the same, in different ways: CCvCaC syllabic variants marked as verbs may become variable with CiCCaC variants; CCvCa(C) dialectal variants marked as nouns become variable with CaCaCa(C) variants. A syntactic distinction, in other words, is becoming morphophonemically marked. Compare the literate and illiterate data in the relevant verb and noun stem-categories.

Illiterate System		MSA equivalents	Literate System
Verbs:			
MV1.1	/drisat/	/darasat/	CCvCaC (NO CHANGE)
1.2	/lbisat/	/labisat/	CCvCaC → CiCCaC (CHANGE)
1.3	/kbarat/	/kaburat/	
1.4	/ṭla9at/	/ṭala9at/	
Nouns:			
MV3.2	/brika/	/baraka(tun)/	CCvCa(C) → CaCaCa(C) (CHANGE)
3.3	/smiča/	/samaka(tun)/	

Table 35: Restructuring in the 'Arab dialect of CCvCa(C) forms: general scheme

These trends become clearer by comparing the actual dialectalness scores for 'Arab literates and illiterates in these categories.

Verbs	Illiterates d-score	Literates d-score		Morphophonemic status
MV1.1	.98	.95		/a/-stems verbs
1.2	.69	.59	}	/i/ or /u/-stem verbs and guttural-stem verbs
1.3	.80	.60		
1.4	.59	.45		
Nouns				
3.2	.77	.33	}	nouns
3.3	.80	.20		

Table 36: Restructuring in the 'Arab dialect of CCvCa(C) forms: quantified data

Clearly the illiterates' data does not show the same pattern of variation as the literates'. Like the literates, the illiterates have a high dialectalness score on MV1.1, but they do not make such a sharp distinction between their treatment of MV1.1 and the other verb-stem categories; nor do they appear to be treating nouns and verbs differently, as the literates do.

Turning now to the other noun category, MV3.1, we can see below (Table 37) how much more likely literate 'Arab are to replace the dialectal variant by the non-dialectal than they are in the equivalent verb category. The dialectal variant in the nominal category MV3.1 is of the /mgharb/-type (compare MSA/B/maghrib/); and in the verbal category MV2.1 of the syllabically identical /y9arf/-type (compare MSA/B /ya9rif/, /yi9ruf/)

	Illiterates	d-score	Literates	d-score
Verb				
MV2.1	/y9arf/	1.00	/y9arf/	.85
Noun				
MV3.1	/mgharb/	.91	/mgharb/	.50

Table 37: Restructuring in the 'Arab dialect of CGaCC forms

The illiterates make virtually no distinction between verb and noun; but the literates are much more likely to replace /mgharb/, the noun, by /maghrib/-type forms, than they are /y9arf/, the verb, by /ya9rif/-type forms. Even so, MV3.1, relative to the other noun categories, is the most likely, for both literate and illiterate speakers, to show the highest proportion of dialectal forms (cf the scores in Table 36). This is a further illustration of the point already made in the case of the non-past and past verb that where there is general switching away from dialectal syllabic forms in the 'Arab data under MSA pressure, the switch is least favoured in roots where adoption of the MSA-type syllabic variant would throw-up closed CaG syllables in non-final position.

If it is accepted that a general restructuring of the 'Arab literate dialect, as illustrated in Table 35, is going on, we still have to explain why the strength of the trend to replace dialectal variants by MSA-like equivalents is so much more pronounced in the noun than in the verb, as Tables 36 and 37 suggest. This is a difficult question to answer. One possible factor is that in absolute terms, verb forms in our data massively outnumbered syllabically similar noun forms: in the 'Arab case, the literate and illiterate data combined to give a total of 256 tokens for MV1.1-1.4 and only 51 for MV3.2 plus 3.3; and a total of 127 tokens for MV2.1 as compared with 77 for MV3.1. If these figures are representative of ratios in normal speech, we could hypothesise that, in the restructuring process we have described, nouns in some sense represent a "line of least resistance" in the switch away from CCvCaC and CGaCC-type syllabic variants. Certain syllabic variant-types are becoming variable with others in the 'Arab dialect, and, as we have seen, there is a correlation between syntactic function and probability of variation in syllable structure. The strength and speed of the change in each category (nouns/verbs) may be related to the absolute frequency of noun/verb tokens in these categories: there are a greater number of verbs than nouns potentially liable to replacement, and they have a greater variety of morphological variants - therefore they occur more often in speech, and, it seems, are more slowly affected by diffusing change, in general, than nouns.

There is also a feeling among 'Arab that "resyllabicated" variants like /brika/, /smiča/, /mgharb/ are somewhat 'old-fashioned'. But this applies to some lexical items more than others: /mgharb/, 'sunset', for example, generally retained its dialectal form even in literate 'Arab speech, and we shall see below that, where literate Baḥārna switched away from their MSA-like nominal dialectal forms towards the prestige dialect, the switch always occurred in a limited number of lexical items like /mgharb/, where the resyllabicated variant is consistently retained by all 'Arab. On the other hand, 'Arab dialectal /ghawa/ 'coffee', another extremely common word, was almost always realised as /gahwa/ in the mouths of literate 'Arab, and, significantly, no example was recorded of literate Baḥārna switching from their dialectal /gahwa/ to /ghawa/.

It is not obvious why there should be such a marked difference in the treatment of these two nouns. However, the Baḥrainis who participated in this study were quite aware of the difference and able to characterise /mgharb/ as merely A and /ghawa/ as 'old fashioned A'. No similar reaction to CCvCat verb forms was noted: while fully aware that such forms were 'A', 'Arab regarded them as quite normal and, apparently, just as typical of educated as uneducated speech. The analysis of our literate 'Arab sample's speech data bears this out (c.f. the remarks in Chapter 1 on the retention of CCvCaC-type forms in verbs in the 'elevated colloquial' of children's radio programmes).

7.3.3.2 Syllabic variants which have the same communal distribution in the same morphophonemic category

Let us now turn to the case of MV2.3 and MV3.3, the only categories of the noun and verb where the sects share non-standard syllabic variants. Literate 'Arab treat verbal and nominal categories differently, switching to the standard variant in the noun only; literate Baḥārna treat them similarly, switching to the standard variant in both. The explanation for the 'Arab data is based on the principle of 'Arab "dialectal restructuring" already put forward, whereby the resyllabicated variant on MV2.2 and 2.3 (high-vowel stemmed categories in MSA) is not replaced by the non-resyllabicated variant, whereas it *is* replaced on MV2.4-6, where MSA equivalents have a low-vowelled stem.

It also so happens that the verbs in the /i/-stemmed category occur more frequently, in absolute terms, than those in the /a/-stemmed, and are therefore, according to our principle of the 'line of least resistance' likely to retain the dialectal syllabic form, while the /a/-stemmed verbs are replaced by MSA-type equivalents (the ratio of MV2.2 + MV2.3 tokens to MV2.4, 5, 6 in the total 'Arab data base is 31:19). By the same argument, it is the CCvCa(C) *noun* variants which undergo change in the restructuring of CCvCa(C) dialectal forms, because (Table 27), they occur far less frequently (ratio 1:4) than *verbs* of the same dialectal syllabic structure.

Thus, as far as the literate 'Arab are concerned, the differential treatment of parts of their dialectal system which are identically communally marked (+ A + B - MSA) can be explained by the overriding principle of "dialectal restructuring", which operates by evolving syllabic structure contrasts in the A dialect which reflect MSA morphological/syntactic distinctions. This is effected according to the 'line of least resistance' principle. That may be why the *high-frequency* MV2.2 and MV2.3 category verbs, from amongst those non-past categories where a syllabic restructuring from

$$\left\{\begin{matrix} y \\ t \end{matrix}\right\} \mathrm{CvCC} \left\{\begin{matrix} v \\ v \end{matrix}\right\} \mathrm{C}$$

to

$$\left\{\begin{matrix} y \\ t \end{matrix}\right\} \mathrm{vCCvC} \left\{\begin{matrix} v \\ v \end{matrix}\right\} \mathrm{C}$$

could apply, are largely unaffected; and why low-frequency *nouns* in categories MV3.2 and 3.3 which have a dialectal structure of the general form CCvCa(C) are more affected than verbs with the same dialectal syllabic shape.

Literate B variation in the noun categories examined can largely be explained according to the principles developed to explain variation in the non-past verb, which like the noun, shows only 'two-variant variation'. There is no third 'neutral' variant, as in the past verb. The parallelism of the non-past and nominal variables resides also, in particular, in the following facts:

(i) MV2.1 and 2.4-6 match MV3.1 and 2 from the standpoint of communal marking; in all five cases the B dialectal variants agree with MSA and oppose the A variants (and are marked + B - A +MSA).

(ii) MV2.3 on the other hand, is identical to MV3.3 in communal marking: the 'Arab and all Baḥārna share a single dialectal variant which opposes MSA (+ B + A - MSA).

Comparing now the data in Table 33 (MV2.3-2.6), Figure 3 (MV2.1) and Table 34 (MV3.1 - 3), we can see that MV3.1 (case (i) above) is treated by the literate Baḥārna precisely as MV2.1, 2.4-2.6: there is marginal adoption of the high-prestige 'Arab variant which sometimes replaces the dialectal, "MSA-like" B variant. Just as the literate Baḥārna tend to replace, e.g. /yi9ruf/ 'he knows' by /y9arf/, so they replace /maghrib/ 'sunset' by /mgharb/. But on MV3.3, (case (ii)), where B illiterates share forms like /smiča/ with the 'Arab, the literates' switch away to /samača/ or /simiča/ is so marked that the dialectal form is zeroed out. On MV2.3, where the 'Arab and Baḥārna also share a single non-standard variant, the B switch is not quite so strong, but still clearly present. Thus the general principles hold for 'two-variant' nominal as well as non-past verb variables:

1. Where the sects share a non-standard variant in any morphophonemic category, the low-prestige B literates show a much stronger tendency to adopt the 'standard' variant than do the high-prestige 'Arab.

2. In categories where the dialectal variant is not shared, and where the low prestige group's variant actually agrees with the standard equivalent in syllabic structure, low prestige literates show a slight but consistent tendency to adopt the high-prestige group's non-standard variant.

MV3.2 appears to be an exception to principle 2 above, since /baraka/ is the B/MSA form, opposing A /brika/, but no marginal switching to /brika/ occurred in the literate B data as it did in MV3.1 from /maghrib/ to /mgharb/. It is likely that the explanation lies in the literate Baḥārna's extreme treatment of the related category MV3.3: the strength of the switch to CaCaCa (or CiCiCa) from dialectal CCiCa on MV3.3 - the strongest in any morphophonemic category considered - may have <u>prevented</u> the reverse process of marginal switching from dialectal CaCaCa to CCiCa on MV3.2. In effect, the literate Baḥārna seem to have been treating all nouns with a CaCaCa syllable structure in MSA in the same way - <u>maintaining</u> dialectal CaCaCa whenever it occurs (and thus conforming to MSA standards) and replacing dialectal CCiCa by CaCaCa whenever it occurs. It is also probably no coincidence that, where the 'Arab were most likely to maintain a non-standard nominal variant (MV3.1), the B literates marginally switched towards it; but where the literate 'Arab themselves, for the reasons already described above, switched frequently to standard variants (MV3.2 and 3.3), then the literate Baḥārna either maintained these standard variants (when they are syllabically identical to dialectal B forms (MV3.2)) or adopted them even more often than the 'Arab (when they are syllabically different from B dialectal forms (MV3.3.)):

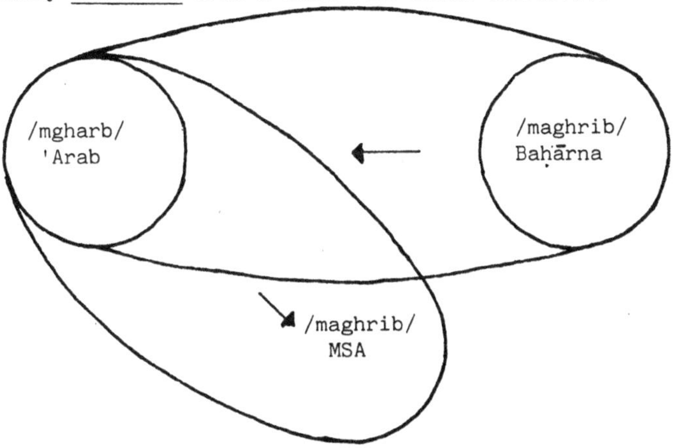

Figure 6: A/B literate switching on 'two-variant' noun variables (variants not shared: A switching to MSA weak, B switching to A form weak) (Type 1)

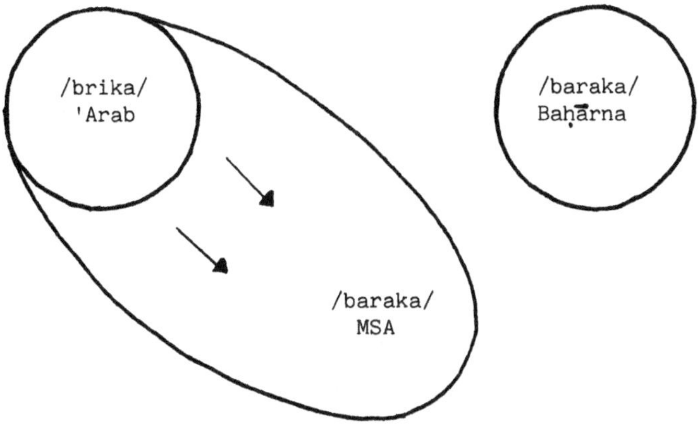

Figure 7: A/B literate switching on 'two-variant'noun variables (variants not shared: A switching to MSA strong, no B switching to A form) (Type 2)

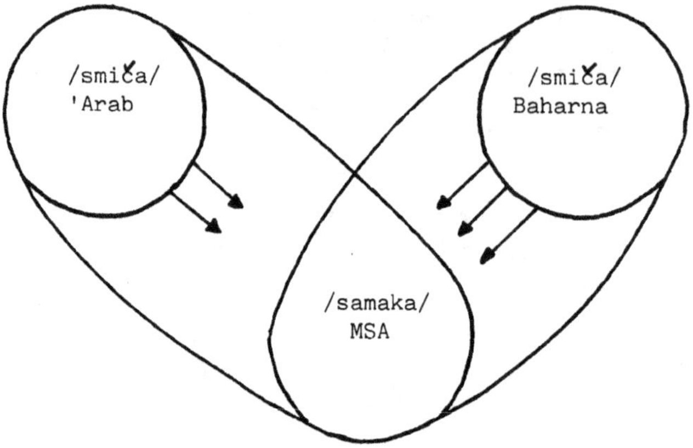

Figure 8: A/B literate switching on 'two-variant' noun variables (variants shared: A switching to MSA strong, B switching to MSA categorical) (Type 3)

7.4 Summary of trends in the data

Before discussing how the type of variable data discussed in this chapter might be handled by rule, we give here a summary of general trends in the data ('high-status' = A, 'low-status' = B):

7.4.1 Three-variant variables (the past verb)

The high-status dialect: the literates are tending to replace the one-variant illiterate dialectal system by a two-variant system in which the syllabic dichotomy reflects MSA vowel height differences in syllabic form. The innovated syllabic form is communally 'neutral'.

The low-status dialect: despite the similarity of the low-prestige dialect system and MSA, the literates tend to introduce the communally 'neutral' form in the verb categories where the high-prestige group introduces it, replacing dialectal variants which are syllabically similar to MSA equivalent forms.

The overall result is the creation of varieties of "literate" BA speech in which there is a high degree of variation, but which show convergence to the extent that literates from both sectarian groups are adopting/preserving the same 'neutral' variant in the same verb-stem categories. Nonetheless, each sectarian group still maintains its own sect-specific syllabic variant whenever the 'neutral' variant is not used. To that extent, it is still possible to pick out a literate speaker as belonging to an 'Arab or Baḥārna community on the basis of the forms he uses.

7.4.2 Two-variant variables

7.4.2.1 The non-past verb

The high-status dialect: as in the past verb, the literates tend to 'restructure' the one-variant dialectal system, in line with MSA stem-vowel-height distinctions. The 'restructuring' is again expressed as a distinction in syllable structure, and is partly conditioned by dialectal phonological factors.

The low-status dialect: where the low-prestige dialect agrees in syllabic structure with MSA, there is a marginal switch to the high-prestige syllabic form; where it does not agree, there is strong switching to an MSA-like form.

The overall effect is that the high-prestige literates seem to be moving to a point where the new dialectal syllabic distinction reflects MSA vowel-height differences; by contrast the low-prestige literates are imitating MSA morphophonemics by adopting MSA-like syllabic structure in all verb-categories. Literate behaviour is therefore partly tending to diverge and partly to converge in the sense that, on /i/-stemmed verbs, the A and B literates seem to be 'nearer' each other, and on /a/-stemmed verbs 'further' from each other, compared with their illiterate fellows. To this extent, the literate dialectal systems are still sect-specific, though to a lesser extent, and in a different way from the illiterate systems.

7.4.2.2 Certain nominal forms

The high-status dialect: norminal forms in the literate A dialect are more affected by restructuring than past or non-past verbs of a similar dialectal syllabic structure. They are more liable to change as the 'line of least resistance' in a general move to a more 'MSA-like' high-status dialect.

The low-status dialect: variation in the noun follows the same general pattern as in the non-past verb, except that the trends are even more pronounced.

8 Morphophonemic rule formulation

8.1 Notational problems

We have argued so far that morphophonemic variation in BA is motivated by consciousness of prestige forms of one kind or another supra-dialectal or local - and arises through the substitution of one for another. But we have not yet broached the subject of how this kind of variation should be expressed in rule-form.

Let us begin the discussion by considering variation in the syllable structure of the past verb. We noted in MV1.1 that the 'Arab showed variation between /drisat/- and /dirsat/-type forms. It seemed arguable, by virtue of the existence of numbers of illiterate 'Arab who had the /drisat/-type categorically, that this was the 'basilectal' form. We noted in the Baḥarna case that a similar situation obtained, but that variation here was between /darasat/- and /dirsat/-type forms. Morphologically, all of these consist of a past stem and an enclitic: -/at/ for the 3rd person feminine, -/aw/ for the common plural, viz.

ROOT:	'to study'	d-r-s	
VOWEL PATTERN:	'past'	a-a	
3 f.s./comm.pl.			at/aw
Underlying structure:		daras +at/aw	

One proposal, then, could be that all three types of surface form - /darasat/, /drisat/ and /dirsat/- could be derived from a single, common underlying form through the operation of different sets of ordered phonological rewrite-rules. This is essentially Abdo's (1969) approach to the description of the phonology of the Palestinian dialect of Al-Mukabbir. Abdo comments on the subject of underlying forms in Arabic phonology in general: "where the differences (between MSA and the dialects) are most obvious, it is striking that in most cases the underlying structures for the spoken dialects....and Classical Arabic are by and large very similar, and almost identical." (1969:5).

But a number of problems arise when we try to account for variation between different syllabic variants such as /drisat/, /dirsat/ by writing variable rules which use normal notational practices.

Consider our 'Arab data. We could account adequately for some illiterates' data (those who have categorical /drisat/-type forms) by making an obligatory rule of vowel-deletion such as:

$$v_1 \longrightarrow \emptyset \ / \ \text{C–C}v_2\text{CaC}$$

operate on an underlying $Cv_1Cv_2C + \begin{Bmatrix} aw \\ at \end{Bmatrix}$. Then, an obligatory vowel-conditioning rule would rewrite v_2 as /i/ or /a/ depending on the consonantal environment: if a preceding or following C + guttural, v_2 = /a/, otherwise v_2 = /i/. Collapsing these two rules, we get in shorthand form the categorical rule:

$$\text{CvCvC} + \text{aC} \longrightarrow \text{CCvCaC}$$

But a difficulty arises in modifying this rule to account for the data of speakers who do not have /drisat/-type forms categorically. It is not the case that, given a CvCvC + aC base form, such speakers' data can be accounted for by simply making them fail to apply either the vowel-deletion rule or the vowel-conditioning rule: if they did, we would get the following 'medial' forms, which, we have already noted, never actually occurred in the data:

*/drasat/ (vowel-deletion but no vowel-conditioning)
*/darisat/ (no vowel-deletion but vowel-conditioning)

That is, it seems that the two phonological rules which we collapsed into one never operate independently of each other to throw up 'medial' forms. They seem, rather, to constitute a single 'rule-system' for the 'Arab community. Could we then account for variation by simply adding angled brackets to the output of this system? Viz.

$$\text{CvCvC} + \text{aC} \longrightarrow \langle \text{CCvCaC} \rangle$$

According to normal variationist notational practice, this would be interpreted as meaning that whenever CvCvC + aC is <u>not</u> rewritten as CCvCaC, it appears on the surface as CvCvCaC (since, as we have noted, the vowel-deletion and conditioning rules either both go through, or neither does). In fact, in every instance where

$$\text{CvCvC} + \text{aC} \longrightarrow \langle \text{CCvCaC} \rangle$$

does not go through, <u>not</u> CvCvCaC, but CiCCaC-type forms show up. CiCCaC-type forms are derivable from the same underlying base by a different pair of interdependent phonological rules which delete v_2 of underlying CvCvC + aC and condition the first obligatorily to /i/ (or to /u/ in certain combinations of velar and labial consonants).

There thus seem to be two alternative rule-systems available to literate speakers, which operate on the same underlying form: the first system ("'Arab" dialect) deletes v_1 and conditions v_2; the second deletes v_2 and conditions v_1. The two systems are mutually exclusive. As pointed out, it is convenient to think of these operations on the underlying form as the action of 'rule-systems', not as the sequential operation of a number of single rules, since the single rules which make them up do not operate independently of each other, and nor is it possible to combine one rule from the first system with one from the second (e.g. */dirisat/ is a non-occurring form). It thus appears that it is rule-systems which are varying with each other, and throwing up surface variation; but it also seems these systems are to be thought of as operating on the same underlying base.

One or other of the following disjunctive rule conventions could be used to capture the facts of the 'Arab data:

$$\text{CvCvC} \quad + \quad \text{aC} \longrightarrow \left\{\begin{matrix}\text{CCvCaC}\\ \text{CiCCaC}\end{matrix}\right\}$$

or

$$\text{CvCvC} \quad + \quad \text{aC} \begin{matrix}\nearrow \text{CCvCaC}\\ \searrow \text{CiCCaC}\end{matrix}$$

Both these formulations are novel. The brace notation is normally used only in the statement of an obligatory "either-or" element in the rule-environment, viz.

$$A \longrightarrow B \quad / \left\{\begin{matrix}C\\ D\end{matrix}\right\} - E$$

states that A is rewritten as B when preceded by C or D and followed by E. Our proposed formulations avoid the need for angled brackets in the statement of rule output, at the expense of adopting either a 'double-rewrite' convention or of extending the use of the brace notation. The disjunctive devices proposed neatly relate both of the types of surface forms found in the 'Arab data to a CvCvC + aC underlying form - the CvCvC stem being independently required as the base for all past tense forms.

The justification for the proposed formalism is to avoid making what would amount to arbitrary and unprovable claims: there is, in principle, no way of deciding whether CCvCaC should be derived from CvCvC + aC and then form the input to a rule which converted CCvCaC to CiCCaC, or whether CiCCaC should be derived first, and then converted to CCvCaC. Any system of rules should be ordered or non-ordered. If rules are ordered, then the ordering should have some independent, testable status. In this case, to order rules which generate CCvCaC and CiCCaC in grammars which show both kinds of form would be entirely arbitrary and have no such status. To escape this dilemma, and to avoid forcing the data into a mould into which it does not naturally fit, all that needs to be done is to relax the ordering constraint on *some* rules - one way of representing such islands of un-ordered rules is our proposed disjunctive rule schema. In short, the point we are making here is similar to that made in Chapter 5: no formalism should force us to make a decision in the way we represent data, without there being empirical evidence to justify that decision. (See Lass 1984: 211-14 for a summary of the arguments against abstract solutions to problems of phonological description.)

In what follows, the term 'disjunctive morphophonemic rule' (DMR) will be used for the type of rule proposed above. In the case cited, the DMR states that underlying CvCvC + aC must be realised in the 'Arab community as either CCvCaC or CiCCaC. In this limited sense, it accurately describes the relationship between what must be presumed to be base forms and surface variants for the 'Arab community as a whole. But it is less precise than it could be: it does not reflect the fact that the category of the verb-stem and the literacy of the speaker influence the likelihood of the 'triggering' of one of the constituent rule-systems which make up the DMR. We could, on the basis of the data, more accurately state the conditions on our DMR as follows:

```
                       → CCvCaC    //  ⟨ 1.1.    ⟨ -lit     [ +'Arab ]
(DMR 1)  CvCvC + aC                      1.3.
                       → CiCCaC          1.2.      +lit ⟩
                                         1.4. ⟩
                                      verb cat.    speaker
```

In order to interpret this we need a reading convention: the *upper* output of DMR 1 - CCvCaC - has the greatest likelihood of occurring in the context of the *upper-most* verb category (1.1.) and the *least* in the *bottom-most*. The converse also therefore holds: the lower output of the rule has the *greatest* likelihood of occurring in the context of the *bottom-most* verb category, and the least likelihood in the *top-most*. The influence of the extra-linguistic factors are interpreted as follows: whenever a speaker is [-literate] the probability of the *upper* output of DMR 1 showing up is greater in every verb category than its probability of showing up whenever a speaker is [+literate], and conversely, whenever a speaker is [+literate] the probability of the *lower* output of the rule occurring is greater than its probability of occurrence whenever a speaker is [-literate] , in every verb category.

The first DMR of 'Arab community variation thus states that all Theme 1 strong verbs having an underlying morphological form of stem plus vowel initial enclitic are realised by surface forms derived through the operation of mutually exclusive sets of vowel-deletion and conditioning rules. The rule environment states that the general likelihood of one output rather than the other occurring is determined by a ranked hierarchy specific to the 'Arab community: stems marked in the lexicon as "1.1." (to use the formulation of

Chapter 7) have a greater probability of occurring, for all speakers, as surface CCvCaC than have those marked "1.3.", which in turn have a greater probability of showing CCvCaC than those marked "1.2.". The contents of the first set of angled brackets thus represent, in a Labovian sense (though not a Labovian form), the communal aspect of the DMR: the hierarchy captures relationships between the lexical conditions for rule operation which pervade the whole community. The contents of the second set of angled brackets refine this generalisation: although, for all speakers, the relationships between lexical sets are the same, the actual likelihood of the upper or lower output occurring is related to whether a speaker is literate or not. This is illustrated below (scores taken from Table 31).

Lexical Categories (hierarchical)	OUTPUTS: CCvCaC [-lit]		CCvCaC [+lit]	CiCCaC [-lit]		CiCCaC [+lit]
↓ 1.1. ↑	.98	$>$	.95	.02	$<$	.05
	$\vee$		$\vee$	$\wedge$		$\vee$
1.3.	.80	$>$	.60	.20	$<$	.40
	$\vee$		$\vee$	$\wedge$		$\vee$
1.2.	.69	$>$	.59	.31	$<$	.41
	$\vee$		$\vee$	$\wedge$		$\vee$
1.4.	.59	$>$	.45	.41	$<$	.55

Table 38: Ranked rule-outputs in the 'Arab speech community on DMR 1

Thus in every lexical category, [-lit] speakers have a greater likelihood ("$>$") of producing CCvCaC than [+lit] speakers have; conversely, in every category, [+lit] speakers have a greater likelihood of producing CiCCaC than have [-lit] speakers ("$<$").

Looking now down the columns of figures, we note that for all speakers, the likelihood of CCvCaC showing up in category 1.1. is greater ("$\vee$") than its probability of showing up in the next category down (1.3.), which in turn has a greater probability of showing CCvCaC than the category below it (1.2.), etc. By the same token, the likelihood of CiCCaC showing up in verb category 1.4. is greater ("$\wedge$") than it is in category 1.1., etc.

The rule-systems which comprise DMR 1 must be presumed to operate only on verb forms. We have seen (Chapter 7) that feminine nouns like 'blessing' have the alternative forms /brika/ and /baraka/ in 'Arab speech, but not */birka/. Morphologically, the underlying form of such nouns is similar to that of some of the past verb forms we have been considering (the 3rd person feminine singular). Nouns like /brika/~/baraka/ can be thought of as having the underlying form:

CvCvC + a (C)
(stem) (enclitic)

The feminine nominal enclitic -/at/(c.f. MSA -/atun/) only shows up in certain genitival nominal constructions, or when a possessive enclitic is suffixed to the noun. Otherwise, the final /t/ or /at/ is deleted:

/brika/ or /baraka/ 'a blessing'
/brikat ə̈l̤lah/ }
/barakat ə̈l̤lah/ } 'God's blessing'

How can we ensure that nominals like */birka/ are not generated by the application of our DMR to underlying CvCvC + at forms which are not verbs? One solution is to make the rule sensitive to the syntactic status of the underlying form. If a lexical item which has an underlying CvCvC + a(C) structure is selected, it only qualifies as a potential input to DMR 1 if it occurs under a VP node in its derivation. If it occurs under NP (i.e. in subject or object position), a different DMR (DMR 2) operates on it. Using the same reading conventions as before, we can write this rule as follows:

$$\text{(DMR 2)}\quad \text{CvCvC + at} \begin{array}{l}\nearrow \text{CCvCat}\\ \\ \searrow \text{CvCvCat}\end{array} \Bigg/ \underset{\text{noun cat.}}{\left\langle \begin{array}{l}3.2.\\3.3.\end{array}\right\rangle} \quad \underset{\text{speaker}}{\left\langle\begin{array}{l}-\text{lit}\\+\text{lit}\end{array}\right\rangle} \quad \left[+\text{'Arab}\right]$$

Condition: CvCvC + at is dominated by NP

Final -/t/ is obligatorily deleted by a late rule, unless the specific conditions described above (suffixation or genitival construction within the NP) are met.

Alternatively, variation in CvCvC + at forms marked as nouns could be accounted for by a straightforward variable rule such as

$$\underset{[+\text{NOUN}]}{\text{CvCvC}} + \text{at} \longrightarrow \langle \text{CCvCat} \rangle \;/\; \ldots\ldots.$$

Here, if the rule fails to go through, CvCvCat appears on the surface, as the data requires. In this case, as in others which we examine below, the data does not provide any principled way of selecting between DMRs and ordinary variable rules. However, the DMR format also seems preferable in this case because it graphically suggests how an originally general phonological process in the 'Arab community which we represented in shorthand form as

$$\text{CvCvC + aC} \longrightarrow \text{CCvCaC}$$

and which operated indiscriminately on all forms having a CvCvC +aC base, whether noun or verb, seems to have become fragmented under the influence of MSA (Ch. 7). CvCvC + aC gives three possible outputs, depending on the morphological status of the base. Diagrammatically, then, while

CvCvC + aC ⟶ CCvCaC

can still account for all the nominal and verbal data of some (mainly illiterate) 'Arab, we need a device like

(DMR 1) CvCvC [+VERB] + aC ⟶ CiCCaC
 ⟶ CCvCaC

(DMR 2) CvCvC [+NOUN] + aC ⟶ CCvCaC
 ⟶ CvCvCaC

to underline the complete regularity of the correspondence between surface form and underlying morphological structure in all the variable data. As a device, ordinary variable rules would fail to reveal the fragmentation of an originally unitary rule into a number of linked and partially overlapping rule-systems. To summarise: where we are dealing with data which *could* be captured within a standard variable rule format, it seems that DMRs nonetheless provide a better notation because they display the data in a way which suggests how dialectal restructuring (Ch. 7) is proceeding.

A similar approach can be used to account for the Baḥārna data. Simple, non-disjunctive rules of an obligatory kind account for the data of those speakers for whom the correspondence between verb-stem type and surface syllabic structure is non-variable. Here, the syllabic forms we have to account for are

	B I (town)	II (village)
1.1.	daras/darasat/w	daras/darasat/w
1.2.	labas/labasat/w	libis/libsat/w
1.3.	kubar/kubrat/w	čubur/čubrat/w
1.4.	ṭala9/ṭala9at/w	ṭala9/ṭala9at/w

The categorical rules which would account for these forms, on the basis of presumed underlying forms are as follows:

(a) *illiterate town Baḥārna*

/i-a/ and /u-a/ stems (marked [-trans] in the lexicon)

(1) CiCaC + aC ⟶ CiCaCaC } rule-system
(2) V ⟶ Ø /CiC-CaC }

(/i/ and /u/ are in complimentary distribution in v_1 position: /u/ occurs only in certain environments involving combinations of velar and labial consonants)

/a-a/ stems (all stems not marked [-trans])

(3) CaCaC + aC ⟶ CaCaCaC

These three rules can account for the data of any B I speaker who has the forms exemplified as /darasat/, /labasat/, /kubrat/, etc. categorically: that is, any speaker for whom the stem category-syllabic variant correspondence is perfect.

(b) illiterate village Baḥārna

/i-i/ or /u-u/ stems

(4) CiCiC + aC ⟶ CiCiCaC } rule-system
(2) V ⟶ Ø / CiC-CaC }

(/i/ and /u/ are in complimentary distribution in v_1 position, as in the case of the town dialect, and v_2 automatically agrees in height and roundness with v_1).

/a-a/ stems

(3) CaCaC + aC ⟶ CaCaCaC

Problems arise in formulating rules to account for data where the correspondence between stem-type and surface syllable structure is not perfect, in just the same way as we noted for our 'Arab data. Literate urban speakers, we note from the data, maintain Rules (1) and (2) categorically: all verbs marked [-trans] in the lexicon undergo the v_2 deletion rule. But /a-a/ stems show variation: sometimes CaCaCaC and sometimes CiCCaC (or CuCCaC in some stems) show up in the data. Rule (3) is thus not categorical for many urban Baḥārna (mainly literates). The CiCCaC/CuCCaC-type forms which show up where Rule (3) fails to go through can be accounted for within the framework of a DMR of the type already illustrated. One of the rule-systems which comprises this rule is, of course, identical in form with one of the systems contained in the 'Arab past-tense DMR. We would again claim that as a data-displaying device this DMR is superior to the variable rule which could also, though in a less revealing way, account for it. Thus:

CaCaC + ac ⟶ CiCCaC / CaCaCaC // ⟨1.4 / 1.1. / 1.2⟩ (verb cat.) ⟨+lit / -lit⟩ (speaker)

The reading conventions for this rule are exactly as in the 'Arab case, and the hierarchy of verb categories, which is specific to the urban Baḥārna, is obtained from Table 31. If this DMR is now generalised by representing the consonantal skeleton of the stem as devoid of a specific vowel pattern (c.f. the 'Arab DMRs), it provides an accurate statement in a single DMR of urban Baḥārna variation in all verb-stem categories, including 1.3.:

$$\text{DMR 3}\quad \text{CvCvC + aC} \rightarrow \left\{ \begin{array}{l} \text{CiCCaC} \\ \text{CaCaCaC} \end{array} \right. \Bigg/ \quad \begin{array}{c} [1.3.] \\ \left\langle \begin{array}{l} 1.4. \\ 1.1. \\ 1.2. \end{array} \right\rangle \end{array} \quad \left\langle \begin{array}{l} +\text{lit} \\ -\text{lit} \end{array} \right\rangle \quad \left[\begin{array}{l} +\text{ Baḥārna} \\ +\text{ urban} \end{array} \right]$$

verb cat. speaker

Condition: CvCvC is dominated by VP

This DMR states that a verb of the underlying form CvCvC + aC is rewritten obligatorily either as CiCCaC or CaCaCaC; that CiCCaC is invariable for all Baḥārna in category 1.3. (enclosed in square brackets); that the likelihood of CiCCaC rather than CaCaCaC is greatest for all speakers in category 1.4. and least in 1.2.; that the likelihood of CaCaCaC rather than CiCCaC is, conversely, greatest in 1.2. and least in 1.4.; and that literate speakers have CiCCaC-type forms, the uppermost output, more often in any verb category in which variation occurs, than do non-literates. (Again, it should be noted that CuCCaC not CiCCaC occurs in some verb stems involving the combination of certain consonants; this however, is irrelevant to the discussion here). Table 39 provides the data base, extracted from Table 31, by which the urban Baḥārna hierarchy of environments in DMR 3 was determined.

OUTPUTS:	CiCCaC [-lit]	CiCCaC [+lit]	CaCaCaC [-lit]	CaCaCaC [+lit]
verb categories (hierarchical)				
↓ 1.3. ↑	1.0	1.0	0	0
	∨	∨	∧	∧
1.4.	.13	< .75	.87	> .25
	∨	∨	∧	∧
1.1.	0	< .40	1.0	> .60
		∨		∧
1.2.	0	< .10	1.0	> .90

Table 39: Ranked outputs in the urban Baḥārna group on DMR 3

Turning now to the village communities, we note in Table 31 a much smaller degree of difference between the literate and non-literate data. On MV1.1-1.3 all speakers had the 'basilectal' variant categorically, while on MV1.4 there was a degree of variation for both literates and non-literates. In fact, Rules (4), (2) and (3) could handle the data produced by the majority of village Baḥārna. But for those who do not maintain an absolute correspondence between stem-type and surface syllabic structure, the same DMR, DMR 3, which we proposed to account for the urban variable data, will also account for the village variable data. This may well be a linguistic reflection of the blurring of social distinctions between village and town which has resulted from the spread of an urban, literate culture. The only way, in fact, in which we need to distinguish between the town and village DMRs is in the ordering of the environment hierarchy. We accordingly designate the village DMR, DMR 3':

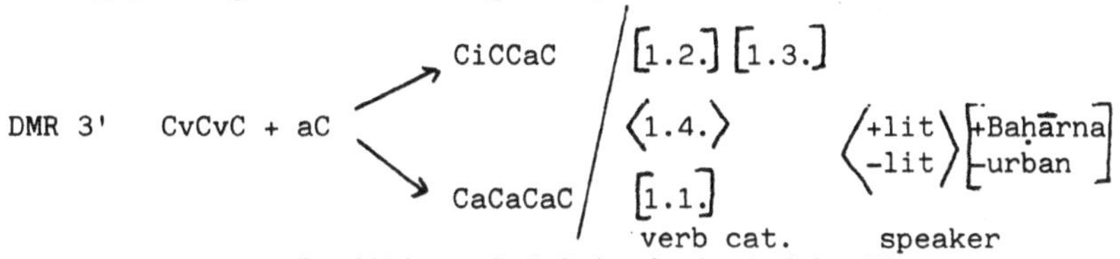

$$\text{DMR 3'} \quad \text{CvCvC} + \text{aC} \begin{array}{c} \nearrow \text{CiCCaC} \\ \searrow \text{CaCaCaC} \end{array} \Bigg/ \begin{array}{c} [1.2.][1.3.] \\ \langle 1.4. \rangle \\ [1.1.] \end{array} \quad \left\langle \begin{array}{c} +\text{lit} \\ -\text{lit} \end{array} \right\rangle \left[\begin{array}{c} +\text{Baḥārna} \\ -\text{urban} \end{array} \right]$$

verb cat.   speaker
Condition: CvCvC is dominated by VP

The square brackets indicate that in verb categories 1.2., 1.3. and 1.1. there is no variation at all in the community. According to our reading convention, this means that CiCCaC-type forms are categorical in 1.2., 1.3., while CaCaCaC is categorical in 1.1. Variation between CiCCaC and CaCaCaC occurs only in MV1.4. Speakers who are [+lit] show a greater likelihood, in this one variable environment, of showing CiCCaC-type forms than do [-lit] speakers: hence [+lit] appears above [-lit] in the statement of 'speaker context'.

DMRs are, then, proposed as data-displaying descriptive devices which express aspects of ordered communal variation of a type which is less insightfully accounted for by the usual type of non-disjunctive variable rule. They specify community-wide limits on which kinds of surface form may vary with which, and in which environments a given surface form is more or less likely to occur. The latter environments are arranged in the form of a set of hierarchical quantitative relationships. The grammars of individual speakers clearly differ in the degree to which they incorporate variability, and in the particular environments in which variation occurs; DMRs specify and summarise the gross relations between these environments which apply to all speakers.

DMRs seem to 'freeze' and display change in the community from one categorical rule-system to another. We need another device – the implicational scale – to illustrate how that change seems to be spreading. In 8.2. below, we present evidence that:

(a) non-random ranked relationships can be shown to exist between the alternative outputs of different DMRs within a single community, and not merely between the constraints on a single DMR.

(b) the procedure of letting individuals' data 'scale itself' – that is, without an a priori division of speakers according to literacy – sometimes leads to a ranking of DMR output –

constraints different from that arrived at by calculating them on the group basis which we have employed so far. A high degree of regularity ('scaleability') of patterning is also revealed. The community's linguistic repertoire in fact manifests itself as a relatively small number of scaled, interlinked grammars. Generally speaking, for all communities, the correlation between which of these grammars a speaker uses and certain apparently relevant social facts about him is quite loose - it is quite possible to find widely different combinations of literate/illiterate, old/young, male/female speakers sharing the 'same' grammar.

(c) quantification of variation in individual cases does not show any regular patterning to justify the further refinement of a three-valued scale, though it is possible to argue that a much bigger data base might have provided a justification for such a refinement.

8.2 Implicational scales and DMR constraints

In the non-past verb, the 'Arab 'dialectalness' scores - that is, the global percentage of tokens showing the resyllabicated variant - were as follows (extracted from Table 27):

	MV:	2.2.	2.3.	2.4.	2.5.	2.6.
Literates (N=17)		.98	.83	.75	.65	.47
Illiterates (N=17)		.98	.92	1.0	1.0	.65

The probability of the resyllabicated variant occurring progressively decreases in the literate data from MV2.2. to 2.6., but no such pattern is apparent in the illiterate data. Thus, whereas a particular verb's membership of one or other stem or categories is related in general to the likelihood of a particular output of a DMR occurring, it would appear at first sight from these global scores that the <u>ordering</u> of constraints in a DMR expressing variation in the suffixed, non-past Theme 1 verb is not the same for literates and illiterates in the same community: that is, the ordering of constraints is <u>not</u> communal. However, if we simply assign to each <u>individual</u> speaker a + (resyllabicated variants only), a - (non-resyllabicated variants only) or a 0 (variation between the two types of form) we obtain Scalogram 6.

The apparent difference between the relative strengths of the constraining environments as between literates and illiterates, which is suggested by the global scores, is shown by the scalogram to be more an artefact of the mode of analysis than a real feature of the situation: as soon as the individual speaker becomes the focus of attention, the irregularities in the data disappear for the most part and the majority of speakers, literate and illiterate alike, can be accommodated within a single, three-valued scaled matrix.

Speaker	Sex	Age	Literacy	Verb-stem categories				
				/i/-stems		/a/-stems		
				MV: 2.2.	2.3.	2.4.	2.5.	2.6.
118	m	30	L	0	-	-	-	-
150	m	45	NL	0	0			-
104	m	20	L	0	0		0	-
93	m	19	L	0	0	0	0	
100	m	18	L	0	0	0	0	0
144	m	26	L	0	0		0	0
13	m	17	L	+	0		0	
119	m	20	L	+	+	0	0	0
122	f	26	L	+	+		0	0
101	f	19	L	+			0	0
95	m	20	L		+	0	0	
103	f	21	L	+	+		+	0
10	f	40	NL	+	+		+	0
18	f	40	NL	+	+		+	0
2	f	50	NL	+	+	+		
21	f	40	NL	+	+		+	0
116	m	40	L	+	+		+	+
145	f	48	NL	+	0	+	+	+
147	f	46	NL	+	0		+	+
120	f	20	L	0	0	+		+
85	f	19	L	+	0	+	+	
7	m	60	NL	+	+	+		+
6	m	55	NL	+	+	+	+	+
146	m	70	NL	+		+	+	+
14	f	21	L	+	+			+
105	m	20	L	+	+	+	+	
22	f	45	NL		+	+	+	+
19	f	40	NL		+		+	+
8	m	55	NL			+		+
109	f	17	L		+		+	
1	f	60	NL			+	+	
5	m	60	NL	+				+
134	f	45	NL	+			+	+
4	m	70	NL				+	

Scalogram 6: Non-past suffixed forms - 'Arab speakers

% cells filled: 73%. Unfilled cells = no data.

Scaleability: 97%

If speakers' choice between +, -, and 0 were not internally constrained - that is, if choice between categorical presence of the resyllabicated variant, categorical absence of it, and variation between the 'resyllabicated' and 'non-resyllabicated' variants were a purely random matter - then the number of possible 'grammars' that is, combinations of +, - and 0 over the five stem-categories MV2.2 to 2.6 would be $3^5 = 243$. In fact, including the grammars of the few individuals which do not scale, only 8 grammars actually occur for the 34 speakers. Choice between +, -, and 0 is clearly non-random - in fact it is powerfully constrained: "0" in any given environment implies "0" or "-" in the cell to its right; "+" in any environment implies "+" in all environments to its left; "-" implies "-" in all environments to its right. These constraints hold across the whole 'Arab community.

The advantage of the scalogram is that it can show in tabular form the communal constraints on variation at a particular moment in time, as well as suggest what the past history, and future direction of change in a community may be. Scalogram 6, for example, shows that the change from a grammar which has the resyllabicated variant categorically (+++++) in all environments, to one which has the non-resyllabicated variant categorically (-----) involves a number of intermediate grammars: reading from the bottom of the scalogram to the top, variation begins with /a/-stemmed verbs (MV2.4.-2.6) and spreads from right to left across the scalogram. The change from variability to the complete zeroing out of the resyllabicated variants ("0" to "-") also proceeds in the same manner: from left to right (from /a/-stems to /i/-stems) and from bottom to top. An individual 'grammar', in the implicationalist sense of the term being used here, means any possible row of "+", "-", and "0", whether or not any actual speaker fits it. In this sense, implicationalists would claim (De Camp 1971:35) that the scale which relates the grammars to each other specifies the theoretically possible range of individual grammars within the community. We have some reservations about this claim which are explained in 8.3 below.

Interestingly, Scalogram 6 suggests that the correlation between a speaker's social identity, in terms of the criteria we have been using, and the grammar he 'occupies', is quite loose: although there is a tendency for the literate and younger 'Arab to occupy positions at the top of the scalogram (that is, they occupy grammars in which the resyllabicated variant occurs less often, or hardly at all), the relationship between social identity and grammar-type is not very clearly defined. This confirms our earlier finding for the 'Arab community (5.10) that the literates feel less need to distance themselves from the illiterates: as the dominant social group, the 'Arab tend to preserve their linguistic homogeneity quite strongly, despite the influence of MSA.

Although the calculation of global scores of "dialectalness" in the way described in Chapters 5 and 7 may give an approximate idea of the relative strengths of constraints on rule-outputs for whole groups, as a method it necessarily obscures some types of internal structuring which the scaling of data on an individual basis highlights. A simple example will illustrate the point. If four speakers each operated a variable rule in a given environment 60% of the time, we could say that the constraining strength of the environment was the same for each individual and for the group as a whole. But if four other speakers happened to operate the same rule respectively 100%, 80%, 60%, and 0% of the time, the average constraining strength of the environment for the group would be the same as in the first case: 60%. Such a 'group' approach clearly falsifies individual data in this second case: individuals are arbitrarily depicted as varying from a group norm.

The scalogram gives a more accurate picture of the latter four speakers' data by assigning a "+" to the speaker who applied the rule 100% of the time, a "-" to the one who failed to apply it at all, and a "0" to the other two. It is generally assumed by implicational theorists that quantified levels of variability have no significance in the set of grammars which are represented in an implicational scale. Hence there is no ordering principle to distinguish between the grammar of a speaker who operates a rule 80% of the time, and one who operates it 60% of the time, except by reference to the grammars of other members of the same community. For example, in Scalogram 6, speakers 93. 100, and 144 all have, on the implicational analysis, grammars which are in no significant respect different from each other. If we had to construct a scalogram of ordered grammars on the basis of their data alone, we would not be able to do it: since all three speakers have variable outputs in all environments, there is no possibility of ordering these environments with respect to each other. But in fact it is possible to arrive at an ordering because there are other speakers from the same community whose grammars differ from those of speakers 93, 100 and 144 in relevant respects. If synchronic variation is visualised as the product of on-going change from the categorical application of a rule or set of rules to categorical non-application thereof, often via variability; and if it is accepted that such change, which takes place in real time, may affect members of a community in a non-simultaneous manner for social or geographical reasons, then the internal structure of the grammars of speakers other than 93, 100 and 144, who are from the same community, will provide a principled basis for ordering the constraints in these three speakers' cases. This is because, given a large enough speaker sample, there will be some speakers who have not yet been affected by changes which have affected 93, 100 and 144. Specifically, the grammars of speakers 13, 119, 95, 103, 10, 18 and 21 differ from those of speakers 93, 100 and 144 in the following respects:

(a) S 13 orders MV2.2 with respect to MV2.3 (+ 0)

(b) S 119 order MV2.3 with respect to MV2.4 (+ 0)
S 95

(c) S 103
S 10 order MV2.5 with respect ot MV2.6 (+ 0)
S 18
S 21

As for the ordring of MV2.4 and 2.5 with respect to each other, the data is neutral: the order of these two environments could be reversed without any overall loss of scaleability. This fact suggests that for the 'Arab community, there may after all be no real basis for distinguishing between these two verb-stem types in the statement of the DMR constraints: a possibility which was obscured by treating the data 'globally'.

The principle involved in implicational scaling is that of achieving maximum internal regularity in the set of grammars which the scalogram represents without recourse to recording quantified levels of variation in individual grammars. According to implicational theorists, it is the mere fact of individual variation which is sociolinguistically significant - that is, whether a rule-change has reached an individual or not - and not whether, if it has reached him, it happens to go through 15%, 50% or 80% of the time in the data collected from that individual. If, in our particular case, we were to substitute actual frequencies of rule application for the "0"s in Scalogram 6, the level of scaleability would be considerably reduced, in whatever way we rearranged the order of speakers or environments. It is, however, quite possible that where the degree of non-scaleability is increased, the reasons are fortuitous: some of the speakers in Scalogram 6 were assigned a "0" on the basis of only 3 or 4 tokens. An extra token or two might have considerably altered the percentage of times they are depicted as applying/not applying the rule in certain more rarely occurring environments. Despite the relatively large size of our data base, we are therefore not in a position to judge whether a more finely grained scale (such as that demonstrated in Wolfram 1969:59-69) would work with our data: there is simply not enough of it for certain speakers in certain environments. This being so, we stick to a three-valued scale in what follows, since it at least enables us to construct a gradatum which embodies a regular and plausible change from categorical rule application across five environments (+++++) to categorical non-application.

We are now in a position to revise the original formulation of the scope of, and notational devices used in, our DMRs in the light of the following considerations:

(a) The ordering of environments should be determined by individual data-scaling (three-valued or quantitative, if sufficient data is available) rather than by calculating global figures for the community. The latter procedure risks obscuring some types of internal regularity, and depicts individuals as 'varying' with respect to a group mean.

(b) Scalogram 6 indicates that the following types of grammar can be distinguished in the community:

(i) grammars which show categorical application of a single rule-system in all environments. (Examples: Speakers 116, 7, 6)

(ii) grammars in which this rule-system sometimes applies and sometimes does not, in one or more environments (Examples: Speakers 21, 95, 100)

(iii) grammars in which this rule-system never applies (No example of such a grammar in the scalogram, but Speaker 118 has a grammar which has almost reached this point).

We do not need a DMR to account for cases (i) and (iii): speakers who have non-variable grammars apply one of two different rule-systems to produce surface forms, but never vary between the two. But DMRs are needed to account for all the cases where speakers have grammars which show variable application of the 'rival' rule-systems for the same reasons as those advanced to account for the past-tense data: it would be quite arbitrary to 'derive' the output of one of these rule-systems from the other by an empirically untestable ordering principle - and such an ordering of outputs with respect to each other is precisely what is implied by the linear format in which standard variable rule notation is cast.

Individual grammars are, as we have seen, minimally different from each other, and represent the gradual spread of change from case (i) above to case (iii). A single DMR will account for all the ranked grammars described by case (ii), correctly depicting the differences between them notationally, as marginal changes in the scope of each of the constituent rule-systems of the DMR. We give a detailed account of how this would work below.

Case (i): grammars with categorical rule-system application (+ + + + +)

The outputs of this grammar (perhaps more accurately 'grammar fragment') can be generated by a single rule-system which converts all occurrences of underlying

$$\left\{\begin{matrix} y \\ t \end{matrix}\right\} \mathrm{vCCvC} + \left\{\begin{matrix} v \\ \bar{v} \end{matrix}\right\} \mathrm{C}$$

into surface

$$\left\{\begin{matrix} y \\ t \end{matrix}\right\} \mathrm{(v)CvCC} \left\{\begin{matrix} v \\ \bar{v} \end{matrix}\right\} \mathrm{C}$$

This rule system consists of the following four phonological rules, which operate together in an all-or-nothing way. Again, the complete absence of 'medial' forms involving the application of some but not all of these rules suggests they are treated as a single unit by all speakers:

1. $$\underset{\text{non-p.stem}}{v} \longrightarrow \emptyset \ / \ C\text{–}\$$$

   'The vowel of a non-past stem is deleted if it occurs in open syllable'.

2. $$\emptyset \longrightarrow v / C\text{–}CC$$

   'An epenthetic vowel is inserted between the first and second consonant of a three-consonant cluster'. This rule feeds off the output of Rule 1 (see below). The height of this vowel is automatically determined by the consonantal environment: if C_1 or C_2 of the cluster is a 'guttural' v is [-high], otherwise it is [+high].

3. (a) $$\underset{[+\text{long}]}{v} \longrightarrow [+\text{stress}]$$

   (b) $$v \longrightarrow [+\text{stress}] / \ C\text{–}C\$$$

   'Long vowels are always stressed; in the absence of long vowels, short vowels in non-final closed syllables are stressed.' (These two rules are sub-routines of the general stress rule for BA.)

4. $$\underset{[-\text{stress}]}{v} \longrightarrow (\emptyset) \ / \ C\text{–}\$$$

   'Short unstressed vowels in open syllable are optionally deleted.'

Following this schema, the derivations for two sample surface forms - /ykit'bu:n/ (/i/-stemmed verb, stem category 2.3) 'they write' and /t'la9bah/ (/a/-stemmed verb, stem category 2.6) 'you (m.s.) play it' are:

underlying:	yaktib + u:n	til9ab + ah
delete morpheme boundaries:	yaktibu:n	til9abah
by Rule 1:	yaktbu:n	til9bah
by Rule 2:	yakitbu:n	tila9bah
by Rule 3 (a):	yakit'bu:n	-
by Rule 3 (b):	-	ti'la9bah
by Rule 4:	ykit'bu:n	t'la9bah

(Note: surface /t'la9bə/ is also possible through the optional raising of [a] to [ə] and the deletion of final h, as exemplified throughout Chapter 7).

Speakers who show the resyllabicated variant categorically can then be regarded as operating a rule-system which collapses Rules 1 to4. In shorthand form, this rule-system is

$$\begin{Bmatrix} y \\ t \end{Bmatrix} vCCvC + \begin{Bmatrix} \underline{v} \\ v \end{Bmatrix} C \longrightarrow \begin{Bmatrix} y \\ t \end{Bmatrix} (v)CvCC \begin{Bmatrix} \underline{v} \\ v \end{Bmatrix} C$$

Case (iii): grammars with categorical non-application of the resyllabicating rule-system (- - - - -)

No perfect example of such a grammar occurred in our data. The nearest to it was Speaker 118 who had (0 - - - -). A (- - - - -) grammar would be one which had completely lost the 'Arab basilectal rule-system which produces categorically resyllabicated forms. All instances of forms whose underlying morphological structure is

$$\begin{Bmatrix} y \\ t \end{Bmatrix} vCCvC + \begin{Bmatrix} v \\ \bar{v} \end{Bmatrix} C$$

would, in such a grammar, simply fail to undergo the 'resyllabicating' rule-system and their surface syllabic structure would be the same as that which is postulated to underlie them.

Case (ii): grammars in which the application of the resyllabicating rule-system is variable in one or more environments

Variation refers to variation between morphophonemic rule-systems and not, as pointed out, to the variable application of one or more of the constituent phonological rules of those systems. To use our DMR notation:

$$\begin{Bmatrix} y \\ t \end{Bmatrix} vCCvC + \begin{Bmatrix} v \\ \bar{v} \end{Bmatrix} C \quad \begin{array}{l} \nearrow \begin{Bmatrix} y \\ t \end{Bmatrix} vCCvC \begin{Bmatrix} v \\ \bar{v} \end{Bmatrix} C \\ \\ \searrow \begin{Bmatrix} y \\ t \end{Bmatrix} (v)CvCC \begin{Bmatrix} v \\ \bar{v} \end{Bmatrix} C \end{array}$$

This DMR will generate, for the whole community, the output of grammars which are intermediate between the categorical application of the rule-system which generates the lower output (+ + + + +) and its categorical non-application (- - - - -) from the same base forms. An inspection of Scalogram 6 shows how these intermediate grammars are ranked. Speaker 116's data can be accounted for by assuming that the DMR may be constrained as follows:

$$\begin{Bmatrix} y \\ t \end{Bmatrix} vCCvC + \begin{Bmatrix} v \\ \bar{v} \end{Bmatrix} C \quad \begin{array}{l} \nearrow \begin{Bmatrix} y \\ t \end{Bmatrix} vCCvC \begin{Bmatrix} v \\ \bar{v} \end{Bmatrix} C \\ \\ \\ \searrow \begin{Bmatrix} y \\ t \end{Bmatrix} (v)CvCC \begin{Bmatrix} v \\ \bar{v} \end{Bmatrix} C \end{array} \quad \Bigg/ \quad \begin{array}{c} [\emptyset] \\ \langle 2.6. \rangle \\ \begin{bmatrix} 2.5. \\ 2.4. \\ 2.3. \\ 2.2. \end{bmatrix} \end{array}$$

That is, the resyllabicated variant occurs categorically in verb-stem categories MV2.5 - 2.2. Only in MV2.6. does Speaker 116 show variability - hence the position of this verb-stem category between the lower and upper outputs of the DMR, and the angled brackets arount it. The symbol $[\emptyset]$ against the top output means that this output was never produced categorically in any one verb-stem category by Speaker 116. For Speaker 119, by contrast, the scope of the constituent rule-systems of the DMR is different: that is, the <u>ordering</u> of the constraining environments is the same as for Speaker 116 (as it is for all speakers in Scalogram 6, except for Speakers 145, 147, 120 and 85), but the <u>locii of variation</u> are different. For Speaker 119, the order of constraints on the DMR reads:

$$
\begin{array}{c}
\ldots\ldots\ldots\ldots\ \ [\emptyset] \\
\left\langle \begin{array}{c} 2.6. \\ 2.5. \\ 2.4. \end{array} \right\rangle \\
\ldots\ldots\ldots\ \ \left[\begin{array}{c} 2.3. \\ 2.2. \end{array} \right]
\end{array}
$$

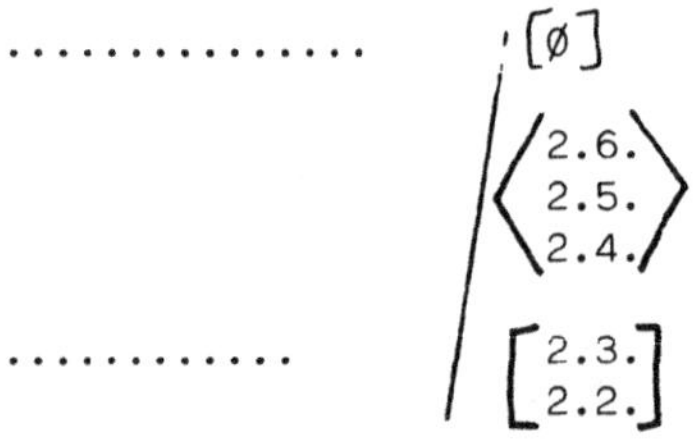

Compared to Speaker 116, Speaker 119 has 'moved' two verb-stem categories into the 'variable' bracket.

In Speaker 104's case, the constraint on the operation of the resyllabicating rule-system has become categorical in MV2.6, and all other verb-stem categories have moved into the 'variable' bracket:

$$
\begin{array}{c}
\ldots\ldots\ldots\ \ [2.6.] \\
\left\langle \begin{array}{c} 2.5. \\ 2.4. \\ 2.3. \\ 2.2. \end{array} \right\rangle \\
\ldots\ldots\ \ [\emptyset]
\end{array}
$$

The symbol $[\emptyset]$ now appears in the environment, level with the non-resyllabicated output, since in no verb-stem category is this output produced categorically by Speaker 104. Turning now to Speaker 118, the scope of variation in the DMR is

$$
\begin{array}{c}
\ldots\ldots\ldots\quad \begin{array}{c} 2.6. \\ 2.5. \\ 2.4. \\ 2.3. \end{array} \\
 \\
\quad\quad\ 2.2. \\
\ldots\ldots\ \ [\emptyset]
\end{array}
$$

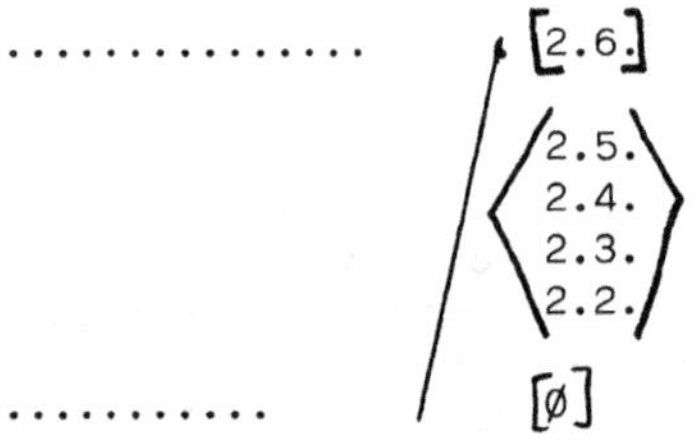

Here the DMR has reached the point where the resyllabicating rule-system almost fails to apply at all: it only applies, variably, in one category of verb-stem. Although we have no

example in the data, it is tempting to surmise that there may be some speakers in the 'Arab community who have gone one stage further, and do not resyllabicate suffixed non-pasts at all. The existence of such speakers is strongly suggested by the scalogram.

The scaling of data can be seen as a heuristic device for arriving at a communal ordering of constraining environments on the outputs of DMRs by reference to individuals' speech data. The DMR itself is a 'summarising' statement of communal variation, and not a model of individual cognition. From the point of view of sociolinguistic description, the formats of data-display we have proposed perspicuously represent both individual differences in the scope of variation in the community, at the same time as highlighting what are clearly communal trends.

8.3 Implicational relationships between DMRs

In this section, we illustrate the fact that the outputs of different DMRs - those for suffixed past verbs and suffixed non-past verbs for example - are themselves implicationally scaled. That is, variability/non-variability in the output of one DMR, is regularly related to variability/non-variability in the output of another. This is perhaps unsurprising: the DMR is no more than a way of displaying communal change-in-progress in one small part of the language, which is part of a more general process of change affecting many parts of it at the same time. A scalogram showing the implicational relationships which exist across DMRs can be considered a specification of communal co-occurrence restrictions: it specifies, for example, which type of syllable structure in a given non-past verb-stem category, may co-occur with which type of syllable structure in a given past verb-stem category, across the whole community. We illustrate how this seems to work in practice below, using the 'Arab data for pasts and non-past verbs.

(i) The DMR for suffixed non-pasts

We designate this DMR, DMR 4. As already noted, it has the form

$$\begin{Bmatrix} y \\ t \end{Bmatrix} \text{vCCvC} + \begin{Bmatrix} \text{v} \\ \bar{\text{v}} \end{Bmatrix} \begin{cases} \nearrow \begin{Bmatrix} y \\ t \end{Bmatrix} \text{vCCvC} \begin{Bmatrix} \text{v} \\ \bar{\text{v}} \end{Bmatrix} \text{C} \\ \searrow \begin{Bmatrix} y \\ t \end{Bmatrix} \text{(v) CvCC} \begin{Bmatrix} \text{v} \\ \bar{\text{v}} \end{Bmatrix} \text{C} \end{cases}$$

From Scalogram 6, we noted that only the following combinations of categorical/variable rule-system applications occurred in the scaleable data:

(DMR 4.1)

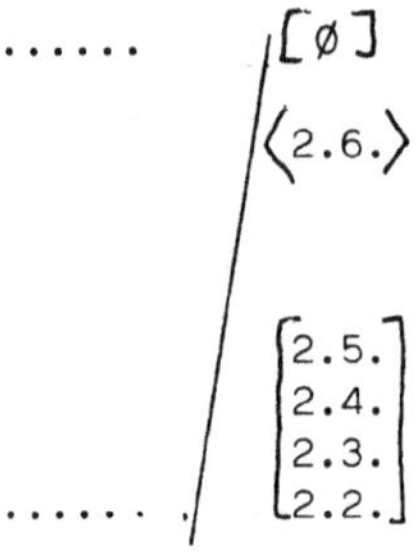

Example: S 21

(DMR 4.2)

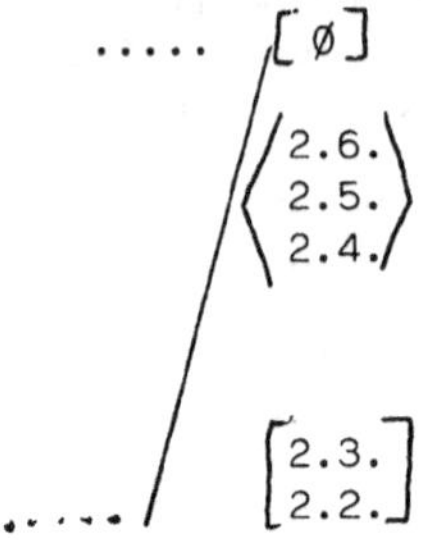

Example: S 119

(DMR 4.3)

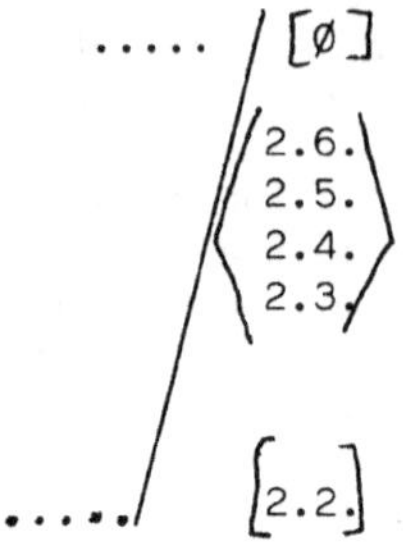

Example: S 13

(DMR 4.4)

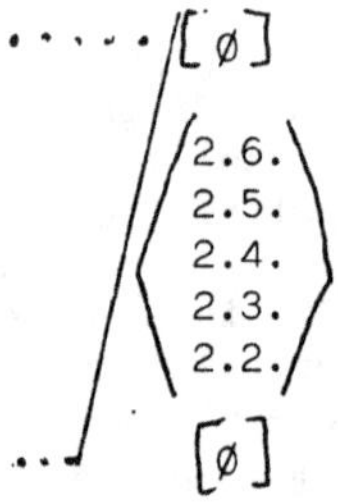

Example: S 100

(DMR 4.5)

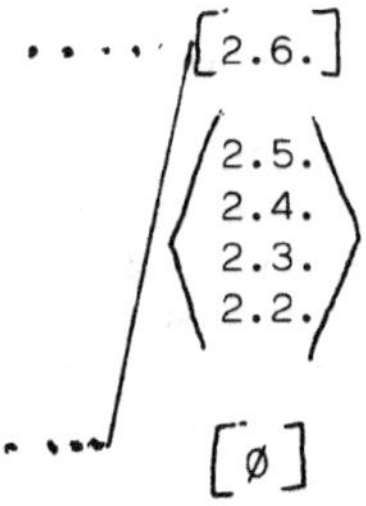

Example: S 93

(DMR 4.6)

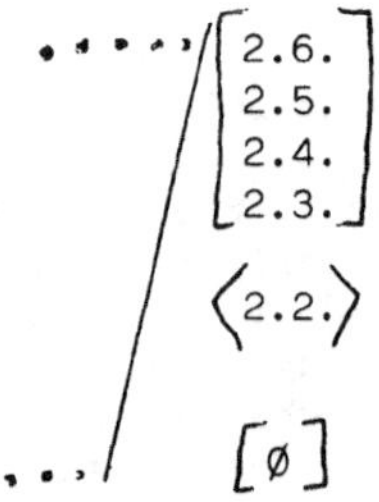

Example: S 118

(ii) The DMR for suffixed pasts

DMR 1 CvCvC + aC → CCvCaC
→ CiCCaC

Condition: CvCvC is dominated by VP

The data shows that only the following combinations of variable/ categorical application of each rule-system occurred:

(DMR 1.1)

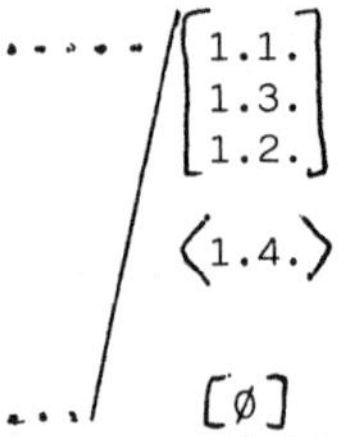

Example: S 10

(DMR 1.2)

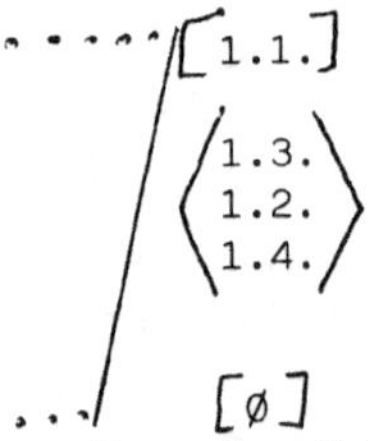

Example: S 119

(DMR 1.3)

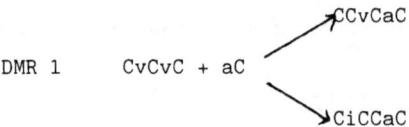

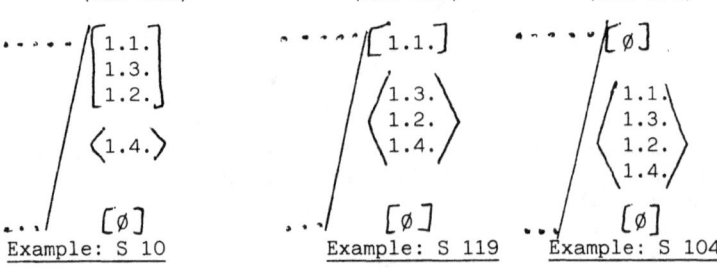

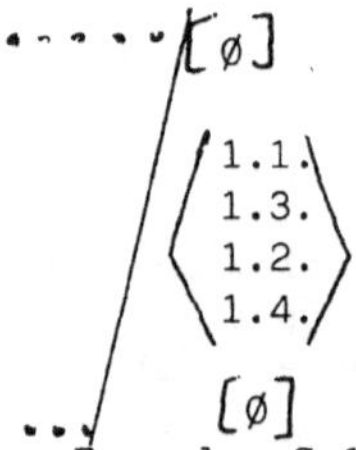

Example: S 104

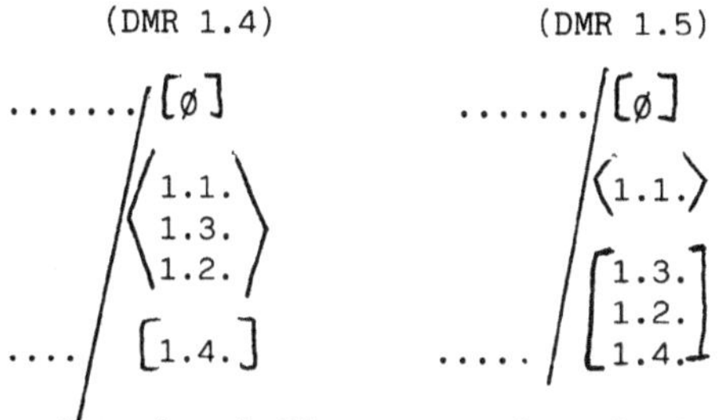

Example: S 85 Example:S 118

Speaker	Sex	Age	Literacy	2.3	1.3	2.6	1.4	Origin	Occupation
118	m	30	L	–	–	–	–	Muḥarraq	teacher
150	m	45	NL	0	–	–	0	Al-Ḥūra	watchman
13	m	17	L	0		–	–	Muḥarraq	teleph'nist
93	m	19	L	0	–		–	Salmāniya	student
147	f	46	NL	0		+	–	Al-Ḥūra	housewife
85	f	19	L	0	0		–	Al-Ḥidd	student
145	f	48	NL	0		+	–	Muḥarraq	housewife
120	f	20	L	0	0	+	0	Muḥarraq	bank-clerk
144	m	26	L	0	0	+		Muḥarraq	technician
104	m	20	L	0	0	0	0	Al-Ḥūra	student
100	m	18	L	0		0	0	Muḥarraq	student
109	f	17	L	+	–		0	Al-Fāḍil	school-girl
119	m	20	L	+	0	0	0	W.Rifāʿ	student
19	f	40	NL	+	0			Salmāniya	housewife
122	f	26	L	+	0	0		Al-Ḥūra	social-w'kr
2	f	50	NL	+	+	0	–	Al-Ḥidd	housewife
21	f	40	NL	+	+	0		Guḍaybiya	housewife
10	f	40	NL	+	+	0	0	E.Rifāʿ	cleaner
18	f	40	NL	+	+	0	0	Gufūl	housewife
103	f	21	L	+	+	0	0	W.Rifāʿ	student
101	f	19	L		+	+		E.Rifāʿ	student
146	m	70	NL	+	+	+		Al-Ḥūra	ex-diver
22	f	45	NL	+	+	+	0	Al-Ḥidd	housewife
8	m	55	NL	+	+	+		Budayyaʿ	ex-diver
7	m	60	NL	+	+	+	+	Muḥarraq	ex-diver
6	m	55	NL	+	+	+		Muḥarraq	ex-diver
1	f	60	NL	+	+	+	+	Al-Ḥidd	housewife
116	m	40	L	+	+		+	Al-Ḥidd	govt clerk
4	m	70	NL	+	+		+	Muḥarraq	ex-diver
5	m	60	NL	+	+			Muḥarraq	ex-diver
105	m	20	L	+	+		+	Al-Ḥūra	student
95	m	20	L	+	+	+		Salmāniya	student
134	f	45	NL		+		+	Budayyaʿ	cleaner
14	f	21	L		+		+	Muḥarraq	bank clerk

% filled cells: 80% (empty cells = no data)
% scaleability: 94%

Scalogram 7: 'Arab data on 4 verb-stem categories

Scalogram 7 shows how these different arrays of variably and categorically constraining environments on these two DMRs are related to each other in a regular way. As in Scalogram 6, "+" represents categorical operation of what we have been terming the 'dialectal' rule-systems. That is to say that, in the case of environments 1.4 and 1.3, "+" means that a speaker always had CCvCaC-type variants; in the case of environments 2.6 and 2.3, "+" means that a speaker always had variants of the $\begin{Bmatrix} y \\ t \end{Bmatrix}$(v)CvCC$\begin{Bmatrix} v \\ \bar{v} \end{Bmatrix}$C - type. The symbol "-" signifies the total absence of these dialectal variants in any environment against which "-" occurs, and "0" signifies variation between these variants and CiCCaC (in environments 1.4 and 1.3), and $\begin{Bmatrix} y \\ t \end{Bmatrix}$vCCvC$\begin{Bmatrix} v \\ \bar{v} \end{Bmatrix}$C (in environemnts 2.6 and 2.3).

The scalogram has been constructed using only four of the ten environments in which the two DMRs operate, for simple lack of space. MV2.3 and 2.6 were selected to represent, respectively, variation in /i/-stemmed and /a/-stemmed non-pasts and, similarly, MV1.3 and MV1.4 were selected as representative, respectively, of past verb stems in which the MSA stem vowel is high, and low.

Scalogram 7 shows clearly how 'simple' implicational scales confined to one set of related environments combine with each other to form complex scales, suggesting the simultaneous but gradual spread of change in different parts of the language system. The scalogram does not, of course explain the motivation for change - the question we dealt with at length in the previous chapter - nor why change seems to have affected some speakers and not others who appear on paper to have similar backgrounds in terms of education, age, geographical provenance, etc. This latter question is dealt with briefly in 8.4 below. What Scalogram 7 does clearly indicate, however, is that co-occurrence restrictions between apparently unrelated rule-systems do exist, and that these restrictions are community-wide: only 7 out of 34 speakers have 'grammars' which fail to fit in with these restrictions, and in each of these 7 cases, the irregularity occurs in only one out of 4 environments.

In some sense, the speakers in Scalogram 7 must 'know' of the existence of the co-occurrence restrictions which the scalogram specifies; but this kind of knowledge is a knowledge of what, in the 'Arab community, is appropriate language use, and not knowledge in the sense of grammatical rules (i.e. cognitive schemata). In other words, an 'Arab speaker knows, and might be able to articulate the fact, that a speaker from his community whom he hears regularly using a certain linguistic item X is likely/bound to use certain other (possibly formally quite unrelated) items Y and Z as well. This does not mean, however, that the relationship between X, Y and Z should be characterised as a 'rule of grammar' which 'Arab 'know' in the sense that it is part of their linguistic competence. It is a 'rule' (if that is the correct term) of community language use.

Leaving aside for a moment the non-scaleable data in Scalogram 7, we can extrapolate Table 40 (below) as a summary of the occurring output-combinations of our two DMRs. For the sake of clarity, these output-combinations will be referred to in the rest of this discussion as 'lects' rather than 'grammars' because of the ambiguity inherent in this latter term. The variant-types are exemplified by four verbs.

	2.3	1.3	2.6	1.4
No variation				
e.g. S 118	yaskinu:n	kubrat	yil9abu:n	ṭil9at
Lects with variability				
(i) e.g. S 13	yaskinu:n/ ysiknu:n	kubrat	yil9abu:n	ṭil9at
(ii) e.g. S 85	yaskinu:n/ ysiknu:n	kubrat/ kbarat	yil9abu:n/ yla9bu:n	ṭil9at
(iii) e.g. S 104	yaskin:n/ ysiknu:n	kubrat/ kbarat	yil9abu:n/ yla9bu:n	ṭil9at/ ṭla9at
(iv) e.g. S 119	ysiknu:n	kubrat/ kbarat	yil9abu:n/ yla9bu:n	ṭil9at/ ṭla9at
(v) e.g. S 10	ysiknu:n	kbarat	yil9abu:n/ yla9bu:n	ṭil9at/ ṭla9at
(vi) e.g. S 22	ysiknu:n	kbarat	yla9bu:n	ṭil9at/ ṭla9at
No variation				
e.g. S 7	ysiknu:n	kbarat	yla9bu:n	ṭla9at

Table 40: Scaled lects in the 'Arab community

It is clear that there are some possible lects which would fit into this scale, but which were not represented by actual data. For example,

	2.3	1.3	2.6	1.4
(a)	yaskinu:n/ysiknu:n	kubrat/kbarat	yil9abu:n	ṭil9at

would fit between lects (i) and (ii) in Table 40. On the other hand, some actually occurring lects (e.g. those of Speakers 150, 147, 145, etc. - see Scalogram 7) do not fit into Table 40. These facts need some explanation.

Where scaleable lects such as (a) above are, as it were,

'predicted' by the procedure of scaling but do not show up in the data, the most likely explanation is that they do in fact occur, but so rarely in the particular circumstances in which the data was collected, or even in an absolute sense, in the community at large, that they escaped detection. There is no reason to suppose that all the lects in a 'polylectal grammar' (to use the implicationalist term for what a scalogram specifies) are equally thickly populated, or that, in a narrow range of data collection contexts, all the lects allowable in that context will be successfully sampled.

Deviant lects pose a more serious problem for the implicationalist, especially if a consistent pattern of deviance, such as is manifested in Scalogram 7 by Speakers 147, 145, 120 and 144 occurs. This gives rise to the suspicion that implicational analysis may fail to capture the full range of permitted lects in the community. A more realistic claim for implicational analysis than De Camp's, who avers it 'generates a theoretical model of polylectal competence in the community, which underlies individual performance' (1971:35), might be that it indicates the most likely route for individuals to follow in moving, stylistically or in real time, from one lect to another. Ideally, what is needed is a complete description of every lect found in the community, including the 'deviant' ones, supplemented by a comparative commentary on the relations between them (Hudson 1980:188). In our case, we are satisfied that Scalogram 7 does indeed capture regular patterns of communal variation, and specifies the ranking of a large number of lects, though some are left unaccounted for. To the practical sociolinguist, the validity of a scalogram is to be judged simply according to the number of exceptional lects and deviant cells it contains: if scaleability drops below a certain level (usually 85%), then further research into the variables which are being related to each other, or into the extent to which the speakers whose data is being examined are really part of the same community, is called for. In this sense too, implicational scaling is a heuristic device.

8.4 Dialect-type and social network

As far as the relationship between sociological factors and lect is concerned, both Scalograms 6 and 7 suggest that it is unnecessary to include a factor such as literacy in the statement of constraints on DMRs, contrary to our original formulation. Although it is true that literate speakers tend to cluster around the 're-structured' lects at the top of each scalogram, and the illiterates around lects, which, we have argued, represent older layers of the 'Arab dialect, the correlation between lect and literacy is by no means perfect. Gal (1979) has argued for the existence of a more subtle relationship between lect and social identity based on the notion of 'speech networks': that is, the group of people with whom a speaker regularly associates and with whom he identifies himself socially (rather than those who, on paper, seem to be his social peers) exercises a powerful influence on his speech which may conflict with what would be predicted by a prima facie 'objective' analysis of his social position. An example will illustrate the point.

Speaker 150, who had one of the least 'basilectal', most 'restructured' lects in the 'Arab group, was an illiterate 50-year-old man from Al-Ḥūra, East Manāma, who was working as a night watchman in an Adult Literacy Centre. As a young man, he had worked as a pearl-diver. Many men of similar background, however, (e.g. Speakers 6, 7 and 8) had quite markedly different 'unrestructured' dialects. A sociological description which simply noted the facts that Speakers 150, 6, 7 and 8 were all poor, aged over 50, illiterate, 'Arab and ex-pearl-divers would fail to explain the socially motivated differences in their speech behaviour.

Speakers 6, 7 and 8 were all leading members of a "dār" - a kind of all-male club specialising in the performance of folkloric arts such as singing, poetry recitation and story-telling. All three were close friends and spent much of their time talking and smoking at the dār, participating in its activities, and reminiscing about the Baḥrain of the pre-oil era. None showed the slightest interest in modern inventions such as cars, television or the cinema, but would discuss for hours on end the merits of various kinds of long-since vanished pearling dhows, and argue about the precise location of pearl-beds which they had not visited for more than twenty years.

Speaker 150, though an ex-diver too, was frank about the hardships of life at sea and how he had hated it. He had given it up after a few years to work for a succession of foreign companies as an odd-job man, driver and so on. He had been particularly anxious to ensure that his sons should not suffer the same fate as himself, and had (unusually for a Baḥraini of his generation) made sure that they all got a good education. One of his children, of whom he was particularly proud, was now a successful heart-specialist. Speaker 150 had many educated friends of his own age (and younger) and whenever his work allowed, he attended literacy classes at the Literacy Centre where he worked as a watchman. While not accepting all the 'blessings' of Western civilisation which have come to Baḥrain in the last 30-40 years, Speaker 150 was unusually outspoken and unromantic about the ignorance and hardships of life during his youth.

Both in his attitudinal set to the modern world, and in the circle of people with whom he habitually associated, Speaker 150 differed markedly from Speakers 6, 7 and 8 - his contemporaries and co-religionists. It is tempting to conjecture that these somewhat intangible but important attitudinal and social differences were indirectly reflected in linguistic differences; Speaker 150 identified with the modernising literate elite by adopting their speech patterns. An 'objective' approach to the sociological characterisation of our four speakers, by limiting itself to noting that they are all old, 'Arab, illiterate, poor, etc. (and on this basis lumping them together as a group) misses sociolinguistic insights of this kind.

I would not argue that the characterisation of the community in some kind of objective sociological terms is in itself poor procedure: in a piece of research of the kind presented here, in which the focus of attention is on the dynamics of dialectal variation and change, some kind of pre-conceived framework has to be brought to bear by the researcher to allow data collection and analysis to go ahead in a systematic manner. As I hope I have shown, much light can be shed on the patterning of variation using a relatively crude system of social categories. Nonetheless, a finer-grained analysis, if this is required, is possible by using a greater degree of participant observation. The difference between the two approaches is basically one of perspective: macro and micro.

8.5 Conclusions

1. In this chapter, it has been argued that variation between syllabic variants in certain categories of the verb and noun in Baḥraini Arabic should be accounted for by a type of rule format (the DMR) which derives these variant types from an independently motivated, 'common-core' base, by means of mutually exclusive, disjunctively ordered sets of morphophonemic rules ('rule-systems'). The constraining environments on these DMRs are community-specific hierarchies of verb-stem categories. The ordering of constraints within a hierarchy is not necessarily the same from community to community.

2. The normal variable rule format is rejected as a satisfactory means of accounting for the type of variation described, since it forces us to depict one syllabic variant as being 're-written', or as 'underlying' another. In practice, there is no way of deciding on what the input, or output of such a variable rule could be.

3. DMRs do not model cognition. They summarise and display the patterns of communal variation (and may suggest the direction of future change). Overlaps between the constituent rule-systems of DMRs from one community to another, reflect the blurring of once-clear, gross, society-language correlations.

4. Implicational scales, as argued in this chapter, can be used as heuristic devices for defining precisely the scope of variation in communal DMRs. That is, they specify co-relationships between DMR outputs, and hence the range of lects in the community. They also suggest how change has spread through the community, affecting different speakers at different speeds, for social reasons.

Bibliography

ABDO D. (1969) "Stress and Arabic Phonology" PhD Thesis, University of Illinois

AL-JISHSHI A.I. (1973) "Min lahjatinā al-maḥalliyya" in Al-Fikr (Journal of Riyād University Faculty of Literature) No. 2 pp 57-9.

AL-TAJIR M. (1982) "Language and Linguistic Origins in Al-Bahrain" Kegan Paul International, London & Boston

AL-TOMA S. (1969) "The Problem of Diglossia in Arabic: a Comparative Study of Classical and Iraqi Arabic" Harvard Middle Eastern Monographs XXI, Cambridge, Mass.

AL-TOMA S. (1974) "Language Planning in Arab Countries" in FISHMAN J.A. (ed.) (1974) "Advances in Language Planning" Mouton pp 279-313

ANSHEN F. (1975) "Varied objections to various variable rules" in FASOLD R.W. & SHUY R.W. (eds)(1975) "Analysing Variation in Language" Georgetown University Press pp 1-10

BAILEY C-J (1973) "Variation in Linguistic Theory" CAL, Washington D.C.

BICKERTON D. (1971) "Inherent variability and variable rules" in Foundations of Language 7 pp 457-92

BICKERTON D. (1973a) "Quantitative versus dynamic paradigms: the case of Montreal que" in BAILEY C-J. & SHUY R.W. (eds) (1973) "New Ways of Analyzing Variation in English" Georgetown University Press

BICKERTON D. (1973b) "The Nature of a Creole continuum" Language 49, pp 640-669

BLANC H. (1960) "Style Variations in Spoken Arabic - A Sample of Interdialectal Conversation" in FERGUSON C.A. (ed) (1960), "Contributions to Arabic Linguistics" Harvard Middle Eastern Monographs III, Cambridge, Mass. pp 81-156.

BLANC H. (1964) "Communal Dialects in Baghdad" Harvard Middle Eastern Monographs X, Cambridge, Mass.

BRAME M. (1970) "Arabic Phonology: Implications for Phonological Theory and Historical Semitic" PhD thesis, M.I.T.

CADORA F.J. (1970) "Some linguistic concomitants of contactual factors of urbanization" Anthropological Linguistics 12 No 1, pp 10-19

CANTINEAU J. (1936 & 37) "Etudes sur quelques parlers de nomades arabes d'orient" Annales de l'Institut d'Etudes Orientales d'Alger (ii) pp 1-118 and (iii) pp 119-237

CEDERGREN H. and SANKOFF D. (1974) "Variable rules: performance as a statistical reflection of competence" Language 50, pp 333-55

DECAMP D. (1971) "Implicational scales and sociolinguistic linearity" Linguistics 73, pp 30-43

DECAMP D. (1973) "What do implicational scales imply? in BAILEY C-J. and SHUY R.W. (eds) (1973) "New Ways of Analyzing Variation in English" Georgetown University Press pp 141-8

DITTMAR N. (1976) "Sociolinguistics: A Critical Survey of Theory and Application" Arnold

EL-HASSAN S.A. (1978) "Educated Spoken Arabic in Egypt and the Levant: a critical review of diglossia and related concepts" Archivum Linguisticum VIII 2

EL-HASSAN S.A. (1979) "Variation in the demonstrative system in educated spoken Arabic" Archivum Linguisticum IX 1

ERWIN W.M. (1963) "A short Reference Grammar of Iraqi Arabic" Georgetown University Press

FERGUSON C.A. (1959) "Diglossia" reprinted in FERGUSON C.A. (1971) "Language Structure and Language Use" Stanford, pp 1-26

FERGUSON C.A. (ed) (1960) "Contributions to Arabic Linguistics" Harvard Middle Eastern Monographs III, Cambridge Mass.

GAL S. (1979) "Language Shift: social determinants of linguistic change in bilingual Austria" Academic Press

GUTTMAN L. (1944) "A basis for scaling quantitative data" American Sociological Review 9, pp 139-50

HAKKEN B.D. (1933) "Sunni-Shi'a discord in Eastern Arabia" Moslem World XXIII, pp 302-5

HANSEN H.H. (1967) "Investigations in a Shi'a Village in Bahrain" Publications of the National Museum, Ethnographical Series, Vol XII Copenhagen

HOLES C.D. (1980) "Variation in Bahraini Arabic: the [j] and [y] allophones of /j/" Zeitschrift für arabische Linguistik 4 pp 72-89

HOLES C.D. (1981) "A Sociolinguistic Study of the Arabic-speaking Speech Community of Bahrain: Language Variation in Relation to Sect-membership, Region and Literacy" PhD Thesis, University of Cambridge

HOLES C.D. (1983a) "Bahraini dialects: sectarian differences and the sedentary/nomadic split" ZAL 10 pp 7-37

HOLES C.D. (1983b) "Patterns of communal language variation in Bahrain" Language in Society 12:4 pp 433-57

HOLES C.D. (1984) "Bahraini dialects: sectarian differences exemplified through texts" ZAL 13 pp 27-67

HOLES C.D. (1986a forthcoming) "The social motivation for phonological convergence in three Arabic dialects" International Journal of the Sociology of Language 61

HOLES C.D. (1986b forthcoming) "Morphophonemic variation in spoken Arabic" Transactions of the Philological Society

HOLES C.D. (1987 forthcoming) "Variation in pronominal enclitic forms as a function of different modes of reference and changing communicative intent in spoken Arabic" Anthropological Linguistics

HOOPER J.B. (1976) "An Introduction to Natural Generative Phonology" Academic Press, New York

HUDSON G. (1986) "Arabic root and pattern morphology without tiers" Journal of Linguistics 22:1 pp 1-37

HUDSON R.A. (1980) "Sociolinguistics" Cambridge University Press

HYMES D. (1967) "Models of interaction of language and social setting" Journal of Social Issues 23 pp 8-28

INGHAM B. (1973) "Urban and rural Arabic in Khūzistan" Bulletin of the School of Oriental and African Studies XXXVI 3 pp 531-53

INGHAM B. (1976) "Regional and social factors in the dialect geography of Southern Iraq and Khūzistan" BSOAS XXXIX 1 pp 62-82

INGHAM B. (1982) "North East Arabian Dialects" KPI, London & Boston

JAHANGIRI N. & HUDSON R.A. (1982) "Patterns of variation in Tehrani Persian" in ROMAINE S. (ed) "Sociolinguistic Variation in Speech Communities" Arnold pp 49-63

JOHNSTONE T.M. (1963) "The affrication of kāf and gāf in the Arabic dialects of the Arabian peninsula" Journal of Semitic Studies viii 2, pp 210-26

JOHNSTONE T.M. (1965) "The sound change j > y in the Arabic dialects of peninsular Arabia" BSOAS XXVIII 2, pp 233-41

JOHNSTONE T.M. (1967) "Eastern Arabian Dialect Studies" OUP

KHURI F.I. (1980) "Tribe and State in Bahrain" University of Chicago Press

LABOV W. (1963) "The social motivation of a sound change" Word 19, pp 273-309

LABOV W (1966) "The social stratification of English in New York City" Center for Applied Linguistics, Washington DC

LABOV W. (1972a) "Language in the Inner City: Studies in the Black English Vernacular" University of Pennsylvania Press

LABOV W. (1972b) "Sociolinguistic Patterns" University of Pennsylvania Press

LASS R. (1984) "Phonology: An Introduction to Basic Concepts" Cambridge University Press

LORIMER J.G. (1908) "Gazeteer of the Persian Gulf" Calcutta

McCARTHY J. (1981) "A prosodic theory of non-contatenative morphology" Linguistic Inquiry 12 pp 373-418

MARTINET A. (1963) Preface to WEINREICH U. "Languages in Contact" The Hague, Monton

MEISELES G. (1980) "Educated Spoken Arabic and the Arabic language continuum" Archivum Linguisticum XV 2 pp 118-143

MILROY L. (1980) "Language and Social Networks" Blackwell

MILROY L. & MARGRAIN S. (1980) "Vernacular language loyalty and social network" Language in Society 9:1 pp 43-70

MITCHELL T.F. (1978) "Educated Spoken Arabic in Egypt and the Levant, with special reference to participle and tense" Journal of Linguistics 14:2

NAKHLEH E.A. (1976) "Bahrain: Political Development in a Modernising Society" Lexington Books

PROCHAZKA T. (1981) "The Shi'i dialects of Bahrain and their relationship to the Eastern Arabian dialect of Muharreq and the Omani dialect of Al-Ristaq" ZAL 6 pp 16-55

RUSSELL J. (1982) "Networks and sociolinguistic variation in an African urban setting" in ROMAINE S. (ed) "Sociolinguistic Variation in Speech Communities" Arnold pp 125-40

SALLAM A.M. (1979) "Gender in the educated spoken Arabic of Egypt and the Levant" Archivum Linguisticum IX 2

SALLAM A.M. (1980) "Phonological variation in educated spoken Arabic: a study of the uvular and related plosive types" BSOAS XLIII 1

SMEATON H.B. (1973) "Lexical Expansion due to Technical Change as illustrated by the Arabic of Al-Ḥaṣa, Saudi Arabia" Bloomington

STATE OF BAHRAIN (1972) Ministry of Finance and National Economy Statistical Abstract

TALMOUDI F. (1984) "The Diglossic Situation in North Africa: A Study of Classical Arabic/Dialectal Arabic Diglossia with Sample Text in 'Mixed Arabic'"Acta Universitatis Gothoburgensis

TRUDGILL P. (1974) "The Social Differentiation of English in Norwich" Cambridge University Press

VERSTEEGH K. (1984) "Pidginization and Creolization: the Case of Arabic" Current Issues in Linguistic Theory No 33, Benjamins Amsterdam

WEINREICH U. (1963) "Languages in Contact" The Hague, Mouton

WEINREICH U., LABOV W., & HERZOG M. (1968) "Empirical foundations for a theory of language change" in LEHMANN W.P. & MALKIEL Y. (eds) "Directions for Historical Linguistics" University of Texas Press pp 95-189

WILSON A.T. (1954) "The Persian Gulf" London

WOLFRAM W.A. (1969) "A Sociolinguistic Description of Detroit Negro Speech" CAL Washington DC

Index

This index is designed to supplement the contents page, and lists topics in Arabic and general linguistics which appear in the text, as well as place names and other local nomenclature. For major headings (e.g. "morphophonology") readers are referred to the Contents page.

affixes: 107-8; lack of susceptibility to variation: 110-1
affrication, as a historical process: 32, 35, 38, 40, 97
age-group and illiteracy: 17-18, 22
age-range of speakers: 29
Agricultural Research Station (Budayya'): 24, 74
'Ajam (Persians): 12
'Āli (village): 16, 39
Āl Khalīfa: 11
'Arab (Arabic-speaking Sunnis): 11-12; linguistic dominance in Baḥrain: 17, 29; prestige dialect of: 38, 44, 149-51, 158; linguistic security: 68; tendency to preserve own dialect: 69, 81, 89, 158, 163, 174, 188; restructuring of morphophonemic system of dialect: 146, 154, 158-9, 164, 174-5; influence of MSA on dialect: 148-9, 154-7, 163-4, 168, 170, 174
archaisms: 50
'Askar (village): 13

Baghdād: 147
Baḥārna (Arabic-speaking Shi'a): 12-13: origins: 39; employment patterns: 13, 17, 24, 38; conservative attitudes: 19, 23; urban versus rural dialects: 30, 38, 39, 72, 150; coalescence of: 152, 185; prescriptivism: 75, 158; linguistic insecurity: 23, 26, 72-3; influence of 'Arab dialectal forms: 39, 72, 75-6, 78, 81, 88, 93, 103-4, 138, 149-50, 163-4, 172, 174; 'standardising' speech of literates: 72, 76, 81, 88, 134, 157; hypercorrection: 73; restructuring of morphophonemic system: 149-52, 158-9, 164, 174-5
Baḥrainis, ethnic origins: 11; 'typical' speech: 16; attitudes to social change: 19
Bani Jamra (village): 39
Bani 'Utūb: 11
borrowingsinto BA: from Persian 35, 53; other languages: 37, 40, 52
brace notation: 178
broken plurals: 37
Budayya': 13, 16

class consciousness: 13
Classical Arabic: 176
classicisation: 57
cottage industries: 13

Dammām: 16
data collection techniques: 1-2, 25-6
Dawāsir: 16
Dēh (village): 38-41, 75
Dēr (village): 108, 110
Dhawāwida: 17
dialects, and Classical Arabic: 4; Eastern Arabian: 32; nomadic/sedentary distinctions: 32-3, 38; of Southern Arabia and Oman: 33; native-speaker value judgements on: 37; of radio programmes: 6; preservation of: 57, 166, 174; 'common-core' items in: 37, 40, 52-3, 57, 64, 76; convergence of: 66, 89-91, 111, 127, 134, 158, 174; 'neutral' forms in: 69-70, 78, 94, 128, 149, 151, 164, 166; markers in: 70, 73, 75, 79, 111, 128; lexical domain of: 76-8, 99, 102, 104; divergence in: 158; strength and speed of change in: 170-1
dialectology, historical: 106
Dirāz (village): 38-40, 75

education system: 13, 16
elections: 16
enclitics: 108
environments of rules: 99-100, 179, 185, 193-4
epenthesis: 118, 192

Fādil (quarter of Manāma): 17

Galāli (village): 13
grammar, types within a speech community: 191 ff.
guttural consonants, effect on syllable structure: 109, 112, 116-7, 121, 132, 147-8, 160

Ḥidd: 13
Ḥiyāch: 17
homogeneity hypothesis: 7, 155

Ḥwala: 11-12

illiteracy eradication: 17-18
implicational scaling: 5, 27, 81 ff, 105, 124, 185, 189-90
indefinite marker: 33
internal passive: 33
intransitive verbs: 113, 125
isomorphism of 'literate' dialects and MSA: 168-9

Jaw (village): 13
Jisra (village): 13

Kuwait: 11, 147
Kuwaiti dialect: 2

lects, individual: 94, 199-200
lexical replacement: 35, 53; analogues: 35-6; 'core-items': 37, 40, 52-3, 57, 64, 76; change, hypothesis of: 100-3, 105; categories in morphophonemic change: 180 ff
linguistic markers: 34, 70, 73; prestige systems: 48, 75-6, 104, 106, 164
liquids: 112-3
literacy centres: 25
literacy, as a social variable: 23-4; factor in speech style: 60, 64, 68, 69, 79, 80-1, 104, 125
literary forms: 79

Madīnat 'Isa: 10, 13
Manāma: 10, 13, 20; accent (of the 'Arab): 34, 38, 40, 45, 149
marriage, between 'Arab and Baḥārna: 16
media: 99
meso (or medial or hybrid) forms: 5, 60, 101-2, 178, 191
Montreal French: 3
morphological patterns in BA: 57-8; inflectional: 111; internal structure of system: 112, 116
morpho-semantic congruity: 42-3, 48, 50, 52, 70, 76, 78, 80, 100
MSA, learning of: 98-9, 102;

neologisms derived from: 35-7
Muharrag, island: 10-17; villages: 29, 93; ('Arab) accent: 34
multilectal grammar: 3
multivalency of dialectal features: 2-3, 106

Nabīh Ṣāleh, island of: 10
North African Arabic: 5
Norwich English: 3
N.Y.C. English: 3

oil, discovery of: 11
Old Arabic: 34
'Oman: 39

panlectal (polylectal) grammars: 27-8, 200
participial constructions: 104, 108-9
pearl-trade: 10-11
phonological merger: 36-7; substitution: 42-3, 48, 60, 176; systems: 70, 79-80; features, bundles of: 101-2; naturalness: 97, 100; rules, historical in BA: 109, 181-2; synchronic in BA: 177-8
population: 10, 13
pre- and post-formatives: 107
prepalatals: 122
proto-forms: 97

Qaṭar: 11
Qaṭīf: 39, 41
Qurānic school: 19

radio, effects of: 16
Ramallah, Jordan: 16
Ras-Rummān (quarter of Manāma): 38, 41, 75, 114, 120, 149
reductional changes: 33
reading conventions (for rules): 179, 181, 183
reading tests: 29
rewrite conventions: 92, 96, 101, 103, 176
Rifā', East and West: 13
rules, disjunctive: 178 ff; of use: 94-5, 198-200; ordering: 178; implicational relationships between: 195-200

Sanābis (village): 38-41, 75
Saudi Arabia: 11, 39
scaleability: 190, 200
sex and literacy: 18-19, 22; and dialect: 22
Shaṭṭ-al-'Arab: 10
Sitra (island): 10
social identity and speech style, correlation of: 188
social network: 200 ff
socio-sectarian affiliation: 22
speech style, gradient nature of: 5; contexts influencing: 26, 28-9; raising: 43, 69, 71, 97
standardisation: 8
stereotypes, dialectal: 8, 31, 43
stress rules: 192
students, British Council: 23; Teacher Training Colleges: 23, 27
Swahili: 3
syllabication in BA, principles of: 109-10, 113-4, 119, 121-2, 125 ff
syllabic templates: 107, 110

technical terms, local: 52, 58, 63
Tehrani Persian: 3
television, effects of: 16
town/village social differences: 22
transitive verbs: 113, 125
tri-literal roots: 57, 59

underlying forms: 96-7, 123, 176-7, 179-81

variable rules: 95-7, 103-4, 177, 182-3
variation: patterned nature of: 7; measurement of: 48-9, 56; factors in the susceptibility of linguistic elements to: 49-54, 71, 79, 124; literacy as a factor in: 75 ff, 88-9, 104; contextual factors in: 7, 73-5, 95; internal regularity of: 91; synchronic versus diachronic: 97-103, 122-3; constraints on: 92-4; inter-rule relationships: 91-2, 155-6; co-occurence restrictions:

102, 139, 198
verb stems in BA: 108, 112-4, 116-7, 131-2; in OA: 113
vowel deletion rules: 118, 177, 192; dissimilation: 116, 119

Yemen: 39

Zallāg (village): 13

Glossary of technical terms

الانفجار الاحتكاكي	affrication
لاحقة	affix
لثوي	alveolar
مماثل	analogue
مساعد	auxiliary
التخليف (تحرك الصوائت من موقع امامي الى موقع خلفي)	backing
تماثل لغوي	congruity (linguistic)
سلسلة متصلة	continuum
هيكل تكونه اصوات ساكنة	consonantal skeleton
تقارب اللهجات	convergence (dialectal)
قاعدة لغوية تمنع من تواجد ملمح شكلي معين في لفظ فيه ملمح آخر لا ينسجم معه	co-occurrence restriction
تبديل ملمح لهجي بملمح لهجي آخر	cross dialectal variation
حذف (الحركة)	deletion
اسناني	dental
تاريخي	diachronic
لهجة	dialect
لهجي	dialectal
غير لهجي (اى فصيح)	supra------
السليلة اللهجية	-----reflex
الانضوائي	enclitic
علم تاريخ الكلمات	etymology
ملمح (لغوي)	feature (linguistic)
صوت احتكاكي	fricative
التقديم (تحرك الصوائت من موقع خلفي الى موقع امامي)	fronting
متكافئ من ناحية الوظيفة	functional equivalent
حلقي	guttural

حركة مرتفعة	high vowel
تحليل لغوي يرتب اللهجات الانفرادية في جدول حسب درجة تشابهها	implicational analysis
(حرف صامت) ينطق بين الاسنان	interdental (consonant)
اللازم	intransitive
تماثل الشكل	isomorphism
لهجة مشتركة تستعمل من اجل التفاهم و لا يتكلمها اى فرد كلهجته الام	koine
لهجة انفرادية	lect
اللهجة القح	basi----
اللهجة المثقفة	acro----
(نحو) يشمل اللهجات الانفرادية	pan----al (grammar)
(كفاءة لغوية) في عدة لهجات متشابهة	multi----al (competence)
التغير اللغوي	linguistic variation and change
(حركة) منخفضة	low (vowel)
علامة اجتماعية	marker (social)
الاندماج	merger
المورفيم/ الوحدة الصرفية	morpheme
مورفولوجيا	morphology
قواعد صوتية وظيفية تنطبق حسب الجنس الصرفي الذي تنتسب اليه كلمة ما	morphophonemic rules
درجة التفاوق الشكلي و المعنوي بين كلمة في اللغة الدارجة ونظيرها بالفصحى	morphosemantic congruity
تعدد الدلالة (او القيمة او الوظيفة)	multivalency (of dialect features)
تنظيم متسلسل (لقواعد لغوية)	ordering (of rules)
حنكي	palatal
اطباق (الحروف)	pharyngealization
الفونيم/ الوحدة الصوتية الوظيفية	phoneme
فوناتيكي	phonetic
الفونولوجيا	phonology
اسم الفاعل	present participle
الرفع (تحرك الصوائت من موقع منخفض الى موقع مرتفع)	raising (of vowels)
(التغير) الاختزالي	reductional (change)
عملية اعادة تركيب المقاطع	resyllabication
(حرف صامت) ينطق في موقع اكثر خلفية من العادة	retracted (consonant)
جدول من اللهجات الانفرادية وهي مرتبة حسب تشابهها الشكلي	scalogram
علم اللغة الاجتماعية	sociolinguistics
احتكاكي	spirant

standardization	تبديل الاشكال اللهجية باشكال مأخوذة من اللغة الفصحى
stem	الجذع
stereotype	صورة عقلية يشترك في حملها افراد جماعة ما من جماعة او شخص آخر
stigmatised	موصوم
stop (consonant)	انفجاري
stress	النبر
structural description	الوصف البنيوي
suffix	اللاحقة
syllable	المقطع
syllabic structure	التركيب المقطعي
syllabic template	الهيكل المقطعي
synchronic	وصفي
transitive	المتعدي
underlying (form)	(الشكل) العميق
uvular	لهوي
variable (n.)	متغير
continuous--------	متغير متصل
discrete ---------	متغير منفصل
---------- rule	قاعدة تعبر عن التغير اللغوي المنظم في جماعة ما
variant	شكل لغوي يختلف عن شكل ثاني يشابهه في المعنى او الوظيفة
velar	حلقي
vowel height	ارتفاع الحركات
vowel pattern	حركات داخل جذع الكلمة

الفصل الثامن والأخير: وفى الجزء الأخير من دراستنا نقوم بمناقشة عدة مشاكل تتعلق بأشكال القواعد اللغوية (linguistic formalisms) التى يستعملها اللغويون المحدثون للتعبير عن التغير المنظم (patterned variation) فى اللغات البشرية وقد اتضح أثناء السنوات العشرين الماضية أن وجود التغير المنظم ظاهرة اعتيادية فى مجتمعات العالم ككل ولكن على ضوء التحليل التفصيلى الذى يقدم فى الفصلين السابقين لهذه الدراسة ، نقترح أن لابد من اعادة النظر فى مبادىء نظام القواعد اللغوية التى يعمل بها حاليا فى مجال علم اللغة بشكل عام.

الاجتماعية العامة التى لاتزال لها أهمية كبيرة فى حفظ الخصائص اللغوية التى تفرق بين الجماعات الطائفية البحرينية : جماعة العرب من جهة ، وجماعة البحارنة من جهة أخرى .

الفصل الثالث : أثبتت البحوث التى أجريت خلال السنوات العشرين الماضية أن أصالة النصوص الشفهية الدارجة قد تتأثر اذا لم يهتم الباحث بالطريقة التى يستعملها فى جمع النصوص . فاذا كان المتكلم الأمى واعيا بأن محادثة يتم تسجيلها مع الباحث أو شخص آخر ، فمن المتوقع أنه يبدل الكثير من الكلمات والألفاظ اللهجية التى يستعملها عادة خوفا من أن يعتبر كلامه همجيا أو غير مثقف ومن هذا قد يأخذ الباحث فكرة خاطئة تمام الخطأ عن طبيعة لهجته . فيجب على كل باحث فى هذا المجال أن ينتبه انتباها كافيا الى كيفية تنفيذ أبحاثه العملية وخاصة الى مايتعلق باختيار المتكلمين ومعاملتهم وتسجيل محادثتهم فى ظروف طبيعية . وهذا الفصل يتناول الاجراءات العملية التى لجأ اليها المؤلف فى جمع النصوص الشفهية التى تشكل أساس التحليل فى الفصول التالية . وقد تم تجميع كمية كبيرة من الأشرطة السمعية تمثل لهجة كل طبقة اجتماعية وكل فئة طائفية فى البحرين .

الفصل الرابع : فى هذين الفصلين تحدد عدة نقاط على المستوى الصوتى الوظيفى الذى لايزال تختلف فى معالجتها الأعضاء غير المثقفين من الجماعات البحرينية المختلفة وتناقش التغيرات والتطورات التى تحدث حاليا فى لهجة المثقفين نتيجة لبرامج محو الأمية وانتشار الثقافة وتوفر نظام تعليمى حديث ولامناص هنا من سؤال يطرح نفسه وهو : ماهى العوامل الاجتماعية التى يمكن اعتبارها مسببات للتغير اللغوى ؟ هل هى تعليمية فقط ؟ ولماذا تتعرض بعض الكلمات والخصائص الشكلية لعملية التغير أكثر من غيرها ؟ وتتأسس الأجوبة لهذه الأسئلة على تحليل دقيق تم اجراؤه على نصوص محكية يبلغ عددها الاجمالى ٣٠٠ر٠٠٠ كلمة .

الفصلان السادس والسابع : ننتقل فى هذا الجزء من دراستنا الى تمحيص مبادىء التغير اللغوى الذى يحدث حاليا على مستوى النظام المفضل لبنية المقاطع (preferred syllable structure) ومايجدر ذكره بهذا الصدد أن لهجة نسبة لابأس بها من المثقفين تختلف عن لهجة أجدادهم الأميين من حيث أنه يبدو أن المثقفين يأخذون فى اعادة تنظيم بنية المقاطع اللهجية ، وخاصة فى الأفعال ، لكى يماثل نظامهم اللهجى الجديد نظام اللغة الفصحى من الناحية الصرفية ولكن الغريب أن هذه العملية لاتتم عن طريق الاقتباس من اللغة الفصحى بل عن طريق اعادة تنظيم الأشكال اللهجية لتشكل نظاما لهجيا جديدا يعكس بنية نظام الفصحى من غير استخدام مركباتها بصورة مباشرة .

مقدمة المؤلف

يتناول هذا الكتاب نتائج الأبحاث اللغوية التى قام بها المؤلف فى دولة البحرين أثناء اقامته فيها فى العام الدراسى ١٩٧٨/٧٧م والتى سبق تقديمها كرسالة الدكتوراة الى قسم علم اللغة فى جامعة كمبريدج فى سنة ١٩٨١م . وكان لهذه الرسالة هدفان أساسيان أولهما وصف لكثير من الخواص اللغوية التى تميز اللهجات البحرينية بعضها عن بعض وثانيهما تقديم مقارنة للنظريات المتضاربة التى جاء بها أساتذة علم اللغة الاجتماعية (sociolinguistics) من أجل شرح التغير اللغوى الذى اكتشفوا وجوده فى كل لغة من لغات العالم . ويمكن القول أن جهود هؤلاء الخبراء لم تقتصر على تحديد الفوارق اللغوية وتمحيصها فحسب ، بل تركزت أيضا على ايضاح الضغوط الاجتماعية التى تظهرها وتبقيها وأحيانا تزيلها . فالدراسة التى بين يدى القارئ تسلط الأضواء على عملية التجدد اللغوى فى دولة عربية نامية لاتزال تتواجد فيها فوارق لغوية ترجع أصولها الى وجود تفرقة اجتماعية قديمة العهد . والغرض الأساس من هذا الكتاب هو شرح عملية التغير اللغوى فى البحرين وتحديد العوامل اللغوية وغير اللغوية التى قد تعتبر مسببات له .

وتنقسم الدراسة الى الفصول الآتية : -

الفصل الأول: يتكون الفصل الأول من مراجعة نقدية للدراسات السابقة التى عالجت مشكلة التغير والهجمات العربية المحلية ، ويمكن تقسيمها الى قسمين متعاكسين : -
أولا: دراسات تقليدية (مثلا Johnstone 1967) تستهدف ادراج الخواص اللغوية وشرحها بصورة تتجاهل مايمكن أن يكون قد دخل فيها من ألفاظ مستحدثة نتيجة لانتشار القراءة والكتابة أثناء العقود الأخيرة . ولاتنتهج دراستنا هذا المنهج بسبب عدم كفاءتها فى توضيح مايلاحظ من تغير لغوى فى كل مجتمع عربى يتعرض للنمو الاقتصادى وماينتج عنه من تغير اجتماعى - أو لنقل كل مجتمع عربى حديث . والقسم الثانى يتكون من دراسات تركز على مايسمى عدم ثبات الملامح الشكلية التى يستعملها المثقفون العرب المتعددو الجنسية عندما يتحادثون بعضهم البعض (مثلا Blanc 1960; Talmoudi 1984) ومع أن مثل هذه الدراسات تعترف بالمشكلة الحقيقية الذى يواجهها الباحث اللغوى عندما يحاول تحليل النصوص الشفهية العربية - مثلا عدم ثبات المميزات الشكلية على مستوى الصوتى الوظيفى (phonological level) - الا أنها لاتوفر قدوة منهجية يعمل بها فى كل الأحوال ويرجع هذا النقص الى ضآلة المواد التى تبنى عليها هذه الدراسات .

الفصل الثانى : يتناول الفصل الثانى العوامل التاريخية والجغرافية والطائفية التى لعبت دورا هاما فى تكوين البناء الاجتماعى البحرينى الحديث . والجدير بالذكر أن كل هذه العوامل غير اللغوية تركت آثارها اللغوية الخاصة التى يعرفها ويدركها أهالى البحرين . وتناقش فى هذا الفصل العوامل

الـدارجـة مستخـدمـاً بعض أساليب رواد المدرسة اللغوية الاجتماعية ومنهم DE CAMP, LABOV, BICKERTON – وتأخذ هذه الدراسة في الاعتبار التغيير اللغوي للأفراد في كل من مجالي اللهجة الدارجة والعربية الفصحى . ويتضح هذا خير وضوح في كلام الكاتب حيث يقول في صفحة (٧) :

«إن التنـوع اللغـوي المنتظم هو في الأسـاس أمـر من أمور الكلام الطبيعي سواء على المستـوى الشخصي أو على مستـوى المجتمـع كله ، ويتطلب معالجة لغوية تتميز بفاعلية مستمرة ولا يحتاج إلى تلك التي تعتمد على أسلوب التصنيف والتبويب» .

ويضيف . . .

«إن التنـوع في اللهجـات الـدارجة يجب ألا يبحث على أنه تدخلاً من الفصحى ، لكنه يجب أن يندرج تحت علم اللهجات العام – وذلك لانه يشكل – من وجهة نظر المتكلم – جزءاً لا يتجزأ من سلوكه اللغوي – تماماً مثل اللهجة التي يتحدثها» .

وتأخـذ هذه الـدراسة بعين الاعتبار عوامل الجنسية ، والانتماء الديني ، والطبقة المهنية وتأثير ذلك كله على التنوع اللغوي وهذا بدون شك يضعها في مجال علم اللغة الاجتماعي .

فإن من المثير للاهتمام أن نلاحظ – كما يشير المؤلف في الفصل الثاني من الكتاب – أنه إن كانت الأراء التي تتعلق بالحكم على نـوع ما من الحـديث على أنـه حديث متعلمين أو غير متعلمين . مبنية على التنوع اللغوي فلابد أن يتم تعريفها في كل إقليم على حدة ، وذلك لأن تاريخ السكان والبنية السياسية والاجتماعية لكل دولة يختلف عن الأخرى حتى في منطقة صغيرة نسبياً مثل منطقة ساحل الخليج

وعلى سبيـل المثـال فاستعـمال حرف الياء بدلاً من حرف «الجيم» في الكلام يشير إلى حديث غير المتعلمـين في الكـويت ، وبـالتـالي فهـو ذات سمة اجتماعية دنيا ، بينما يظهر نفس الحـرف في كلام أهـل السنـة في البحرين ويميزه عن كلام أهل الشيعة لا يحمل ذلك أي صبغـة اجتـماعيـة . والـواقـع أن المجتمعات اللغوية التي تحدث عنها المؤلف في حالة تغيير لغوي واجتماعي سريع – وتحاول هذه الدراسة (ص ٨) أن «تشرح كيف أن مجموعة مختـارة من عوامـل صوتيـة وصـرفية في العربية التي يتحدث أهل البحرين ، قد أصبحت مسرحاً للتنوع وأن هذه العوامل في سبيلها إلى التغيير الشامل في النهاية» .

بروس انغام
محرر

تقديم

يظهر هذا الكتاب في وقت تم فيه نشر دراستين تتناولان الموضوع ذاته - أي التنوع اللغوي في البحرين - أولاهما الدراسة التي قام بها ثيودور بروخاسكا Th. PROCHASKA والثانية هي تلك التي كتبها الاستاذ مهدي التاجر . وتعالج هذه الدراسات الموضوع من نواح مختلفة . حيث تعتمد دراسة الاستاذ التاجر اعتماداً أساسياً على الربط بين التنوع اللغوي وعلم الأنساب التقليدي مستمداً معلوماته من المصادر التاريخية العربية . أما دراسة الاستاذ بروخاسكا فهي مقارنة ثلاثية الأطراف بين لهجات الشيعة في البحرين ولهجة أهل السنة وكذلك لهجة أهل عمان المجاورة ، ملتمساً في بحثه تفاسير تاريخية للوضع اللغوي الحالي في هذه المنطقة .

وتركز الدراسات الثلاثة على التنوع الصوتي والصرفي الكثير الحدوث في اللغة العربية ، وتعتمد في هذا على نفس القواعد التي أسسها حاييم بلانك في كتابه المشهور «اللهجات المتداولة في بغداد (١٩٦٤)» H. BLANC COMMUNAL DIALECTS IN BAGHDAD والذي شرح فيه اللهجات الدارجة للمسلمين واليهود والمسيحيين في مناطق الحضر موضحاً العلاقة التاريخية التي تربط هذه اللهجات بمجموعة اللهجات الموجودة خارج حدود المنطقة تحت الدراسة .

ومن الجدير بالذكر أن الصورة العامة في مجتمع البحرين الذي يتناوله المؤلف بالدراسة ، قريبة الشبه بتلك التي في العراق والتي تناولها الاستاذ بلانك في كتابه الذي أشرنا إليه آنفاً ، أي أن تدفق المهاجرين من أواسط الجزيرة العربية قد تسبب في ايجاد منطقة منقطعة عن نطاقها الأصلي والذي يشمل الأجزاء التي تمارس فيها هذه اللهجات الآن . ولهذا ، فإن لهجة الشيعة (البحارنة) هي اللهجة الأقدم وهي التي ترتبط باجزاء من عمان وبدرجة أقل بالاحساء . بينما ترتبط لهجة أهل السنة بمنطقة نجد .

ويذكر المؤلف في دراسة سابقة (١٩٨٣ (م) ، ص : ١٥) : أن «تصنيف الاستاذ بلانك اللجات العراقية إلى مايسمى «بلهجات الحضر» و«لهجات الرحل» ينطبق في صفاته العامة على اللهجات البحرينية مع كثير من الاختلافات في التفاصيل - وينطبق ايضاً على مناطق اخرى خارج منطقة العراق .

وتختلف الدراسة الحالية اختلافاً تاماً عن الدراستين السابقتين في كل من المعالجة العامة والأسلوب . فالمؤلف من أوائل علماء اللغة الاجتماعيين الذين يعملون في مجال اللغة العربية ، ويأتي بحثه هذا نتيجة لسنوات عدة من الدراسة للهجات البحرين ويظهر بعد مقالاته الأربعة التي كتبها عن نفس الموضوع في أعوام ١٩٨٠ ، ١٩٨٣ ، ١٩٨٤ على التوالي .

وقد طور المؤلف الأسلوب الذي اتبعه بلانك في وصف الاختلافات بين اللهجات

بسم الله الرحمن الرحيم

تأليف
الدكتور كلايف هولز
جامعة سالفورد

التغير اللغوي
في دولة عربية متطورة

الكتاب السابع

مؤسسة كيغان بول العالمية
لندن - نيويورك

مكتبة اللسانيات العربية
سلسلة كتب عالمية في الدراسات اللغوية العربية

هيئة التحرير
د . محمد حسن باكَلاّ
جامعة الملك سعود – الرياض
المملكة العربية السعودية
د . بروس انغام
جامعة لندن

هيئة التحرير الاستشارية

البروفيسور يوسف الخليفة أبو بكر (جامعة الخرطوم) ، البروفيسور آرنه امبروس (جامعة فيينا – النمسا) ، البروفيسور بروس انغام (جامعة لندن) ، البروفيسور السعيد محمد بدوي (الجامعة الأمريكية في القاهرة) ، البروفيسور بوغوسلاف زغوريسكي (جامعة وارسو) ، البروفيسور أحمد محمد الضبيب (جامعة الرياض) ، البروفيسور محمد حسن عبد العزيز (جامعة نيروبي – كينيا) ، البروفيسور بيتر فؤاد عبّود (جامعة تكساس الولايات المتحدة الأمريكية) ، البروفيسور صالح جواد الطعمة (جامعة انديانا – الولايات المتحدة الأمريكية) ، البروفيسور مارتن فورستنر (جامعة جوهانس غونتنبرغ – المانيا الغربية) ، البروفيسور تشارلس فيرستيغ (الجامعة الكاثوليكية في نيجميغن – هولندا) ، البروفيسور مايكل كارتر (جامعة سيدني – استراليا) ، البروفيسور رجا توفيق نصر (الكلية الجامعية في بيروت) ، البروفيسور أوتو ياسترو (جامعة ارلانغن – نورنبرغ في المانيا الغربية) .

التغير اللغوي
في دولة عربية متطورة

مكتبة اللسانيات العربية

الحمد لله وحده . والصلاة والسلام على من لا نبي بعده . أما بعد : فإن هنالك أسباباً عدة دعت إلى إنشاء هذه السلسلة من الكتب في حقل اللسانيات والصوتيات العربية .

أولاً : إن هذا الحقل يمر بتطور سريع في إطار الدراسات اللغوية المعاصرة . كما أن كثيراً من الجامعات العربية والغربية قد بدأت تدخل علم اللسانيات وعلم الصوتيات وبعض العلوم اللغوية الحديثة ضمن مواد التدريس بها . بالإضافة الى الإهتمام المتزايد في الدوائر اللغوية العالمية بهذا الميدان .

ثانياً : ومع ازدياد الاهتمام بالدراسات اللسانية والصوتية العربية بدأت تصل هذه الدراسات إلى مرحلة متقدمة في النضوج ليست مستفيدة من معطيات علم اللسانيات العام والعلوم الأخرى النسبية فحسب . بل وأيضاً من معطيات الدراسات اللغوية العربية القديمة .

ثالثاً : بدأت تظهر في حقل اللسانيات العربية فروع ونظريات مختلفة تشمل الصوتيات والفونولوجيا والنحو والدلالة ، وعلم اللغة النفسي ، وعلم اللغة الاجتماعي ، وعلم اللهجات العربية ، وصناعة المعاجم . ودراسة المفردات . وتدريس العربية أو تعلمها كلغة أولى أو ثانية أو أجنبية ، وعلم الاتصال ، وعلم الإشارات اللغوي . ودراسة المصطلحات . والترجمة . والترجمة الآلية ، وعلم اللغة الإحصائي ، وعلم اللغة الرياضي . وتاريخ العلوم الغوية العربية . وما إلى ذلك .

يضاف إلى هذا كله أن الاقبال على اللغة العربية دراسة وتدريساً وبحثاً يزداد يوماً بعد يوم على الصعيدين المحلي والدولي . ولما لم يكن هناك منبر يرتفع منه نداء لغة الضاد وتعلو منه أصوات الباحثين والمتخصصين فيها لذا وجدت مكتبة "اللسانيات العربية" لتسد هذا الفراغ الكبير والفجوة العميقة وتدفع بالبحث اللغوي العربي قدماً إلى الأمام خدمة للغة القرآن الكريم والتراث العربي الأصيل ، وسيراً بالبحث اللساني العربي للحاق بركب اللسانيات العامة المتقدم . وإثراءً للدراسات اللغوية واللسانية العربية .

وتحرص هذه السلسلة العالميّة على تقديم الجديد من البحث اللغوي وإعطاء الفرصة للبحاثين من العرب وغيرهم للمشاركة في بناء صرح اللسانيات العربية حتى تستعيد الدراسات اللغوية مجدها الماضي العريق .

ولأن هذه السلسلة تعد الأولى من نوعها في الدراسات اللسانية العربية المتخصصة . فإننا نهيب بكل باحث متخصص في مجال اللسانيات العربية بمختلف فروعها النظرية منها والتطبيقية أن يشارك بجهوده وأفكاره وأبحاثه وألا ينجل بتقديم أجود ما لديه من عطاء في سبيل دعم أهداف هذه السلسلة وتطوير مجالاتها الواسعة . والباب مفتوح أمام جميع الأقلام العربية والشرقية والغربية التي تخدم هذه الأهداف الخيّرة .

ونسأل الله العلي القدير أن يحقق لهذه السلسلة ما تصبو اليه من نجاح وتقدم . قال سبحانه وتعالى :

«وقل اعملوا فسيرى الله عملكم» ، صدق الله العظيم . والله الموفق لما فيه الخير والصواب لصالح أمتنا العربية الإسلامية المجيدة ولغتها العريقة الأصيلة . إنه سميع مجيب .

For Product Safety Concerns and Information please contact our EU
representative GPSR@taylorandfrancis.com
Taylor & Francis Verlag GmbH, Kaufingerstraße 24, 80331 München, Germany

www.ingramcontent.com/pod-product-compliance
Lightning Source LLC
Chambersburg PA
CBHW062144300426
44115CB00012BA/2027
9781138974319